SDLC 3.0

Beyond a Tacit Understanding of Agile,
Towards the Next Generation of Software Engineering

Mark Kennaley

Fourth Medium Consulting Inc.

mark@fourth-medium.com

Many of the designations used by manufacturers and sellers to distinguish their products are claimed as trademarks. Where those designations appear in this book, and Fourth Medium was aware of a trademark claim, the designations have been printed with initial capital letters or all in capitals.

Some images from www.bigstockphoto.com

Some images from Wikipedia Commons

Some images from www.openclipart.org

The author and the publisher have taken care in the preparation of this book, but make no expressed or implied warranty of any kind and assume no responsibility for errors or omissions. No liability is assumed for incidental or consequential damages in connection with or arising out of the use of the information or programs contained herein.

Visit Fourth Medium at www.fourth-medium.com

ISBN 978-0-9865194-0-6

Text printed on recycled paper

First Printing January 2010

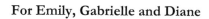

For Emily, Gabrielle and Diane

Foreword: *by Scott Ambler*

Being a firm believer in measured value, I thought I would start with a quick discussion of the two metrics that indicate the value of a book to me. The first one is how much did I mark up the book as I was reading it and the second is how many books or articles did the book reference that I sought out afterwards. I treat my books harshly, highlighting important ideas and writing my observations and thoughts in the margins as I read, and my copy of *SDLC 3.0* is marked up severely. As for the second metric, as I was writing this a shipment from Amazon arrived with seven books which I ordered after this book piqued my interest in them.

The most important question that I can attempt to answer in this foreword is what I believe you will get out of reading this book. First and foremost, this book presents a realistic and reasoned view of agile software delivery. Note how I use the term delivery and not just development – this book goes far beyond the software development life cycle to consider the full delivery life cycle. In fact, it goes further to consider how to apply agile and lean concepts at the enterprise level; more on this in a minute. The book forgoes the marketing rhetoric that is all too common in the mainstream agile community and instead focuses on what works in practice and more importantly explains why it does so through the application of systems theory. Don't worry – although Mark does present a few relatively complex mathematical explanations for why agile techniques work the way they do, he walks the reader through the explanations in a coherent and understandable manner.

The second strength of this book is its solid foundation in IT history. Time and again I see practitioners waste months, and sometimes years, as they relearn lessons from the past. In chapter 2 Mark presents a graph overviewing the historical roots of today's methodologies and in chapter 3 he presents the history of systems control theory. Both of these graphs, and more importantly the discussions around them, will help to give you the background that you need to work your way through the propaganda of the process prosthelytizers among us. These two chapters alone will be an eye opener for the majority of agile developers today.

Mark applies his deep understanding of methodologies, systems control theory, and human behavior throughout the book. Page after page he presents strategies from a wide variety of sources, not just the current process fashion, and explains why and in what circumstances they work. His argument that systems theory provides the underlying explanation for why agile and lean strategies are effective is a strong one, providing IT practitioners a path to move away from superstition and folklore to actual understanding.

Mark argues coherently for what he calls SDLC 3.0, a tailored hybrid of strategies taken from lean, agile, and the unified process. Each of these process camps have their adherents, people who often point out the weaknesses of other process religions without recognizing their strengths. SDLC 3.0 doesn't make that mistake, but instead adopts ideas from each camp and weaves them into a stronger and more coherent whole. The book's name is apt, it truly does represent a third category of software process (the first one being waterfall/serial development and the second iterative and incremental development).

The final strength of this book is the focus on enterprise-level processes. It's very rare to see coherent discussions of project-level issues and enterprise-level issues in the same book, yet SDLC 3.0 pulls it off. Mark combines ideas from lean software development, Information Technology Infrastructure Library (ITIL), and Enterprise Unified Process (EUP) to describe how to be truly agile across your entire IT department, not just within the scope of a single project team. This enterprise view requires a more holistic view, and dare I say a more mature one, than what we typically see in the mainstream agile community today. If you're trying to roll out agile across your entire IT department, or at least a large portion of it, then I suspect this book will be a valuable resource.

The bottom line is that it isn't very often that a software process book comes along that truly impresses me, and SDLC 3.0 is one of the few that has. To put things in perspective, other such books include *Extreme Programming Explained* by Kent Beck, *Lean Software Development* by the Mary and Tom Poppendieck, *Introduction to the Rational Unified Process* by Philippe Kruchten, and *Organizational Patterns of Agile Software Development* by Jim Coplien and Neil Harrison. So yes, I highly recommend that you read this book.

Scott W. Ambler
Chief Methodologist/Agile, IBM Rational
Creator, Agile Modeling and Enterprise Unified Process
March 2010

Preface:

In today's current business climate, it would seem reasonable that the message of "more for less" should be as important, if not more important as that of being "agile". Ironically however, within Enterprise IT *Lean Thinking* has not received as much of a buzz. Instead, it has been *Agile Software Development* enjoying much interest and publicity in recent years. Some argue that the Agile phenomenon is just a natural outgrowth of all prior years of knowledge and experience within the software engineering community. Others, most notably members deeply rooted within the Agile community, argue that all prior approaches are fundamentally flawed and offer no value. More often than not, these arguments claim the lack of applicability of Lean due to its origins in manufacturing. Or they tie strict interpretations of the mis-interpreted Waterfall methodology paper to other methods and experiences. The different perspectives representing a spectrum of views are arguably grounded more from a political ideology than established fact, something that could be described as being akin to religion. These divergent perspectives and associated debates have been termed the "methodology wars". But we know we live in a world that is made up of shades of grey. In other words, the world is not black and white. Wisdom, which is accrued over time, teaches us of such pragmatic realities.

Ultimately, this book is about integration. It is about the integration of competing method-specific communities. It is about the inclusive integration of "Agile" and "un-Agile". It is about the integration of the left wing and the right wing, or at least the incubation of a centrist perspective, independent of any ideology except that of modern software engineering. It is about the integration of diverse experience from many corporations, not just a few. And it is about integration of heterogeneous rather than homogeneous professions and knowledge sets, with a personal contribution from my own profession, Electrical Engineering. As many EE's have followed a similar path into the software engineering field, I suspect that many still have the ability to dust off those old university textbooks and leverage some of the most intense applied science known to man in an effort to go beyond what is "tacitly" known about the state of the practice. The hope is that by "putting out there" certain hypotheses related to why and when various techniques work, more of this type of cross-application of knowledge can occur.

My inspiration for this is in the works of Jay W. Forrester, who first attempted to apply these very same concepts and actionable practices to understanding social dynamics. He did this work as the founder of MIT's System's Dynamics Group and was awarded the IEEE's highest honor. But the roots of such works were incubated in the hard engineering of SAGE – the antiballistic control system that was developed as a result of the cold war. It is arguable that many methodologists have also been influenced by this innovative application of knowledge.

My role in this work is that of an integrator with many years of diverse practitioner experience. Exposure to a broad spectrum of environments has enabled me to draw insights from being "on the ground" in these organizations. Some of these projects have been of extremely large scale and complexity, something that continues to haunt the Agile "sweet-spot." Reflection by practitioners seems to be more and more acceptable within research circles, which increasingly seek joint industry/academic collaboration to further the profession. The book in every section attempts to present unique and practical thoughts and ideas on advanced topics. It goes beyond the typical dogma or vanilla interpretations of Agile and other modern software engineering approaches.

The theme of the book is one of facilitating reflection and discussion surrounding the state of the practice in software engineering. The hope is that facilitating such a discussion will reduce the extremely high-order waste that typifies the *us-vs.-them*, *this method vs. that method* debates. Instead, it seeks to stimulate a discussion related to *this practice vs. that practice for a specific context*, why such a practice fits the context in question, and what basis we can serve up for making this choice credible (as opposed to the typical norm – "just because").

This book is for those who wish to challenge the views contained herein, and constructively contribute to what needs to be a continuous conversation. It is hoped that it will serve to facilitate a coming together by liked minded, reasonable folks who may have observed some of the counterproductive differentiation that has occurred in our field. This issue will be discussed from time to time throughout this work. I have found that these people are colleagues who value pragmatism, straight talk and common sense rather than "maintaining the mystery" of a cottage industry.

Mark Kennaley

Table of Contents

Table of Contents

Chapter 1: "Agile", the Movement

Within the field of Software Engineering, the word "Agile" is spoken at an increasingly frequent rate. Conferences, books, internet articles, and blogs all deal with commentary on what could be described as a bit of a phenomenon. And the current state of Software Engineering has definitely been advanced significantly through the awareness created regarding the values and principles of "Agile".

But when asked whether a team is "being Agile", or whether an organization "is Agile", you sometimes get strange and confusing answers. The terminology that has grown up with the Agile Movement represents jargon that is easily identifiable within the community; but needless to say can be a little foreign to other constituencies. As shown in Figure 1.1, pigs, chickens, sprinting, burning, velocity, muda, and my personal favorite "YAGNI– you ain't gonna need it" all surround how "Agile" is described in conversations around the water cooler.

Figure 1.1 – Agile jargon

When pressed for more concrete explanations, the next stage of an inquisitive discussion typically leads to the only articulation of what Agile "is" - The Agile Manifesto [1]. Published in 2001 as a result of a gathering at a ski resort, it was the result of a set of collective thinking on what was wrong with the state of Software Engineering at that time. It was limited to a set of methodologists that had varying degrees of management and practitioner experience. Each of the 17 male signatories represented experiences from companies such as Tektronix, Chrysler, Dupont, Individual Inc., Borland, PatientKeeper, Easel Corporation, Advanced Development Methods and others.

Figure 1.2 is a screenshot of the webpage that is the Agile Manifesto. It is the only source of doctrine within the Agile community in which all other knowledge traces back to. To be deemed Agile, an approach must be consistent with the Manifesto – which unfortunately is subject to interpretation. Needless to say, this has sometimes caused frustration among IT executives for whom "trust me" rings hollow. For want of something more, risk adverse executives sometimes find themselves trying to understand the scientific origins of this value structure. This is because they are typically required to exercise due diligence in how they spend shareholder funds for such things as large scale process improvement investments. As such, they are required to look beyond anecdotal evidence and individual accounts of success.

Figure 1.2 – Agile Manifesto

Two problems exist with the Agile Manifesto, regardless of the content or philosophical beliefs contained therein. The first is the sentence that appears in the middle of the page. Often overlooked or misinterpreted, it reads: *"That is, while there is value in the items on the right, we value the items on the left more"*. In other words, the drafters of Agile did not intend to engage in a black-and-white debate. The founding fathers were wise enough to understand that we live in a world made up of shades of grey. And when you deal with people and you are attempting to enact change, you have politics. Politics is defined as *the constant application of pressure to achieve an objective*. Objectives are never achieved through purist interpretations, or "bull in the china shop" organizational change strategies. There are always shades of grey, which in the software engineering world means varying context. What might work in one environment/organization will necessarily need to be modified for another, albeit within the essence or spirit of the Manifesto. Agile was intended to bring about change and indeed it has. But as with any political spectrum, ignoring this sentence has enabled various fringes and factions to advance their potentially misaligned agenda.

The second problem with the Manifesto in its physical form is that the first web-page is only half the story. Often overlooked, the bottom of the page serves up a link to a second page – the principles of Agile, which get a little more concrete and explanatory. Figure 1.3 below is the second page of the Agile Manifesto:

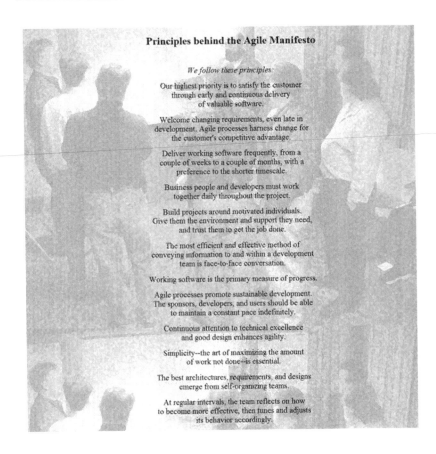

Figure 1.3 – 2nd part of the Agile Manifesto

When one looks at the above "definition" of Agile, one can intuitively understand that these are good concepts. But the important question is why? To explore the nature of this question, we must first understand the nature of "knowing" and how this relates to belief systems.

1.1 – Tacit Knowledge

Two types of knowledge exist – explicit knowledge (also known as "focal awareness" in Cognitive Sciences), and tacit knowledge ("subsidiary awareness") [2]. With tacit knowledge, people are not often aware of the knowledge they possess or how it can be valuable to others. An iceberg metaphor is typically used to describe the distribution of knowledge that people have related to a specific area.

As shown in Figure 1.4, explicit knowledge is the part above the waterline that we see; tacit knowledge is the part below the waterline and much broader and deeper.

Figure 1.4 – Tacit Knowledge Metaphor

The majority of software engineering knowledge remains tacit. Many books have been written on the subject, but these books represent an exception rather than the mainstream of the experience garnered by broad and diverse software developments. Every so often, a "thought leader" will attempt to capture and codify his or her knowledge and experience in a book or paper. But the experiences that are written about typically do not test the extremes of the problem spaces that organizations find themselves confronted. And the vast majority of accrued knowledge remains unpublished, even with the sea of literature to keep up with.

One aspect of tacit knowledge that seems critical, whether it be for the advancement of the state of the practice in software engineering, or the simple conveyance of knowledge about a business problem so that it can be enacted in software, is that the understanding of tacit knowledge and its' transfer among individuals requires <u>trust</u>. This is the essence of the third value statement of the Agile Manifesto *"Customer Collaboration over Contract Negotiations"*. In other words, it is very difficult to extract tacit or intuitive knowledge (the majority of the knowledge possessed) from a business stakeholder in a low trust environment. Documents and other approaches attempt to facilitate the persistence of knowledge. Yet the persistence medium of written documents and models does nothing to address the underlying conveyance dynamics, which with tacit knowledge requires trust, not protocol or structure. This leads to the second value statement of the manifesto which yields a more efficient means of conveying knowledge about the accuracy of demand fulfillment– *"Working Software over Comprehensive Documentation"*.

When one looks at the software engineering body-of-knowledge (BOK) landscape, one finds a plethora of codified knowledge in the form of guidelines, standards, templates, heuristics, patterns, best practices and processes. Figure 1.5 below illustrates what could be termed "method soup". It shows the combination of diverse and sometimes bloated process-ware that exists today.

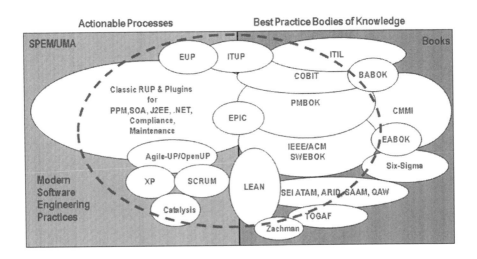

Figure 1.5 – Software Engineering Bodies of Knowledge

Each of the contributions in the above picture offer value to the world of software engineering. It would seem reasonable that integrating what is of value from each of these and discarding the extraneous or inconsistent filler is what is needed. At the very least it would make sense to reconcile overlap such that communities can normalize their perspectives. But unfortunately these bodies of knowledge remain silo's of knowledge. The silo's typically result from various academic or commercial interests, with little profit motive that would result in integration efforts. As if an emotional attachment is developed to the turf that defines the center of gravity of a BOK, the followers within the various communities propagate a differentiation philosophy. Even terms central to the domain model of each doctrine become "owned" by each community. For example, the word "governance" becomes owned by the COBIT (Control Objectives for IT) [3] framework and the auditor following. The word "change" typically is protected by the PMBOK (Project Management Body of Knowledge) [4]; and the word "service" is owned by ITIL (IT Infrastructure Library) [5] and somehow the property of the Government of the UK.

All of this leads to an *us-vs-them mentality* when these practices and bodies of knowledge are all forced to coexist within Enterprise IT. One could argue this is the largest source of waste that exists in organizations today. And with such a competitive environment, it is no wonder that low trust environments ensue. As such, software engineering knowledge transfer is at best slow - let alone collaborative.

When it comes to explaining the Agile body of knowledge, the declaration of what is a good approach to developing software says nothing in relation to business terms – NPV, DCF, IRR, or ROI. Nor does it explain the origins of these core values. In other words, the Agile Manifesto is "superstitiously declared" [6]. This does not mean that it is wrong; it just means that it represents more a value/belief structure than hard management science. Hence, the current state of Agile could best be described in a positive light as a movement. This movement has done much to educate and enlighten some of the universal truths of how software development should occur. It is just that the practices and articulations of principles remain prima-facie descriptions of what to do, and how to do it. But what lacks is the "why" such that a wide variety of contexts are provided the deep insights necessary so as to select the correct approaches at the right time.

With any movement, negative aspects are sure to emerge. These negative aspects could be described as "branding" and "dogma". In the former situation, opportunists block the knowledge transfer among diverse software engineering communities because it is profitable to do so. And the latter situation is where blind faith leads to broad stroke interpretations and purists that are more interested in maintaining the sanctity of the "club". These negative aspects of the movement have the potential to stifle evolutionary progress and free-thinking. It is to mitigate these risks that it is necessary to move Agile beyond a tacit level of understanding.

1.2 – Industry Adoption Perspectives

The IT Industry research firms monitor the progress of various technologies as they emerge at a frantic pace. C-level executives leverage these resources so as to have a fighting chance at keeping up with all that is happening in the world of such things as emerging technologies, application development, software engineering tooling and the like. Firms like Gartner Group, IDC, Forrester Research and the Burton Group all participate in the IT Market Research segment. For Gartner Group as of 2008, this has grown into a $1.3 billion business. The key point is that these researchers are paid to keep up, and their opinion is followed. One research product in particular that is followed diligently by IT Leadership is Gartner Group's *Hype Cycle* [7]. Figure 1.6 below illustrates this research product.

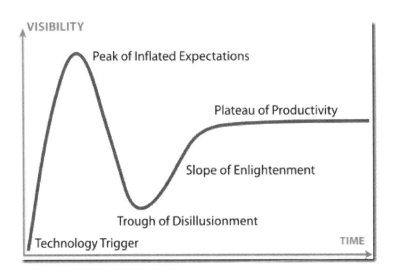

Figure 1.6 – Gartner Hype Cycle

This curve as illustrated is an assessment of the current state of expectations and "hype versus reality" for a particular technology, and shows through the use of symbols on the curve (colored circles, triangles) the opinion of the Gartner research analysts as to the time remaining to mainstream adoption. Included with the chart is an explanation of the technology and the rationale for its position in the Hype Cycle. Many Hype Cycles are published yearly, including Emerging Technologies, Architecture, BPM, Semiconductors, Smart Grid, IT Operations Management - and one for Application Development which is relevant for this book. One of the most notable Hype Cycles was for eBusiness in 1999, which predicted the burst of the dot com bubble. Figure 1.7 describes the meaning of the phases.

Hype Cycle Phases, Benefit Ratings and Maturity Levels

Table 1. Hype Cycle Phases

Phase	Definition
Technology Trigger	A breakthrough, public demonstration, product launch or other event generates significant press and industry interest.
Peak of Inflated Expectations	During this phase of overenthusiasm and unrealistic projections, a flurry of well-publicized activity by technology leaders results in some successes, but more failures, as the technology is pushed to its limits. The only enterprises making money are conference organizers and magazine publishers.
Trough of Disillusionment	Because the technology does not live up to its overinflated expectations, it rapidly becomes unfashionable. Media interest wanes, except for a few cautionary tales.
Slope of Enlightenment	Focused experimentation and solid hard work by an increasingly diverse range of organizations lead to a true understanding of the technology's applicability, risks and benefits. Commercial off-the-shelf methodologies and tools ease the development process.
Plateau of Productivity	The real-world benefits of the technology are demonstrated and accepted. Tools and methodologies are increasingly stable as they enter their second and third generations. Growing numbers of organizations feel comfortable with the reduced level of risk; the rapid growth phase of adoption begins. Approximately 20% of the technology's target audience has adopted or is adopting the technology as it enters this phase.
Years to Mainstream Adoption	The time required for the technology to reach the Plateau of Productivity.

Source: Gartner (June 2008)

Figure 1.7 – Gartner Hype Curve Defined

Figure 1.8 is the Gartner Hype Cycle for Application Development, 2008. This research describes Agile as being stuck in the "trough of disillusionment", where it has been for the last 3 years. According to Gartner, *"because the technology does not live up to its overinflated expectations, it rapidly becomes unfashionable."* To emerge from this level towards broader industry acceptance and realize the full potential of the technology, *"focused experimentation and solid hard work by an increasingly diverse range of organizations lead to a true understanding of the technologies applicability, risks and benefits."*

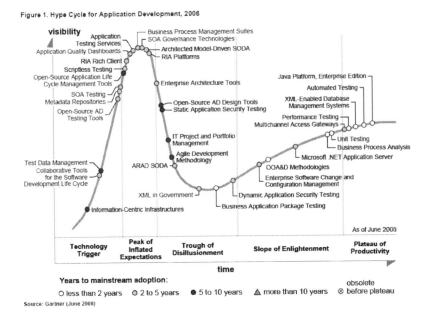

Figure 1. Hype Cycle for Application Development, 2008

Figure 1.8 Gartner Hype Cycle for Application Development, 2008

So in other words, from a business and executive stakeholder perspective, it is time for grounding Agile principles and practices in sound Management Science. This means that an exploration of contextual appropriateness needs to replace broad stroke and over-simplistic application.

1.3 – Software Delivery Project Results

Another longstanding research product followed somewhat more loosely than the previous citation is the Chaos Report from the Standish Group [8]. Every two years since 1994, this publication illustrates the status of IT delivery projects, assessing success, failures and challenges. Figure 1.9 shows the results over the time span that Standish Group has been performing this research.

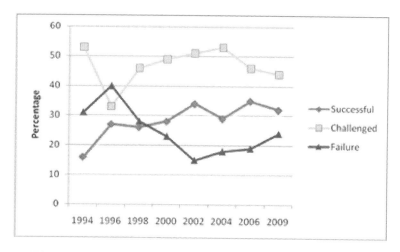

Figure 1.9 – Standish Chaos Report Results 1994 to 2009

In the above data, "Successful" means a project is completed on time and on-budget, with all the features and functions as originally specified. "Challenged" means a project is completed and operational, but over budget, over the time estimated and offers fewer features and functions than originally specified. "Failed" means the project is cancelled at some time during the development cycle.

Along with the data resulting from a large sampling of corporate IT interviewees is the summary of the current perspectives on the causes for the outcome of the projects. It should be noted that even this research work has indicated for sometime that smaller project milestones are key to successful project outcomes, consistent with the Agile Manifesto. Similarly, the top two reasons cited relate to customer collaboration and engagement. Table 1.1 illustrates a sample of these results.

Table 1.1 – Standish Group's Chaos Report

Successful		Challenged		Failure	
Factors Cited	**%**	**Factors Cited**	**%**	**Factors Cited**	**%**
1. User Involvement	15.9	1. Lack of User Input	12.8	1. Incomplete Requirements	13.1
2. Executive Management Support	13.9	2. Incomplete Requirements	12.3	2. Lack of User Involvement	12.4
3. Clear Statement of Requirements	13.0	3. Changing Requirements	11.8	3. Lack of Resources	10.6
4. Proper Planning	9.6	4. Lack of Executive Support	7.5	4. Unrealistic Expectations	9.9
5. Realistic Expectations	8.2	5. Technology/ Incompetence	7.0	5. Lack of Executive Support	9.3
6. Smaller Project Milestones	7.7	6. Lack of Resources	6.4	6. Changing Requirements	8.7
7. Competent Staff	7.2	7. Unrealistic Expectations	5.9	7. Lack of Planning	8.1
8. Ownership	6.3	8. Unclear Objectives	5.3	8. Didn't need it any longer	7.5
9. Clear vision & Objectives	2.9	9. Unrealistic timeframes	4.3	9. Lack of IT Management	6.2
10. Hard working, Focused staff	2.4	10. New Technology	3.7	10. Technology illiteracy	4.3
Other	13.9	Other	23	Other	9.9

When it comes to the next three reasons for success and the similar corollary top reasons for failure, an interesting observation can be made. Central to the success pile is clear requirements, proper planning, and realistic expectations. The first two are at odds with the philosophies articulated with the Manifesto and the nature of tacit knowledge as discussed previously. But the latter reason, "realistic expectations" is core to understanding what is probably the main reason for the perception (and therefore the reality in the minds of stakeholders and customers) of perpetual poor showing by IT delivery. Over 15 years it would appear that all the process improvement ideas, methodologies, innovations, advancements in automation and languages haven't made a dent. But it could also be argued that perhaps it is that expectations are not being set properly; and that prediction of outcomes based on "original scope" as per the definition of Success, Challenge and Failure above is the core reason. Clear statements of requirements are extremely rare and only represent an outlier of the sampling data when it comes to "initial specification". And "proper planning" only occurs when a more deterministic project is undertaken, one that is not unprecedented in its scope. Such deterministic (as opposed to stochastic) projects are rare in software engineering.

1.4 – The Problem with Predictions

The fourth value statement of the Agile Manifesto is *"Responding to Change over following a plan"*. To understand the essence of what was intended with this belief, it is instructive to understand the nature of change outside of software engineering. One such field of study that is subject to rapid change is the weather. The weather has long been studied, with various formulae and models attempting to seek an understanding. Hurricanes, for example, represent a type of weather which one could argue is worthy of prediction. The problem is that the consequences for a wrong prediction can be catastrophic. Even with the multiple computer simulation tracks that are forecasted by the National Oceanic and Atmospheric Administration (NOAA) and the National Hurricane Center (NHC) using supercomputers, at best a 3-5 day cone of uncertainty can be established. But even with this, the cone is quite large. Take hurricane Katrina for example. We know what the result of this massive storm was in hindsight. Figure 1.10 below from NOAA illustrates that as of August 25th 2005, this storm was not a major hurricane when crossing the Florida peninsula.

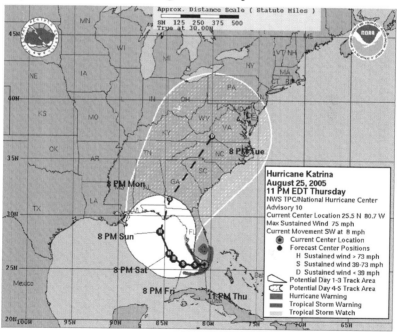

Figure 1.10 – Hurricane Katrina landfall in South Florida [9]

But within the next 48hrs this storm would drastically change course with the entire cone of landfall shifting to the west putting the city of New Orleans directly in its path. Figure 1.11 shows what Katrina looked like after emerging into the warm waters of the Gulf of Mexico where it reached the strength of 175mph or a Category 5 storm a mere 2 ½ days later.

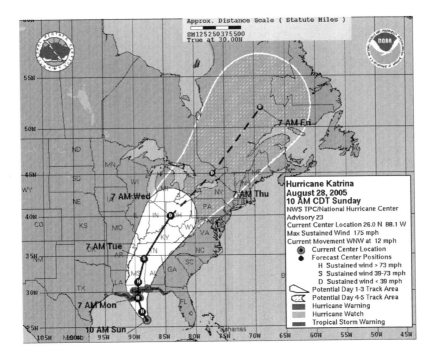

Figure 1.11 – Hurricane Katrina @ Category 5 headed at NOLA

The key point to get from this analogy is that predictions are interrelated to the concept of setting expectations, which is a core issue in software engineering. And it could be argued that the technology environment, changing business conditions, organizational dynamics of a delivery team and the churn in explicit requirements which necessarily stems from the nature of tacit knowledge are at least as complex a dynamic system as that of a hurricane. And we do not have supercomputers to try to predict where projects are going. So instead of trying to predict human beings (the most local and arguably simplest dynamic variable), the founding fathers of Agile suggested embracing the inherent change in software developments and adapting in an efficient and effective manner. Even though a more detailed explanation was lacking in the authoritative doctrine of the Agile Manifesto, one can easily agree that the reasoning is sound. The goal of this book is to explain Agile beyond anecdotal or metaphorical terms. In other words, to go beyond the *tacit* knowledge of what has been shown to work in practice. This book is also intends to put forward an idea of integrating all past knowledge into a holistic system of practices and provide an explicit knowledge foundation of how to continue evolving and improving.

Chapter 2 is focused on uncovering where Agile came from, and how it fits into the overall software engineering "sands of time". Its purpose is to illustrate that Agile is not an end, but rather a beginning. Chapter 3 is intended to provide a sound model for how and why Agile works. Systems theory has only been flirted with in the past as the metaphorical basis for modern software engineering practices. This chapter aims to put forward explicitly the dynamic systems thinking, mathematical models and tools to lay the foundation for the application of this established body of knowledge. Chapter 4 presents a domain model of modern software engineering that serves as a baseline for the third major generational branch of software engineering – SDLC 3.0 (Software Development Lifecycle 3.0). Chapter 5 builds upon this model to explain the common ground of current prominent approaches. In doing so, it seeks to bring communities together by *"calling a spade a spade"* so to speak. Chapter 6 attempts to identify the unique valuable contributions from distinct practices embraced among the various communities, and how these sometimes are de facto synonyms and nothing more. Chapter 7 discusses the topic of agility at scale, and identifies which community contributions can help address the well-known challenges that Agile has historically faced. Chapter 8 addresses how SDLC 3.0 integrates within the larger IT enterprise context that software delivery organizations live. Chapter 9 discusses the controversial first value-statement of the Agile Manifesto – *"Individuals and Interactions over Processes and Tools"*. Specifically, it discusses the realities of modern software engineering that require a softening of the anti-tool and anti-process description stance originally taken within the Agile community.

Chapter 2: Agile Archeology

Contrary to what some may believe, Agile did not just pop out of thin air. Much has been written about the various methods that have been deemed Agile and how to implement the practices contained therein. But when one looks to how these approaches evolved, only a few works describe the origins of these approaches. It is hard to believe that each of the Agile methods originated completely and uniquely from the limited scope of the authors that articulated them. In fact, it would seem reasonable that these authors were influenced by prior experience and works. Figure 2.1 illustrates the long lineage of commonly identifiable software engineering approaches. When one looks at the picture, four distinct "branches" appear which roughly correlate to the various communities that embrace the approaches and philosophies contained therein. These somewhat isolated evolutionary paths are "Waterfall" [10], "Iterative and Incremental Development – IID",

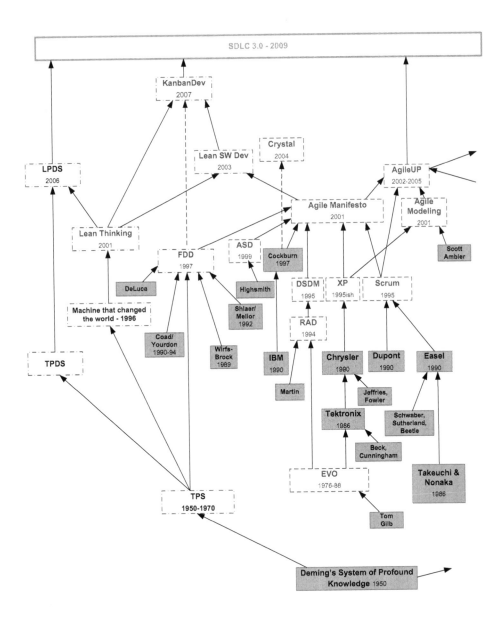

Figure 2.1 – History of Modern Software Engineering Methods

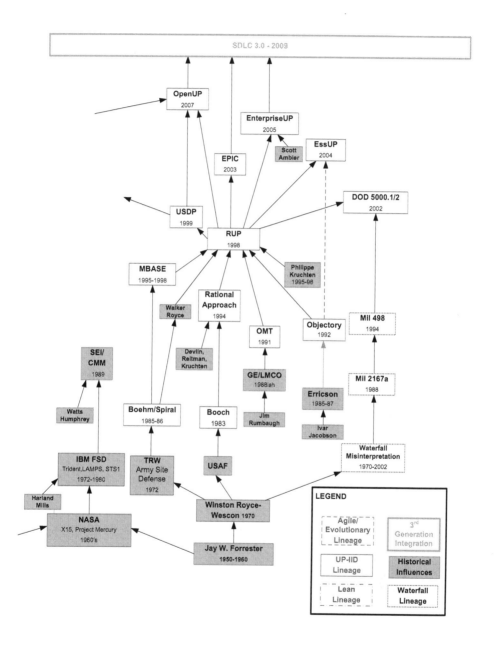

Figure 2.1 – History of Modern Software Engineering Methods

"Agile Software Development" and more recently "Lean Software Development" [11], which represents an instantiation of Lean Thinking[12] and the study of the Toyota Production System (TPS)[13]. From the picture, one can argue that much if not all the experiences codified into methods traces back to much earlier ideas and management principles as indicated by references to the likes of W. Edwards Deming[14] and Jay W. Forrester [15]. And from these earliest roots, one can abstract only two major differentiating generations or "major branches" of software engineering approach (sometimes synonymous with "Software or System's Development Lifecycle – SDLC). The first is "SDLC 1.0 - Waterfall", and the second is what could be termed "SDLC 2.0 – the Iterative Method Wars" which includes all other approaches including Agile.

The point of understanding history is one of context. As one can see, the items in the middle are those that are commonly included within the Agile "family". But these methods share a common ancestry. The question is how and why did a branch occur? Was there a fundamental difference in issues faced by the projects that resulted in the differing articulations of practices, or was it simply personal preference or philosophical/cultural differences. The benefit of looking to the past and the various evolutionary tracks is to concretely form a basis of whether natural selection of the approaches has occurred, with the better approach prevailing, or whether the industry has lost a valuable set of practices in the ensuing competition. It is this latter scenario that is associated with the large order *us-vs-them* waste that must be eliminated.

2.1 – In the beginning there was the "Accidental Waterfall"

It took a while for the conversation to finally hinge around fact when it comes to the notorious "Waterfall" methodology. In fact there wasn't even supposed to be a Waterfall approach at all. This is the accident that ensued from a lack of due diligence by the industry in failing to completely read and properly interpret the seminal paper of Winston Royce in 1970. As is common in the written word, the articulation was taken the wrong way for what one could assume are reasons of simplicity, or worse – the ability to delay the day of reckoning by projects that were doomed to fail. But ironically it is the Waterfall paper that was one of the first published papers that advocated the practice of iterative development, risk reduction and accruing learning value from working software. And so one can rather controversially state that the origins of the Agile movement was the Waterfall – the correct interpretation of the paper. Figure 2.2 illustrates the waterfall approach, which correctly shows the feedback loops that occur in real projects. The dashed lines were historically dropped which led to the accident we now love to mock.

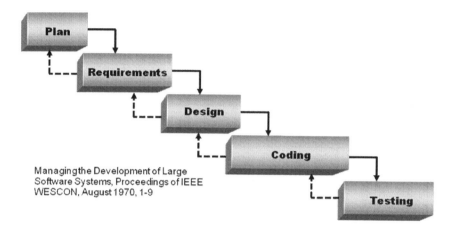

Managing the Development of Large
Software Systems, Proceedings of IEEE
WESCON, August 1970, 1-9

Figure 2.2 – The "Waterfall" Approach

It is amazing how passionate the defense of Waterfall is among what some term "Traditionalists". Certain attempts have been waged to identify when and why this ill-conceived approach makes sense. These can invariably be tied to what the Lean Thinking world calls *Type II muda* – that is waste that is necessary due to the way work is currently performed. If armed with this understanding, insightful managers might make the connection that work doesn't have to be performed this way and therefore waste can be eliminated. To understand the type of waste that is associated with this approach, the body of knowledge known as "Theory of Constraints – ToC"[16] is sometimes referenced. Stemming predominantly from Industrial Engineering, a common approach taken to identify process performance problems in the course of engaging in process improvement is a *VATI analysis*. VATI refers to the different process configuration types that exist in manufacturing. Figure 2.3 illustrates the various process configurations:

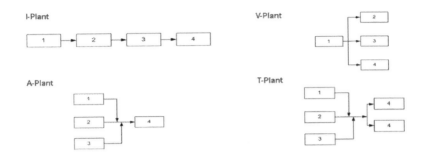

Figure 2.3 – Plant types from ToC

When one looks at the misinterpretation of the waterfall, one can easily see that it represents a single-pass serial and batched method. From ToC, this is called an I-Plant, and represents the slowest and simplest process configuration. This contrasts the other process configurations, which manifest concurrency. So when thinking in these terms, it is hard to argue for the slowest process configuration when the only benefit is its inherent simplicity and lack of integration/coordination complexity. Modern software engineering and the infrastructure supporting it enables more robust process configurations.

Early after the turn of the millennium, the effects of Clinger Cohen (also known as the Federal Acquisition Reform Act of 1996)[17] started to take hold. Commercial and industrial influences began to have more and more effect on the strategies applied to the large scale software engineering endeavours of the US Federal Government, especially the US Department of Defense (DOD). Due to the climate of favouring acquisition of industry "best practices" and approaches over home-grown methodology (which was notorious within DOD circles), study ensued on some of the largest programs on how to introduce and socialize evolutionary and iterative practices. These early transformational efforts would lead to admonishment by the Under Secretary of Defense to stop using single-pass, serial and batch oriented acquisition strategies[18]. Figure 2.4 captures the tone of this communication.

THE UNDER SECRETARY OF DEFENSE
3010 DEFENSE PENTAGON
WASHINGTON, DC 20301-3010

APR 1 2 2002

ACQUISITION,
TECHNOLOGY
AND LOGISTICS

MEMORANDUM FOR SECRETARIES OF THE MILITARY DEPARTMENTS
CHAIRMAN OF THE JOINT CHIEFS OF STAFF
UNDER SECRETARIES OF DEFENSE
ASSISTANT SECRETARIES OF DEFENSE
INSPECTOR GENERAL, DEPARTMENT OF DEFENSE
GENERAL COUNSEL, DEPARTMENT OF DEFENSE
DIRECTORS OF THE DEFENSE AGENCIES

SUBJECT: Evolutionary Acquisition and Spiral Development

Since the publication of DoD Directive 5000.1 and DoD Instruction 5000.2, in which the Department established a preference for the use of evolutionary acquisition strategies relying on a spiral development process, there has been some confusion about what these terms mean and how spiral development impacts various processes such as contracting and requirements generation that interface with an evolutionary acquisition strategy. The purpose of this memorandum is to address those questions.

Evolutionary acquisition and spiral development are methods that will allow us to reduce our cycle time and speed the delivery of advanced capability to our warfighters. These approaches are designed to develop and field demonstrated technologies for both hardware and software in manageable pieces. Evolutionary acquisition and spiral development also allow insertion of new technologies and capabilities over time.

Figure 2.4 – Effective Death of the Waterfall Misinterpretation

In essence, the habits that took so long to cease were finally "ordered". This was significant, as DOD programs were one of the largest sources that perpetuated the Waterfall accident. Large Defense contractors and the inherent contractual basis for the organizational relationships that ensued are at the heart of the *"Customer collaboration over contract negotiations"* value statement of the Manifesto. The contractual nature of DOD programs is typically cited as the fundamental reason for the tendency towards the big specification, big plan, firm commitment and the command and control style of management. The funny thing is that a contract is supposed to be a formalized relationship of trust – but nothing of the sort results in these programs. Instead of trust, GANTT charts that surround entire floors of buildings resulted to provide "visibility" into the programs. You can envision teams of highly priced consultants running around multiple times a day with scotch tape to update their "big visible charts".

2.2 – SDLC 2.0: Different branches of Iterative / Incremental Development

What could be termed the "second generation" of software engineering methods or "SDLC 2.0" evolved from the experiences of early software development and (mis) application of the Waterfall approach. Well published failures and poor results in software engineering in contrast to the advancements in the complementary computing hardware world led to research study. One of these centers of funded study was at the University of Southern California (USC) and the research agenda of Barry Boehm. One early pre-cursor to commonplace Agile methods was the Spiral [19], risk-driven approach developed through experience and study at TRW. It should be noted that Winston Royce and his son Walker Royce were heavily involved with TRW in the Defense contractor space. Figure 2.5 illustrates the Spiral model.

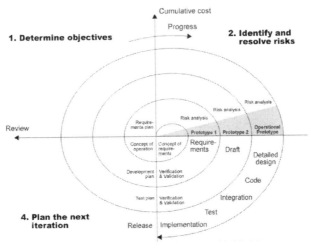

Figure 2.5 – Spiral Model

Another early iterative development method is Evo[20], in which Tom Gilb articulated and amplified on the original incremental intentions of Winston Royce's waterfall. Figure 2.6 illustrates the lifecycle of Evo.

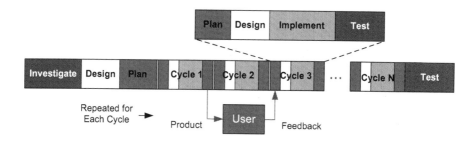

Figure 2.6 – EVO

Evo is often seen as the early origins of Agile, as it focuses on a high frequency, value-centric approach to prioritizing the chunks of software growth. This emphasis is in contrast with the early risk reduction theme of the Spiral articulation, and more in line with the Agile works which did not contemplate the issue of "technical debt" and what can ensue when customers/product owners overly skew value over risk due to limited insight into technical complexity. But notice here that there are up-front "Investigate", "Design", and "Plan" periods of time, similar to the up-front risk mitigation approaches stemming from the Spiral approach.

Each of these approaches zeroed in on critical aspects that are now common in the various offshoots. From these early origins, many method descriptions resulted from over 25 years of studying the root causes of why software engineering could not establish the kind of performance results that other industries have achieved in relation to process improvement. Expansion into studying componentization, modifiability and extensibility of software quickly followed. With the maturing of the mechanisms and paradigms for the actual construction/fabrication of the basic elements of software maturing and consolidating, the industry then evolved to focus on management aspects of the software production problem.

With all the fragmentation of describing processes and practices, two distinct instances of consolidation have occurred during the Iterative and Evolutionary period. These are important in that they were attempts to integrate prior knowledge. However in both instances, these were arguably driven by commercial interests rather than for advancing the industry.

The first example where we can see integration in modern software engineering and iterative development history was the consolidation strategy at Rational Software Corporation. Faced with fragmentation, especially within the Object Oriented Analysis & Design method subset space, and driven arguably by the commercial interests of selling CASE tools (computer assisted software engineering) tools, integration of three prominent approaches to software engineering – OMT (Object Modeling Technique) [21], the Booch Method[22] and Objectory[23] were bound into a novel web-delivered mechanism that we now know as the Rational Unified Process (RUP) [24]. This product for sale was quickly followed by a non-productized articulation in the book The Unified Software Development Process[25] (USDP or Unified Process-UP for short). Both represent the integration of a large amount of experience from the leading consultants (called Tech Reps at Rational) such as CEO Mike Devlin, CTO Rich Reitman, Chief Scientist Grady Booch, well known methodologist and linguist Jim Rumbaugh, and acquired Objectory AB founder Ivar Jacobson (these latter "three amigos" credited with the UML – Unified Modeling Language[26]). The RUP web-delivered product development would be led by Philippe Kruchten with practice content contributions from other acquired company thought leaders like Dean Leffingwell (Requisite Inc.) and Brian White (Pure Atria).

These two complementary works – the Unified Modeling Language and the Unified Process would achieve mindshare dominance in the late 1990's and early 2000's. But this would not last forever, as a group of methodologists from non-Rational circles left out of the party would arguably emulate the same strategy and form the "Agile Alliance". This non-Rational club would highlight what they disliked from the heavily commercialized thrust and the recurring failure patterns such as the blind usage of heavyweight CASE-tools. What would also be articulated within the Agile Manifesto would be a reference to bloated process-ware, a perception that could directly be attributed to the RUP product, which unlike its underlying meta-model and book would grow rather unwieldy, with over 35 overly specialized roles (due to the object-oriented decomposition that was the result of its architected nature), 99 or so artifacts/work products which were commonly manifested as documents, and a work breakdown structure (WBS) that contains over 174 or so activities and tasks, commonly interpreted as prescriptive and overly sequenced.

As we will discuss later, each of these two major consolidations were similar and yet different, representing valuable experience from different corporations. Yet they have devolved into competitive forces that one could argue has been less than productive for the industry.

2.2.1 – Unified Process / MBASE

Coincidental with the strategic objective of consolidating the fragmenting Object-Oriented Analysis & Design methodology communities in the late 1990's, the adoption of USC's Model Based Architecting and Software Engineering – MBASE[27] phase structure was intended to make explicit the IT Investment Governance structure. Contrary to incorrect interpretation as a work-product based waterfall, the MBASE phases were intended to enforce themes of effort on a timeline that would enable investments to be abandoned if unfeasible, either technically or economically. As a natural progression of the Spiral approach, this risk confrontive approach to work-breakdown-structure was focused on achieving stability early such that a reasonable certainty of investment outcome could occur. To achieve this, Software Architecture as a centerpiece feature of the approach leverages a specialized stakeholder community to exercise investment governance. To make potentially large-scale stakeholder community governance feasible, discrete phase assessments and associated gates are leveraged. This contrasts with the fluid governance frequency effected through a single governance authority as seen with Agile approaches. Figure 2.7 is commonly how the RUP or the underlying Unified Process is articulated at a high level.

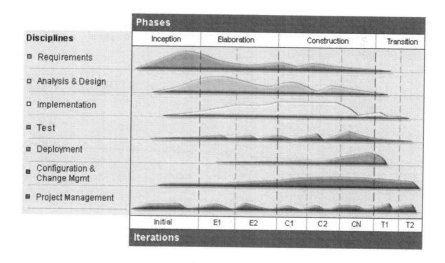

Figure 2.7 – Unified Process "Humpty-back" Chart

The introduction of the word "phases" is typically ammunition for Agilist's that claim that UP is a Waterfall variant. But as discussed, the phases and the iterations contained within these themed periods of time are no different than Agile approaches, except for that they are explicit. Each iteration still results in tested, working software for use in feedback by business representatives (or at least that is what is supposed to happen). The disciplines on the left represent cohesive specializations of labor and associated project effort types and work output. Each discipline collaborates with other disciplines to yield working software per iteration. This effort expenditure is articulated at the intersection of the iterations through the use of intensity charts (the colored humps). These specialized "swim-lanes" of collaboration are also in conflict within some Agile community circles, as a generalist-only, developer centric mentality typically accompanies the decomposition of work and therefore articulation of Agile processes.

As discussed earlier, the approach to take the MBASE approach was expanded with the Rational Unified Process commercial product. As a product for sale, much elaboration of the core attributes of a Unified Process based approach ensued to attempt to add more "features" and obviously sell more copies. This resulted in the RUP evolving towards a framework/scale-down strategy of practices, roles and work products. In essence, the RUP was to be treated as a framework, where instantiation of practices and process elements was intended to be performed to match the context. But achieving this *development case* for a project became too unwieldy and confusing for most apprentices to the method. As a process framework, it gained a reputation as being bloated method-ware which was prescriptive, similar to prior large-scale method-ware examples from the 1980's.

More recent efforts have attempted to accentuate the core value proposition of the UP with the creation of OpenUP[28]. The efforts of the Eclipse Foundation have attempted to reverse the top-down tailoring strategy into a minimal core approach to leveraging the core architecture-centric features. Reduction of specialization has resulted in less fragmentation of the work product base and therefore the perception of the method as being document-centric. Figure 2.8 illustrates the high-level visual articulation of OpenUP.

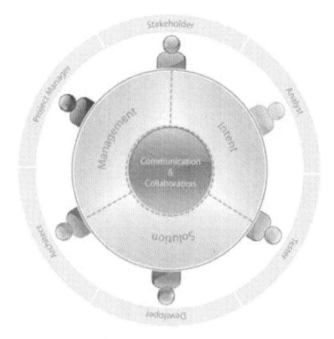

Figure 2.8 –OpenUP

Efforts to stop the prescriptive myth have occurred through the Essential UP (EssUP)[29], which tries to promote a practice-orientation as opposed to a process-centric WBS. And valuable contributions related to integrating UP into the broader enterprise have resulted in the Enterprise UP (EUP)[30].

2.2.2 – Agile Methods (Scrum, Extreme Programming)

The two dominant Agile approaches resulted from developer-centric frustrations with tool vendors and a perception of heavyweight ivory tower methodologists who had never developed a line of code in their life. Scrum[31], stemming originally from PatientKeeper with a little help from Dupont, and eXtreme Programming (XP) [32] arising from Techtronix and Chrysler IT, were intended to be a lobby against non-value add anti-patterns like command & control project management and big requirements up-front typical of the Waterfall approach. It established a community which attained critical mass and an effective voice for change from established circles intent on developing ancillary stuff at the expense of delivering real and lasting IT value.

XP was arguably the first method deemed to be "Agile". Figure 2.9 illustrates the meta-model of practices that make up the approach.

Figure 2.9 – Extreme Programming (XP)

The key tenets of this approach that were unique was a focus on increasing the frequency of feedback from working software into 2-week intervals. And it focused on waste reduction in the form of lightweight requirements engineering practices while favoring co-location with the business, focus on the core value-adding activities delivered by developers, and Theory Y Management[34]. The approach was articulated to be holistic in that it required all practices to be performed as a "system of practices", each working together [33].

Scrum, albeit articulated around the same time as XP, gained popularity afterwards. As an empirical Project Management approach, Scrum sought to focus on simplified approaches to the Project Management topics of planning, estimation, progress monitoring and reporting. Iteration frequency was defined as fixed at 30-day durations, presumably in an effort to linearize the feedback-loop to enable a simple first derivative metric based on scope. The Scrum approach first used the term velocity. Recent practice within the Agile community is to apply Scrum as the project management framework, with XP practices leveraged for the other disciplines. Figure 2.10 illustrates the central concepts of Scrum.

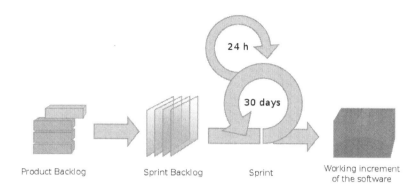

Figure 2.10 – Scrum

One of the most notable elements of Scrum is the use of lightweight queue-based scope management and work breakdown mechanisms. Typically implemented in low-tech form, the *Product Backlog* serves as a customer managed queue of demand requests for the product. When a *Sprint* is launched (the term for the 30 day fixed time-boxed iteration) just-in-time planning occurs (also known as rolling-wave planning) in a similar queue-based approach. The queue for work management for the Sprint is called a *Sprint Backlog*. Also notable and very visible within Scrum is the notion of the *Daily Scrum* meeting. This meeting is another term for a daily standup, except that it is the team that is participating and sharing coordination information, not a central project manager. In Scrum, the closest thing to a Project Manager who would typically hold daily standup meetings is called the Scrum Master, who acts more as a facilitator and runs interference for the core team when blocks or issues arise.

2.2.3 – Lean Software Development - FDD

Another modern software engineering approach commonly branded as being Agile actually has affinity closer to the principles and practices of Lean Thinking. Feature Driven Development (FDD)[35] emerged out of the experiences of Peter Coad, Jeff Le Luca and others in 1997, before the Agile term and the Agile Manifesto were even created. They were tasked to salvage a project to build a large commercial lending system in Singapore (50 people, 15months, $20M). This project was leveraging a waterfall lifecycle and was in trouble. Incremental development practices were incorporated, as well as engineering techniques like domain modeling to resurrect the effort. Ultimately the project was turned around, and success was attributed to what is commonly known as FDD. Figure 2.11 illustrates the core FDD approach:

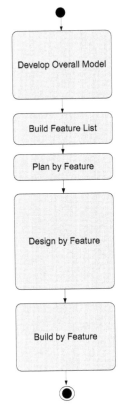

Figure 2.11 – Feature-Driven Development (FDD)

The linkage with Lean comes in the form of the advocacy to perform "micro-incremental" development in a one-piece flow manner. In other words, make development increments small and minimize batching. As such, it is sometimes referred to as "iteration-less" development, as there is no concept of iterations in FDD, only increments. Features serve as the user identifiable chunks of the desired system, and the goal is to arrive at features that are minimal or can stand on their own and are valuable by themselves. After a reasonably short period of time to set the stage by establishing the team, identifying an overall solution approach, and collecting enough understanding of the desired features, an ongoing focus to establish a rhythm and flow of completing and delivering features occurs. Monitoring of progress also leverages the typical Lean Manufacturing Cumulative Flow Diagram.

As with anything in the continuous evolution of software engineering techniques, Features as the central requirements/scope elaboration mechanism share a common minimalist philosophy with the Agile approaches when it comes to Requirements Engineering– most notable XP User Stories. Features are written using a simple grammatical structure with the following template used for their construction:

<action> [a | the] <result> [of | to | for | from | ...] <object> [with | for | of | ...] <parameters>

An illustrative example might look like the following:

verify the 2a-7 compliance for a given trade order (for a 7/7 municipal bond)

Features leveraging this approach lead to the construction and mapping to a problem domain model, which can be thought of as a visual glossary and the beginnings of the design.

The term "Lean" stems from the study of the works of the MIT International Vehicle Program. This program studied the emerging competitive dominance trends of the Japanese auto manufacturers, especially Toyota, and resulted in the books *The Machine that Changed the World* by James Womack, Daniel Jones and Daniel Roos[36], and *The Toyota Way* by Jeffrey Liker[37]. These books later resulted in the book *Lean Thinking* by James Womack and Daniel Jones. This latter book represents the abstraction of a set of core principles that can be applied to industries beyond manufacturing, and is a direct result of the study of what is known as the Toyota Production System. Figure 2.12 illustrates Taiichi Ohno's TPS "House".

Figure 2.12 – TPS House

The first usage of the term "Lean Software Development" was articulated in the book of the same name by Tom and Mary Poppendieck. It represents an application of the Lean Thinking principles that were abstracted to software development. The resulting Lean Thinking abstraction applied to Software Development resulted in a description of 22 management tools:

Eliminate Waste

Tool 1: Seeing Waste

Tool 2: Value Stream Mapping

Amplify Learning

Tool 3: Feedback

Tool 4: Iterations

Tool 5: Synchronization

Tool 6: Set-based Development

Decide as Late as Possible

Tool 7: Options Thinking

Tool 8: The Last Responsible Moment

Tool 9: Making Decisions

Deliver as Fast as Possible

Tool 10: Pull Systems

Tool 11: Queuing Theory

Tool 12: Cost of Delay

Empower the Team

Tool 13: Self Determination

Tool 14: Motivation

Tool 15: Leadership

Tool 16: Expertise

Build Integrity In

Tool 17: Perceived Integrity

Tool 18: Conceptual Integrity

Tool 19: Refactoring

Tool 20: Testing

See the Whole

Tool 21: Measurements

Tool 22: Contracts

Following the trend of the study of Lean, recent innovations have occurred in what loosely has been termed "Kanban Development"[38]. Promoted by methodologists such as David Anderson and driven partly by experience of usage at Microsoft, this approach represents a renewed study of Feature-driven development in conjunction with the Work-in-

Progress (WIP) limiting mechanisms leveraged within TPS. Figure 2.13 illustrates a conceptual view of how WIP is limited through the use of the "Kanban" or card mechanism at Toyota. As will be discussed later in Chapter 7, different physical manifestations of this concept are possible while still leveraging the queuing theory that is the basis for why it optimizes productivity.

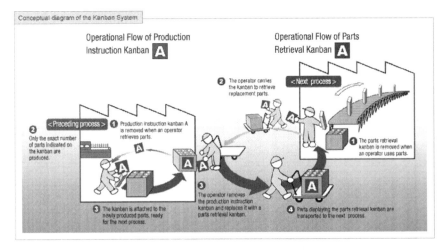

Figure 2.13 – Conceptual Diagram of a Kanban System[39]

2.2.4 – The Hybrids (Agile-UP & Lean-Agile)

Even within a climate of considerable fragmentation, with participants trying to "out iterative" or "out Agile" each other, examples of pragmatism have actually occurred within the SDLC 2.0 period. Driven by experiences on-the-ground from various practitioners typically at the fringes within any one of the above communities, hybrid approaches have emerged. These branded approaches attempt to leverage different practices that span two differing communities in an attempt to address project needs. Such a pragmatic strategy typical forms when practitioners are faced with project realities in which pure or "normal" practices just won't work. These challenges have typically been problems of scale, management or business culture or geographical distribution.

The first articulation of a hybrid approach was with the Agile-UP by Scott Ambler[40,] , which attempts to reduce the role, work product and discipline count while still retaining UP's core practices, something similar to the efforts of Open-UP. The Agile-UP approach advocates leveraging any Agile practice that makes sense for the project context, like Test-driven Development, or Continuous Integration. And from its origins in Agile Modeling, it infuses the practice of lightweight visual reasoning.

A second articulation of an Agile-UP was leveraged by Valtech and Craig Larman[41]. This approach seeks to leverage the architecture-centric governance structure of the Unified Process and the Use Case practices for driving iterative and incremental development. But it attempts to improve upon the Objectory-based OOAD approach that is within the pure Unified Process incarnations with a Catalysis-based approach[42] in an effort to improve the interaction between Analysis and Design. And this instance of Agile-UP also infuses Scrum project management, such that its practices and specifically time-boxed iterations as opposed to deliverable-based iterations are favored.

Another example of a hybrid approach emerging is Lean Agile. One articulation of this combination has been branded "Scrum-ban" by Corey Ladas[43], which seeks to enhance throughput by leveraging most Scrum practices within an iteration that has a batch size of one. It is called Scrum-ban because it leverages the Lean practice of Kanban to limit WIP and therefore minimize cycle time.

2.3 – SDLC 3.0: Time for a Rebase

A "re-Base" is a term that is common within configuration management circles. It represents a syncing of a branch or codeline from another branch. Typically, code on a mainline branch is labelled, and then everyone syncs or reBase's to that stable set of elements or "configuration" periodically so as to not run into integration breakage. The longer that code can drift / diverge in isolation, the more the chance of breakage upon re-synchronization. Resolving merge conflicts is the price that is paid for the benefits of parallel development, and the longer isolation occurs without a merge, the more complex and costly is the synchronization.

In the case of the world of software delivery methodology, the 1.0 generation branch (Waterfall) is long overdue to be retired. It has run parallel to the 2.0 generation branches (iterative/incremental development) for a long time. Additionally, the second generation branching is long overdue for re-synching. Figure 2.14 below illustrates the suggested parallel development strategy for software delivery methodology (SDLC).

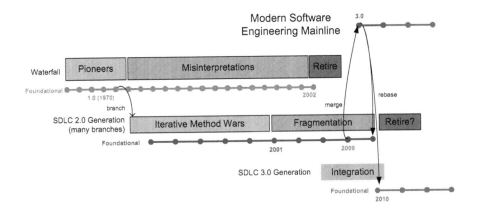

Figure 2.14 – Software Engineering Method Branching

The net result of this high degree of *isolation* and lack of *integration* is the pedantic debates, the rampant *us-vs-them mud-slinging*, and the tunnel-vision that is hindering the advancement of the profession. And all of this amounts to extremely high-order waste, Type 1 (unnecessary) muda. Pedantic debate about the various approaches is of no value to the customer. The mainline value-stream is software engineering, not one of the generational branches or sub-branches (the various flavours within a community). It is time to reduce the "code drift" that has resulted from the SDLC 2.0 iterative method wars, and also it is time to formally retire SDLC 1.0 – the accidental Waterfall misinterpretation.

"SDLC 3.0" is intended to inspire the notion of a third generation label on the mainline of SDLC approaches. As a major release identifier, it indicates that something fundamental warrants a new major release branch. This fundamental value proposition is the integration of all the past experience within a foundational environment of software engineering management science. No one lineage provides all the proven practices and experience. But modern IT environments are faced with all the problems that are addressed by the various practices/patterns. So instead of selecting an entire method to solve a delivery process problem, selecting the more atomic practices from multiple methods would seem to be a more reasonable approach.

SDLC 3.0 integrates all this past experience into a coherent new baseline for future evolution to occur. It encapsulates a focus on integration within a holistic IT value-stream; a focus on acquisition leveraging real-options theory; a focus on organizational system dynamics to apply the correct negative-feedback strategy during the various stages of a products lifecycle; focus on pull and flow; a focus on waste reduction; and a focus on Theory-Y management. Instead of having locally optimized genre's or cliques of evolving software engineering expertise, a reBase to SDLC 3.0 seeks to integrate, harmonize and heal the competitive wounds of the past.

Software engineering has evolved (in some strange and interesting ways) over the past 50 years, and it will evolve for the next 50 years. By establishing a baseline in the year 2010, the hope is that constructive innovations, enhancements and defect resolution can occur in a way that adds to a single body of knowledge. The purpose of the label SDLC 3.0 is for instilling the notion that additions to software engineering should be identified in a similar fashion as to how we identify versions of software. One could envision SDLC 3.1, 3.2, 4.0 and so on. This leads to a core principle of SDLC 3.0 – **Evolving**.

The next chapter will attempt to underpin the essence of modern software engineering with concrete explanations as to why various practices work. This includes most notably Agile, but is equally applicable to the other modern communities of practice. By taking Agile beyond the anecdotal and tacit level of understanding, this book seeks to enable all modern software engineering communities to rally around an indisputable basis for why various aspects of their heart-felt practices work.

Chapter 3: Understanding Agile using System's Theory

"I think you should be more explicit here in step two."

from *What's so Funny about Science?* by Sidney Harris (1977)

Within the software engineering community, the application of other bodies of knowledge from other industries is accelerating. Agile implicitly leverages insights from such areas as organizational psychology, sociology and cognitive sciences. Similar to these areas of insight, dynamic systems theory, queuing theory, industrial engineering and real options theory have remained implicit or are just emerging in their use to explain the origins of the Agile belief structure. This is probably due to a lack of diversity among those participating within the community. What is needed is not homogeneity of thought, but rather participation from people having differing knowledge backgrounds. Only recently have people started engaging from outside the Agile community, challenging the established dogma in search of deeper meaning and explanation. Only through this critical study of Agile will the practices achieve widespread acceptance as per the Gartner lifecycle.

To address the industry research perspective that Agile is somehow stalled, it is important to explain modern software engineering in a way that is not bound to philosophical differences, political agenda or commercial interests. The IT industry generally agrees that Agile works. But debates still rage over which approach is better, what is "deemed" Agile and what is not. If someone would just explain in a credible way the "why" of the deeming rules, a great amount of lost productivity could be eliminated and adoption would accelerate.

This chapter attempts to ground the definition of Agile using a longstanding mathematical basis and applied science (engineering) metaphors to help enable Agile to address some of the outstanding questions and issues.

3.1 – The Problems with Existing Models

Frederick Winslow Taylor introduced the Scientific Management philosophy through his time studies [44] going as far back as the late nineteenth century. The intent was to provide rigor and structure through empirical methods around how to approach management and improve labor productivity. While some of the beliefs are controversial related to the deterministic nature of the metaphors applied, the focus on explaining process improvement through study and empirical data is generally agreeable. Sometimes referred to as being the first management consultant, his work would be continued with the likes of Henry Gantt which later led to the Gantt Chart and the Critical Path Method (CPM) [45]. Somehow along the way, Scientific Management took on an objective that was laced with the ability to predict outcomes – deterministically. This is the root of the raging debate between "Traditionalists" and "Agilists". While the outgrowth of Taylors work has not proven successful, the ideal of grounding management practice in science remains sound.

One of the areas that is the result of the outgrowth of the CPM and techniques based on predictive planning is Earned Value Management (EVM) [46]. EVM emerged from the United States Government and over time has become a contracting requirement of the Office of Management and Budget. This oversight organization of government procurement made EVM a requirement for anyone who wished to do project delivery contracting with the United States government. In

1998, it was codified into a standard - ANSI/EIA 748. It is now extremely widespread and common within project management discipline, and a central practice underpinning the Project Management Institutes' PMBOK. Figure 3.1 illustrates the key elements of EVM.

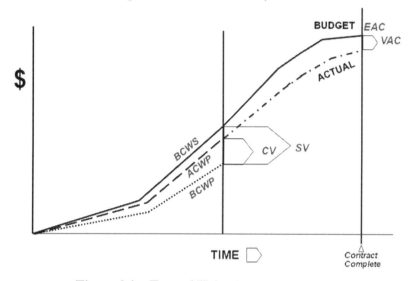

Figure 3.1 – Earned Value Management

Earned value management calculates the Budgeted Cost of Work Scheduled at the outset of the project, and tracks Actual Cost of Work Performed (ACWP) and Budgeted Cost of Work Performed (BCWP) to determine project health - Cost Variance (CV) and Schedule Variance (SV). At the end of a project we are left with Variance at Completion (VAC) which is assessed against a baselined Estimate at Completion (EAC). The calculation of these values is based on a detailed project schedule and plan established and baselined at the onset of the project, with the expectation of project health based on these predictions. This planning is established for the *entire* project, not the *horizon of visibility*, and has a funny way of being cast in stone by the stakeholders who approve the project using it as the basis for investment.

One of the main contributors to this approach and standard was Northrop Grumman. As an extremely large defense contractor, their methodologists were heavily motivated to actively participate in shaping the standard practice around progress status reporting. But even this organization has observed something that is problematic with the standard [47]. Specifically, Earned Value Management does not include logical scope (features and functionality) in its definition (the value that customers are paying for). Budgeted Cost of Work Performed (BCWP) tracks work, not realized logical scope. Work is not the same as features or functionality. The team could be busy performing tasks that have no real relevance to what the customer is paying for – muda in Lean terms. Doing busy work is not the same as delivering working software. And if following a "Waterfall" approach, this fact does not become apparent until the Cost Variance and Schedule Variance begin to widen drastically. Northrop suggests integrating scope into EVM through the integration of EIA 731 – Systems Engineering Capability Model [48]. Specifically inclusion of Technical Performance Measures (TPMs) is advocated.

EVM could be described as a "model" used for understanding the execution of software projects. It includes mathematical formulae which are intended to provide insights into project dynamics. However as will be discussed, the model does not take into consideration feedback. It is an Open-Loop system model.

Another parametric model of IT delivery projects is the Constructive Cost Model (COCOMO-II) [49]. Figure 3.2 illustrates this mathematical model of software engineering economics and effort estimation.

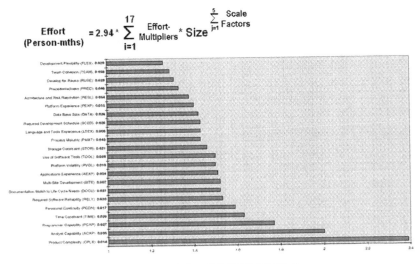

Figure 3.2 – COCOMO II [49]

This model is leveraged for the estimation of projects and was developed through the research activity at the University of Southern California – Center for Software Engineering by Barry Boehm and his research team. The model contains 22 parameters which attempt to define the nature of the project context which is being studied. The parameters are configured into a simple algebraic formula which shows some degree of correlation to actual observed project results. This evolving data set is leveraged through Bayesian techniques to continually calibrate the parameters as more data is collected through completed projects.

Whether you believe the nature of the parameters accurately captures the complexity dimensions of modern software development projects, or whether it just represents an extremely oversimplified model of reality (which is what models are anyways – representations of reality), another problem exists with this very popular model. When looking at the model for usage in proactively determining project health, the one central variable of a dynamic system is missing – time. Nowhere does "t" exist in the model. However, it is implicit in the model, and this concept has been alluded to in some of the accompanying graphs regarding estimation accuracy. Figure 3.3 shows the notion of the confidence intervals related to the usage of the COCOMO II model.

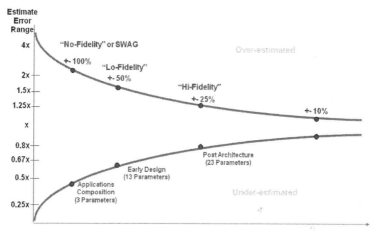

Figure 3.3 – COCOMO II Confidence Intervals

Time is discretely accommodated through the use of the three different models that are based on information accrued at a point in time during the project delivery. The slope of the accuracy boundary illustrates the convergence on the stable estimate between the three discrete points where the model is leveraged. Too often however, project stakeholders misuse the models, and a "fire and forget" estimate up front ends up being the only one leveraged, often with misrepresented estimate ranges presented to win the work.

In both of these two "models", the overlying theme is one of trying to understand how projects work so that proactive measures can be taken to influence/improve project outcomes. But projects are much more complex than these simple models would indicate. And herein lies the problem. While modeling is necessary to better understand and influence software delivery projects, the expectations that are set by using such trivial models and formulae can cause more harm than good. They give the impression of accuracy and predictive capability. Instead, what is needed is a new model that embraces the inherent complexity of modern software engineering. And it just so happens that these very models exist from other fields of study.

3.2 – Systems Theory

Once you recognize that a modern software engineering project is indeed a system, one can begin to immerse in the extremely broad body of knowledge that some call "systems thinking". Systems theory has a very long history, originating formally in 1920 through what is known as the Bertalniffy General System Theory [50]. In this seminal work, systems are studied through four integral domains:

- Philosophy, the ontology, epistemology and axiology of systems

- Theory, as set of interrelated concepts and principles applying to all systems

- Methodology, the set of models strategies and tools that instrument systems theory and philosophy

- Application, the application and interaction of the domains

This was reiterated as per Steiss & Buckley in 1967, *"Interdisciplinary perspectives are critical in breaking away from industrial age models and thinking, where history is history, math is math segregated from the arts and music separate from the sciences and never the twain shall meet."* [51] The evolution of Systems Theory has taken many branches in the course of its application. Figure 3.4 illustrates the long history of the study of systems and the diverse application of Systems Theory.

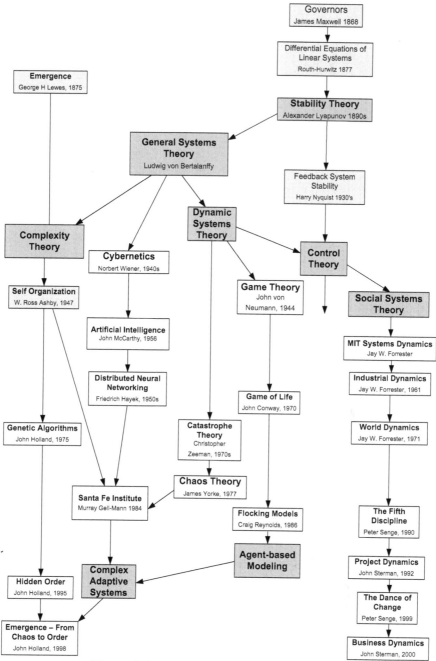

Figure 3.4 – History of Systems Theory

One branch within this evolution that deserves special mention is that of Jay Wright Forrester of the Massachusetts Institute of Technology – MIT. This IEEE Medal of Honor recipient founded the MIT System Dynamic's Group in the early 1960's, after a career working within his profession of Electrical Engineering within the US Navy. During his early works, he assisted Gordon S. Brown who is accredited with modern Control Theory. He designed the Whirlwind aircraft simulation computer, which eventually became SAGE – Semi-Automatic Ground Environment which was responsible for North American Missile Defense in response to the USSR's ballistic missile program. At MIT he later delivered works surrounding the application of his experience with Control Systems to organizational dynamics. This cross-disciplinary application of knowledge served as the basis of MIT's Systems Dynamics Group where he published books on *Industrial Dynamics, Urban Dynamics and World Dynamics* [52, 53, 54].

One of the faculty within the Systems Dynamics Group at MIT is Peter Senge, author of the book *The Fifth Discipline* [55]. Mentored by Jay W. Forrester, Senge articulates the concepts of Systems Dynamics thinking as applied in learning organizations. A second follower of Forrester's pioneering work is John Sterman, who is the Professor of Management at the Sloan School of Business, director of the System Dynamics Group and author of *Business Dynamics* [56]. The thought leaders from within this thread of research definitely have an engineering background, as does John Holland (discussed later in this chapter) who is a professor of Electrical Engineering at the University of Michigan. There seems to be a strong underpinning of thought from this discipline that is leading to organizational management innovation. Historically, the Agile community has looked to systems thinking, but mostly focused on the Complex Adaptive Systems [57] and Emergence thread. One area that seems absent however is the thread of application of Control Systems Theory. Given the history of Agile, it is probably due to the name of the field. However, if the two threads of investigation could somehow be integrated, perhaps additional insights could be achieved. In other words, there appears to be an opportunity to leverage the body of knowledge of Control Systems in conjunction with Complex Adaptive Systems.

A system is defined as "a set of interacting or interdependent entities forming an integrated whole. Systems share common attributes including structure (defined by the parts of their composition), behavior (which involves inputs, processing and outputs), and interconnectivity (structural and behavior relationships between each other)" [58].

Examples of the types of systems include living systems, mechanical systems, celestial systems, political systems, sociological systems, economic systems and information systems. And systems are either open (interact with their environment), or closed when they are isolated from their environment. But one trait shared by all systems is they exist in time. The term for this is "dynamic systems".

Dynamic Systems, whether they be mechanical, electrical or social have one common feature – they exhibit a dynamic response to input. Figure 3.5 illustrates a typical response of a dynamic system to a unit step input.

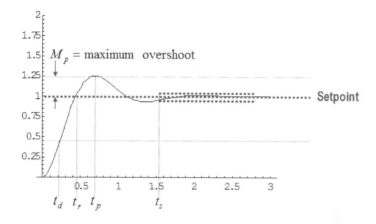

t_d : Delay until reach 50% of steady state value

t_r : Rise time = delay until first reach steady state value

t_p : Time at which peak value is reached

t_s : Settling time = stays within specified % of steady state

Figure 3.5 – Dynamic System Response to Unit Step Input

Given a setpoint input (in this case a unit step function), the transient response of the system generally exhibits the above relationship, where t_{rise} is the time it takes to first reach the new equilibrium, t_{delay} is the amount of time to reach 50% of the setpoint, t_{peak} characterizes the amount of overshoot, and $t_{settling}$ is the amount of time it takes for the output to reach a stable point that is its effective steady-state.

Three dynamic curves are possible for this response – an under-damped response, which oscillates to a large degree before arriving at the steady state; an over-damped response, which never crosses the setpoint level (no overshoot) and takes the longest to arrive at steady-state; and a critically damped response, which arrives at the steady-state value the quickest with little overshoot. Figure 3.6 illustrates the three possible dynamic response curves that indicate the performance of settling to a chosen setpoint level.

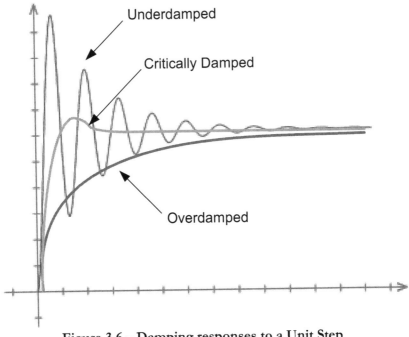

Figure 3.6 – Damping responses to a Unit Step

From the above three curves, it would seem logical that if one were to view a project as a dynamic system, then the best or optimal performance of a project delivery would be the critically damped response. This is equivalent to specifying a minimum error and is optimum in terms of gain or effort expended. The next section makes the case for treating a project organization as such a dynamic system.

3.3 – The Project Organization – A Complex Adaptive System

Certain systems adapt to their environment. In the case of a Hurricane, it adapts to changing water temperatures, steering wind currents and land masses. Hurricanes have been described as "Complex Adaptive Systems - CAS" [59]. A Complex system by definition is one in which the number or the types of parts in the system, and the number of relations between the parts is non-trivial. Adaptive systems are ones which can react to changing conditions in the environment in which they exist. Organizations, including Software Development Projects, have also been described as Complex Adaptive Systems [60].

When one hears Agilists discuss the linkage with CAS, the flock of bird's example inevitably comes up. The interesting thing however, is that while the interplay among the agents within the flock is not centrally controllable or predictive, ironically there is order at the macroscopic level of flight – at the system level. It is described as "Order emerging out of Chaos" [61]. Some have articulated an Agile project as being "at the edge of chaos". Indeed the seminal Scrum paper describes the project organization using these terms. Even predating the term Agile by over 20 years, there are references to this identification at an anecdotal level through the description of historical project deliveries as "Chaordic Systems" [62]. Some have even used the term "herding cats" as a metaphor [63]. From a Systems Theory perspective, CAS and complex systems occupy a space between Chaos and Order [64], so it would appear a valid linkage.

Whatever the "proper" categorization of projects in terms of today's level of understanding of Systems Thinking, the key point is that they are difficult if not impossible to fully understand at a system level in a detailed white-box sense. But as we shall see later in this chapter, such a detailed model is unnecessary in terms of influencing the system. Treating the project organization as a very complex black-box of dynamism is all that is needed in aggregate, as long as we can observe the results or output from that very busy network of self-organizing agents. We will never be able to fully understand all the motivations, emotions and intellectual processes of the individuals that make up a project, let alone understand a complex network of these sentient beings.

With all the attempts to apply a label to the system known as a software project, the fundamental question is whether the investor has any control over outcomes. Is each project a random roll of the dice; or is it pre-determined based on initial conditions and only known after the fact (the definition of Chaos). In essence this argument suggests that the results of an investment will only be known for certain after the fact (true), but that no insight or influence of the outcome can occur (not true). Take for example a vessel crossing the Gulf Stream. While elements of the system are linear and deterministic (like the rudder, motor, blocks, winches), the overall behavior is stochastic and non-linear. And the environment is likewise non-linear. But we can still influence our passage. Our selection of vessel type and its "patterns of behavior" influence how we will interact with the environment. For example, the configuration of our "project" will be different if we sail a single hull vessel than if we cross with a catamaran/multi-hull. And even though our crew are highly stochastic with different skills, can experience difficulties at sea (sea-sickness, scurvy), the common goal under the leadership of a captain enables order in what can easily become chaos. And indeed the system can become unstable, like in the event of a storm.

Another example has recently emerged related to attempting to control/influence a CAS. Bill Gates and the Gates Foundation is funding research and has submitted patent applications that aim to influence something that is an enormous CAS – a Hurricane [65]. The idea is to attempt to steer Hurricanes away from densely populated areas or areas that contain critical infrastructure. The innovation is to modify the environment and establishing enormous system dampeners by welling up cold water to the ocean surface. The technology hopes to alter the behavior of the CAS. While not without controversy, it suggests the ability to control the CAS at the system level.

3.3.1 – Influencing the CAS

From the previous discussion, it is suggested that the Complex Adaptive System that represents modern software engineering projects can indeed be influenced (as opposed to deterministically controlled). That is to say, there are certain levers that can influence the macroscopic behavior of the CAS. To suggest that IT investment is just a random, uncontrollable outcome is to suggest that CIO's have no means to exercise *due diligence*. This is not a reasonable or practical position.

Steering a CAS implies either influencing the behaviors of the agents within the system itself directly (highly controversial), or influencing the system through changes in the environment (perhaps not so controversial). The latter has been likened to "Co-Evolution", where evolution of the environment leads to an evolution of the agents of the CAS [66]. Either way, with Software Development projects, the input is knowledge or "pure thought stuff" as described by some methodologists [67]. If one views the production of software as having only one input (or control variable as will be discussed later) then the model becomes much simpler. If we aggregate complex interactions of a team of knowledge workers into a single input that results through a complex and non-linear relationship to the output from the system (the software), then we begin to have a model in which to explore the ways in which steerage is possible. The question is can a software development CAS be influenced through the application of knowledge such that the delivery is perhaps optimal (rather than predictive) within the stability region of the system?

Figure 3.7 represents a model for the CAS in relationship to its influence – in IT terminology the project governance.

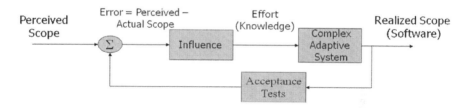

Figure 3.7 – Model for Software Development Projects

In this model, the goal is what is perceived to be the scope of the project. The perception of the requirements of the project is moving and changing as more is learned about reality. In effect, the requirements are just an imperfect model of the actual intended scope, which will be uncovered through the extraction of explicit knowledge. Resources are applied as input to the project (the raw material is actually knowledge as result of effort expended) and this is applied within the complex adaptive system of people, process and technology. The output of this system is realized scope – software in the case of a software development project. The feedback comes in the form of acceptance tests of the features/functionality delivered. The results of executing these tests results in an understanding of the delta between perceived and actual scope. The error represents the gap between where the team currently is and where it needs to go to meet the goals of the project. Based on the error signal, influence in the form of adjustment/adaptation occurs. These adjusting influences on the knowledge input to the CAS focus on converging on the end goal in as quick a fashion as possible.

3.3.2 – Making the Connection with Control Systems Engineering

It just so happens that this model is common in one of the sub-fields within Systems Theory. This subfield is Control Theory and Control Systems Engineering as practiced in Mechanical and Electrical Engineering. Figure 3.8 is the simple canonical block diagram form of the abstract model presented in Figure 3.7.

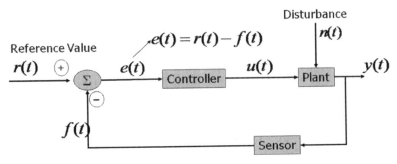

Figure 3.8 – Canonical Block Diagram

In the model above, a sensor observes the output of the system over time and feeds this information back to a comparator such that the difference between the desired setpoint r(t) and the actual output y(t) can be determined (the error function e(t)). This delta serves as the basis for the input signal applied to the plant. This input signal is shaped based on applying gain u(t) designed from one of a number of control strategies to enable a stable and rapid convergence on the setpoint.

The model in the above figure is leveraged for such seemingly uncontrollable things as aircraft through flight control systems and autopilots, process flow control of fluids (highly dynamic), thermostats, communications flow control, and car cruise-control systems. The common theme in all of these is that they are all highly complex and dynamic systems that are indeed controllable (i.e. can be influenced) through the use of negative feedback.

The question that invariably will be passionately exalted by both the traditional command and control management types and Agilist's alike is "who is the controller"? And this is the key point. Many control strategies exist in the world of Control Theory, each to different effect and results. Nothing in articulating that a "controller" exists suggests that this is a single person or "overlord". In fact even with such a simplified abstraction as projects being a SISO (Single Input, Single Output system – a single variable control problem with the input being knowledge and the output being working software), nothing in this suggests a single person controller. The Agile movement has embraced the notion distributed leadership (situational leadership) – which in Control Theory would seem to be similar to *Distributed/Networked Adaptive Control* [68]. This is one in a series of many control strategies which has benefits and liabilities in dealing with a certain class of control problems.

The remaining sections of this chapter explore how the body of knowledge of Control Systems Engineering might be applied to gain insights into how and why Agile works, and how we can further the advancement of modern software engineering.

3.4 – Control Theory Issues

In the field of Control Theory, three issues are commonly tackled when defining a strategy for compensating a system. With the assertion that that software engineering projects are Complex Adaptive Systems, the questions of linearity, controllability and stability will affect how we approach the various mathematical tools and indeed the sub-fields necessary to consider. At face value, each of these would appear to be at odds with the emergence/chaos school of thought. However, even if we exhaust some of the "simpler" techniques and mathematics, we can then turn to other recent topics of Control Theory including *Non-linear Control, Stochastic Control, Bifurcation Control and Chaos Control* [68].

3.4.1 – Linear Time Invariance

A **time-invariant** system is one whose output does not depend explicitly on time. Having equated project systems to Complex Adaptive Systems, it would seem that projects do not fit with this definition. The project organization evolves over time and changes its behavior depending on the time varying conditions of the environment in which it exists. This means changing business conditions, changing technology, changing membership in the project and the like. So it would seem that the techniques of Control Systems Engineering do not apply to understanding Agile projects. But there is one area of control that attempts to cope with the fact that the parameters of the system being controlled are time-varying or uncertain. This is *Adaptive Control* [68]. Adaptive control involves modifying the control law used by a controller to cope with the fact that the parameters of the system being controlled are slowly time-varying or uncertain. This body of knowledge is used for example, in accommodating changes in an aircraft in flight as the process under control undergoes changes like changing mass due to fuel changes. One simple technique for Adaptive Feedback Control is called *Gain Scheduling* [68], in which linear control techniques are applied within a time region of operation, followed by other controller parameters/design for differing time regions. So in other words, the dynamics of the plant are treated as time invariant within differing bounds of operation, and therefore Control Theory can be applied. As will be discussed in a later chapter, this might imply that different dynamics and control strategies for a software project might apply during different scheduled stages of the delivery (like the engineering or architecture stage and the construction or build-out stage).

The second issue to confront is the non-linear nature of a CAS. A **Non-Linear** system is one in which the principle of superposition does not hold or where the output is not proportional to the input. While the interactions with the software development environments (IDE's) appear to be linear (and time-invariant), and the feedback mechanism (testing tools) are linear, the interactions among the agents within the project organization are non-linear in nature. You can think of this as being no different than flying a aircraft or sailing a vessel where a team is involved. The mechanisms which steer the vessel towards its' destination are effectively linear. But the crew can behave in strange ways (or non-linear ways), so the track of the ship is by no means guaranteed. The same holds for software development.

For a non-homogenous system of agents which is linear apart from the presence of a function of independent variables, it is possible to perform approximations of linear systems with multiple variables. Such an approach is the subject of research, an example of which is the mathematical proof of the separation of the organizational non-linearity's such that linear techniques apply [69]. In this study of project organization dynamic performance, the probability distribution of non-linearity's represents a shift that averages to that of *Markovian* variances (also known as "white" or random noise). Luckily, Non-Linear Control Theory deals with the realities of non-linearity in the physical world such that Linear Control techniques and the tools for their analysis apply. One technique that is typically applied is feedback linearization, where isolation of the static non-linear portions of the model from the dynamic linear portions of the model is a common linearization technique. These techniques result in model approximations known as *Hammerstein-Wiener* [70] models.

One could view examples of such linearization within software development projects as being modifications of organizational structure. The larger the team, the higher the non-linearity effects; so if the organization can be structured such that they are approximately linear, then we can effectively apply control theory. Other techniques to reduce the non-linearity's include pairing, and acquisition-orientation.

The key point to take away from this is that just because a project system may exhibit properties of a CAS does not mean that recent innovations in *Adaptive Non-linear Control Engineering* do not apply. These advanced topics deserve study, but are beyond the scope of this book. For now it is sufficient to state that we can still gain useful insights by making certain simplifying assumptions for the purpose of explaining certain aspects of why "Agile" works.

3.4.2 – Controllability & Observability

For control techniques to apply (meaning influencing the system/project), the system must be observable through measurements of the output. Obviously, working software output from development activity is observable and testable, which represents the desired element that must be measured to understand the error component. Without knowing the gap between the actual realization of output with the desired setpoint for the project, control or influence is not possible. This would appear to be ironically the essence of why waterfall projects fail. The SISO system is made up of knowledge as the aggregated input to achieve software as the output. And yet with the open-loop configuration that effectively represents a waterfall, closure of this knowledge gap is left until too late, when controllability is no longer possible.

3.4.3 – Stability and Convergence

A system is stable if for a bounded input the output is bounded (sometimes called BIBO stability). This is a simple definition of stability; others exist including "practical" stability and Lyapunov stability [68]. We wish to converge on a goal in as fast as a manner as is stable. Control theory provides us the means to determine the relative stability and also the margins of stability (robustness); this in addition to our interest in the rate of convergence. Current traditional practices predicting health based on measures of resource expenditure and schedule should be discarded, as these measures are not directly related to the desired setpoint output (working software). Additionally, stability should be leveraged alongside performance to understand if the best possible delivery is resulting or whether the project is experiencing a risk of a lack of convergence on the desired outcome (becoming unstable).

3.5 – Proportional-Integral-Derivative Control

One approach to control that is by far the most implemented in industry is *Proportional-Integral-Derivative (PID) Control* [68]. This approach is designed to compensate an open-loop system such that system stability is assured, and the overshoot/error and transient response of the system are within desired specifications. For a given setpoint, the typical goal is to track to that value as quickly as possible. This is similar to software project deliveries and the desire to deliver on a set of objectives in an environment where error is present. As such, the implication is that study of this applied science should be of value.

One important feature of this control strategy is that a detailed model of the plant is not necessary, and reasonable results are achieved without such a white-box representation. Only an approximation is required. This is compatible with the observation of modern software development projects being Complex Adaptive Systems with a high degree of uncertainty in the model. We will never know all the time-varying complexities of the agents making up this system type.

Introducing a PID Controller in the feed-forward configuration delivers performance compensation. Not only does it improve stability, but it also can be used to improve the dynamic response of the system. And when the cumulative error is minimized for the transient response to a setpoint from an initial condition, we approach optimization.

Figure 3.9 illustrates the configuration of a PID controller within a negative feedback control system.

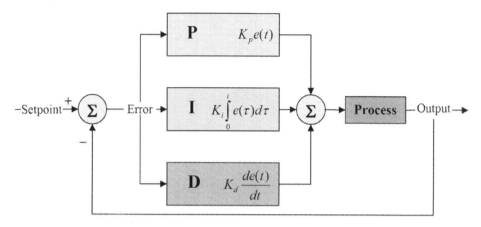

Figure 3.9 – PID Controller

The proportional control component enables rapid advancement towards the goal or setpoint. Gain is applied to the instantaneous or current error between the current state and the desired setpoint. This approach when applied alone has two problems; notably that the controller cannot speed up correction in response to a rising error (destabilizing); and it cannot keep track of the corrections lost over the time period over which the instantaneous error is corrected.

The integral control component applies gain or compensation to the sum of past error. An integral controller accumulates error in its memory, which continues to apply a correction even when the proportional control has waned due to the reduction in the instantaneous error. Thus, it speeds up the correction while also overcoming the steady state error.

Derivative control applies gain or compensation based on the rate of change of the error. It can accelerate correction when the error grows at a fast rate. When used together with proportional and integral control, it can speed up the movement to the new equilibrium, although, not on its own.

Figure 3.10 describes the equation of the input to a plant under control as a result of applying a PID control strategy.

$$u(t) = K_P e(t) + K_I \int e(t)dt + K_D \frac{d}{dt} e(t)$$

Figure 3.10 – Time Domain Input to the Plant from PID Control

Designing a PID controller entails selecting appropriate values for the respective gains K_P, K_I and K_D such that performance is optimal and the system remains stable.

3.6 – The Mathematical Tools from Classical Control Theory

It was suggested earlier that two important elements were missing from two of the most recognizable mathematical models within the world of software engineering. The first of these is scope. From control theory, this is the tracked variable "y". The second of these missing variables is "t", meaning that the common IT mathematical functions as articulated do not depend on time. If we elevate functions like these such that they are dynamic and depend on time, the result is a *Differential Equation* [71]. Solving these equations is nothing like EVM or COCOMO-II. Therefore, it is no wonder we have had problems with prior models – the math is a little oversimplified.

One mathematical tool that is leveraged within classical control theory and application to dynamic systems for continuous time is the *Laplace Transform* [68]. This tool is used to solve differential equations (equations that depend on time and derivatives of time/rates of change). It is used for analysis of linear time invariant systems. It represents a transformation from the time domain into the frequency domain where inputs and outputs are functions of complex angular frequency in radians per unit time. Given a simple mathematical formula for the input and output of a system, performing a Laplace Transform provides an alternative functional description which makes solving the temporal equations much easier. What requires complex integral calculus in the time domain only requires solving simple algebraic equations in the frequency domain, the conjugate of the time domain. Figure 3.11 is the definition of a Laplace Transform.

$$\mathbf{L}[f(t)] = F(s) = \int_0^\infty f(t)e^{-st}dt$$

where *s=α + jω* (α and ω are real numbers, j is imaginary)

Figure 3.11 – Laplace Transform

The Laplace Transform is also known as an "s-transform", in that it converts time into the complex plane. A complex number is one which has real and imaginary parts. Figure 3.12 illustrates the complex plane in mathematics.

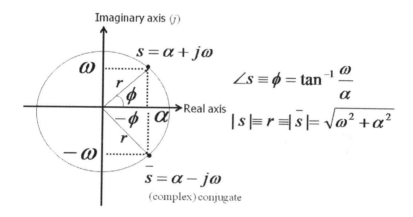

Figure 3.12 – Complex Plane

Laplace Transforms convert inputs and outputs that are functions of time into the same inputs and outputs that are functions of the complex angular frequency in radians per unit time. The complex angular frequency is the measure of the rotation rate. So in our negative feedback system, it is the number of cycles or "iterations" per unit time.

Figure 3.13 illustrates common Laplace transforms for simple functions in the time domain.

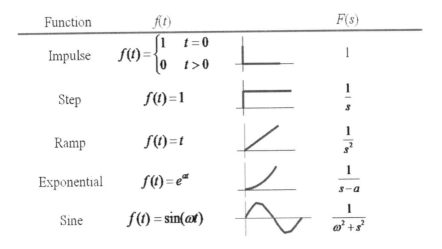

Function	$f(t)$		$F(s)$
Impulse	$f(t) = \begin{cases} 1 & t=0 \\ 0 & t>0 \end{cases}$		1
Step	$f(t) = 1$		$\dfrac{1}{s}$
Ramp	$f(t) = t$		$\dfrac{1}{s^2}$
Exponential	$f(t) = e^{at}$		$\dfrac{1}{s-a}$
Sine	$f(t) = \sin(\omega t)$		$\dfrac{1}{\omega^2 + s^2}$

Figure 3.13 – Common Laplace Transforms

3.7 – Modeling and Analysis of the Software Project Control System

To analyze our model such that we can explore interesting attributes of modern software engineering project dynamics, we need to piece together our model for the project organization using the PID control strategy. Our model for the system can be condensed into the following algebraic form.

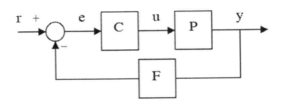

where...

- r(t) is the reference signal (the scope of the project),

- P(t) is the plant (the complex adaptive system that is impossible to model precisely as it deals with human beings) ,

- C(t) is the controller for the project (the entity/entities who exercise influence over the project by applying gain),

- y(t) is the output that is observable and measurable,

- F(t) is the function that represents the sensor

- e(t) is the error function

Figure 3.14 – Project System Model

To analyze this system, we will leverage classical Control Theory and Laplace Transform's to convert each model element into the frequency domain. The following relationships exist as illustrated in figure 3.15.

$$Y(s) = P(s)U(s)$$
$$U(s) = C(s)E(s)$$
$$E(s) = R(s) - F(s)Y(s)$$

Solving for Y(s) in terms of R(s) gives…

$$Y(s) = \frac{P(s)C(s)}{1 + F(s)P(s)C(s)} R(s)$$

$$\frac{Y(s)}{R(s)} = H(s) = \frac{P(s)C(s)}{1 + F(s)P(s)C(s)}$$

$$H(s) = \frac{Open\,loop\;Transfer\;Function}{Characteristic\;equation}$$

Figure 3.15 – Closed-loop Transfer Function

The portion of the above equation H(s) is called the *Closed-loop Transfer Function*. The numerator is referred to as the open loop transfer function going from **r** to **y**, and the denominator is referred to as the

Characteristic Equation, and is one plus the gain going around the feedback loop. It is called this because the roots of this equation determine the dynamic characteristics of the closed-loop system.

Control is established through an understanding of the values for **s** which make the numerator zero (the zeros), and that make the denominator zero (the poles). PID control techniques enables us to design optimal control into the system with what is known as "pole placement". Note that solving the characteristic equation does not involve the R(s) or E(s) components. And from control theory, we know that the system will respond for a unit step or impulse the same for more complex inputs, so we can simplify the reference signal in this manner.

3.7.1 – Understanding the Reference and the Error Function

Analysis of system dynamics begins with the concept that we do not need to understand the input function **r(t)** in detail. Control Systems Analysis and Design typically leverages the unit step function as it is sufficient to understand the meaningful attributes of the system. We can think of the input to a project however as being like a step function. The controversial question is whether that desired setpoint is fixed or changing. If we think in terms of actual scope versus perceived scope however, a step function makes a lot of sense.

The scope for the effort within a certain time horizon is fixed. It is just that no one truly *knows* what that scope is. What we know from practice is that our knowledge of scope is dependent on the customer, and their knowledge is mostly tacit. Therefore, at the outset of a project, only a perception of scope exists. As we learn more and more about the delta between perceived and actual scope through testing, we will see the actual scope curve emerge. But instead of having a complex reference signal input to the project, we can accommodate the non-linearity and stochastic nature of the realization of this perceived scope through the error function.

Therefore,

Actual Scope = Perceived Scope - Error in Knowledge

The error that results as we attempt to converge on the actual scope of the project is made up of many components including the following as illustrated in Table 3.1:

Table 3.1 – Components of the Error Function

Changing business conditions
Error in Explicit Knowledge
Errors in realization of knowledge
Errors in development interaction communication
Errors in development skills and knowledge

In any event, the above discussion only serves to validate our notion of the project system as it relates to knowledge as the input. As we will see, given certain simplifying assumptions, we do not need to know the exact model of the input (which makes sense because all projects are different) to be able to explain why negative feedback works.

3.7.2 – Understanding the Influence of the PID Controller

The controller is modeled after a PID control strategy, and as such we have the following in the frequency domain:

$$U(s) = K_P E(s) + K_I \frac{1}{s} E(s) + K_{DS} E(s)$$

$$U(s) = \frac{K_{DS}^2 + K_P s + K_I}{s} E(s)$$

$$U(s) = \frac{K (s + z_1)(s + z_2)}{s} E(s)$$

Figure 3.16 –Frequency Domain Representation of PID Controller

Therefore we can see that a PID controller introduces two zeros and a pole at the origin into the system's transfer function. In Section 3.8, we will see the mathematical effects of this on the system. Metaphorically, however, we can think of each of the compensation terms as follows:

Proportional Compensation Term –

This type of control is consistent with the typical project management strategy of adding more and more resources to a project to get the desired rise characteristics towards a goal. But as we know from classics like "The Mythical Man-month" [72], just throwing bodies at the problem does not translate to faster response. From control theory, we know that beyond a certain point we run into instability. Meaning that there are limits to how much gain we can apply to a system before it becomes unstable. Proportional-only compensation of a project is the simplest yet most ineffective control strategy that exists. This type of influence must be used in concert with other compensation policies.

Integral Compensation Term –

This component of control can be thought of as leveraging the history of the gap that should have been closed in terms of the currently perceived scope and realized scope. By integrating this gap historically, we are effectively assessing our effectiveness and compensating accordingly with increased effort (gain) from practices that can improve this convergence. During the transient period of the project, this can include introducing more effective communication techniques like co-location, where learning from history accelerates closure on the setpoint or goal in extracting tacit knowledge from our stakeholders. As such, we equate our practices related to stakeholder interaction and organizational learning to integral control. Any practice that effects knowledge extraction improvement represents integral control.

From Control Theory, we know that the most significant effect of including the Integral term in PID control is to ensure that the Steady-state error approaches zero. As we approach steady-state and our setpoint goal, integral control manifests itself as enabling the remaining gap to be closed within tolerances. This "last mile" convergence can be effected through such practices as regression testing and release rehearsals. Steady-state gap tolerances in a web-based eCommerce application may be less than with a safety-critical real-time application, so the degree of "ceremony" used to implement late stage integral control should be commensurate.

Derivative Compensation Term –

The derivative control term is made up of gain based on the current rate of change of error. This effect is one of acceleration and deceleration in nature and provides anticipatory action. Various practices can be seen to implement derivative control. Early risk reduction has an acceleratory effect, as more resources can be applied earlier if investment feasibility is proven. Similarly, reuse and Asset-based development supplies a high level of K_D gain during the transient period.

Derivative control is also central to Agile in the form of leveraging *velocity* to determine the scope tackled within a iteration. Assessment of *done-done velocity* ensures stable delivery of working software at the end of each iteration. This longstanding Agile practice prevents attempting to tackle too much scope per timebox which can result in instability. Derivative control also supplies a optimizing effect when convergence action is supplied for overshoot that occurs in less than optimal knowledge extraction (underdamped). Similarly, it has the effect of preventing negative effects related to a lack of committal for the duration of an iteration on scope, or poor stakeholder participation in the process of tacit knowledge transfer.

3.7.3 – Model Approximation for the Plant

The classic dilemma with Control Systems Engineering and modeling physical systems is the tradeoff between model accuracy and tractability. While Agent-based system models are statistically more accurate and account for such phenomenon like imperfect mixing, heterogeneity and emergence, the differences are shown to not be *practically* significant with respect to decisions on how to influence the system [73].

Earlier it was mentioned that one of the benefits of PID Control is that a detailed model of the plant/process is not necessary. Even so, recent study into the dynamic behavior of projects has emerged from research circles, which builds upon the early pioneering efforts of Jay W. Forrester. Through these works, models of the project organization related to cooperative problem solving (like software development) are emerging [69]. The conclusions of one such paper suggest that the non-linearity's or fluctuations of the plant can be treated as Markovian, which is consistent with Non-Linear Control strategies. And, for the intrinsic stochastic nature of cooperative problem solving projects like software development, it is also suggested that linearization can be effected through reduction in organizational size through modular structure. Figure 3.17 describes the differential equations (in matrix form) from this study which form a model of the project.

$$dx = [(A_0 + M - I)dt + dS(t)]x(t),$$

where $dS = S(t)dt$ is a matrix of independent mean-zero Wiener processes
I is an interaction matrix.
M is the matrix of the mean value of fluctuations.
A_0 is the unperturbed effort matrix.

assumed that the noise is white (fluctuations are Markovian)

Figure 3.17 – Project Organization Differential Equation

Analysis of this research is beyond the scope of this text. But it seems to reduce to an exponential function of time based on the overwhelming Eigenvalue in the interaction matrix. Therefore, for study purposes, we will leverage a similar yet simplified model of the plant. This model can be seen in such works as Putnam's SLIM cost estimation approach [74], and in the typical resource expenditure curve from EVM – the so called "Rayleigh curve". The time domain format of this equation is shown in Figure 3.18.

$$p'(t) = 2Kate^{-at^2}$$

where...

- p'(t) is the effort expended as a function of time,
- K is a scale factor,
- a is a shape parameter.

Figure 3.18 – First Order Linear Simplification for the Plant

Taking the Laplace transform of the simplified first-order approximation of the plant/project model, we arrive at the following for P(s) in Figure 3.19.

$$P(s) = \frac{1}{(s-a)(s-a)}$$

Figure 3.19 – Frequency Domain Representation of Plant

The interpretation of this simplification of the CAS is that knowledge is cumulatively added in the production of output in an exponentially growing fashion. While this model of the plant represents a drastic simplification as a first-order Rayleigh differential equation and necessarily removes non-linearity, it represents a useful start in yielding insights as to why certain practices work.

3.7.4 – Resultant Model in the Frequency Domain

Each of the model elements are combined into a feed-forward configuration (also called cascade compensation). Figure 3.20 illustrates the resultant project organization system model in the frequency domain as a result of taking the Laplace Transform on the individual components and assuming a unity constant for the feedback signal F(s).

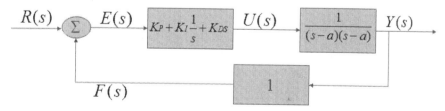

Figure 3.20 – Model of Project System in Frequency Domain

The characteristic equation for the closed-loop transfer function H(s) is described in Figure 3.21.

$$Characteristic\ Equation = 1 + \frac{K(s + z_1)(s + z_2)}{s(s - a)(s - a)}$$

Figure 3.21 – Characteristic Equation of the
Closed-loop Transfer Function

So what can we do with this? Even with an oversimplified model of the project CAS, and even with the linear, time-invariant control strategy of PID control, performance analysis from classical control theory can tell us about general aspects as to the transient response, steady-state error and stability behaviors. As a start, we will attempt to answer the following questions:

1) What are the effects of changing the iteration duration (aka frequency) on a project, and how can we use this knowledge to select the "correct" iteration practice?

2) If we desire a critically damped response for the project (the optimal performance curve to converge on scope), what values for proportional control, integral control and derivative control should we choose?

3) What are the limits in which our application of gain (resources) remains stable?

3.8 – Analysis of System Performance

The world of control system design is all about making tradeoffs based on the desired system response to input. Assuming that a common tenet in modern software engineering is to deliver to market as fast as possible, it would be reasonable to want to understand the fastest response that can be achieved while operating within a "sustainable pace". In other words, a mode in which the project delivery is stable. And if we could understand what the gain profile would look like to have the fastest possible convergence, we could identify the optimum response to stakeholder demand rather than setting some unrealistic expectation for a delivery response. We would also like to know the nature of the damping and feedback loop frequency (resonance frequency) for this response, which will affect our resource expenditure and the amount of cumulative error (overshoot). In control systems engineering, this is called a performance index, the most basic being called *IAE – Integral of the Absolute-value of Error* [68].

Different tools are available to the control engineer in designing the desired response to a dynamic system. These include longstanding mathematically rigorous techniques such as Laplace or s-plane techniques like Root Locus analysis, *Fourier Transform* or jω frequency analysis like Polar Charts based on something called the *Nyquist* stability criterion or Magnitude and Phase analysis using *Bode Plots* (Logarithm Charts) [68]. We will discuss just two of these techniques to understand how to design the project control system, a process called *loop shaping*.

3.8.1 – Root Locus Analysis & Design in the s-Plane

A technique commonly used in control systems engineering is the *Root Locus* method, created by Walter Evans in 1956 [68]. This approach remains popular among practitioners. The response of a system to any input can be derived from its unit step response. The closed-loop poles of the system determine completely the natural of the unforced response of the system. The root locus is the curve created from the roots of the characteristic equation of the closed-loop transfer function as the loop gain of the feedback system is increased from zero to infinity. The roots are the locations in the s-plane where the transfer function becomes infinite, which are the points where the characteristic equation becomes zero (called poles, as opposed to zeros which cause the numerator or the open loop transfer function to equal zero).

Its' main utility is in analyzing the transient response and stability of SISO (single-input, single-output) dynamic systems. A system is stable if all the poles of the transfer function are in the left hand side of the complex plane. Poles for the system located further from the origin have more rapid response. Where poles are located on the real axis in the s-plane, the response is exponential, either decay if in the left side of the complex plane, or exponential growth in the unstable right-hand side. Pole-pairs that exist in the direction of the imaginary axis bring either decaying or increasing oscillatory responses with frequencies higher the further from the origin. Figure 3.22 illustrates the stability regions of the s-plane, and the effects of pole locations on the convergence rate.

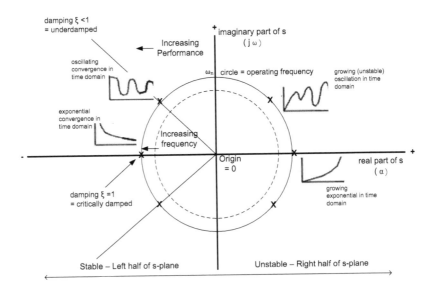

Figure 3.22 – Effects of Pole Placement on Dynamic Response

To construct a root locus plot, we use the fact that the characteristic equation must equal zero, or KCP = -1. Varying the gain K removes amplitude and means that the polynomial C(s)P(s) in the complex plane must have a net phase of 180 degrees where there is a closed loop pole. When performing manual geometrical construction from this fact, we add angle contributions from the vectors extending from each of the poles of KC to a prospective closed loop root (pole) and subtract the angle contributions from similar vectors extending from the zeros, requiring the sum be 180. According to vector mathematics the angles add (or subtract, for terms in the denominator) and lengths multiply (or divide). To test a point for inclusion on the root locus, all you do is add the angles to all the open loop poles and zeros. While this used to be performed with pencil and paper, tools like Mathworks-Matlab will automatically perform this calculation to produce the plot.

The root locus approach is used to design the damping ratio and natural frequency of feedback system. It gives the pole locations for every possible closed loop system configuration that can be created from the open loop plant and any positive gain. This is achieved by establishing radial lines out from the origin in the s-plane at the desired damping ratio and drawing a radius circle at the constant natural frequency, we can select the appropriate gains for K_P, K_D and K_I that form an intersection such that stability is ensured (all poles existing in the left half of the complex plane).

3.8.2 – Effects of adding a PID Controller

We can influence the project such that instability cannot occur, and such that we have the fastest response possible. Also, we can affect our error performance index by identifying the resonant frequency and gain necessary for a critically damped response. The approach to achieve this in control engineering is called *pole placement*. To influence the dynamic response of the project organization being influenced, the resultant transfer function of adding a PID controller in the feed-forward position of a closed loop system adds a pair of zeros and a pole at the origin.

Figure 3.23 illustrates the Root Locus plot for this configuration supporting our approximated model for the plant (the Agile Project System) .

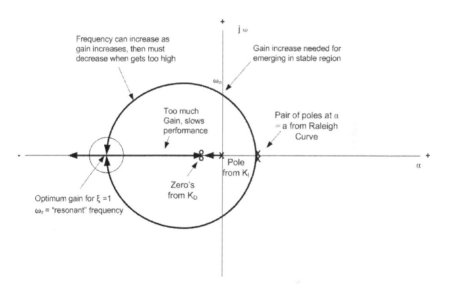

Figure 3.23 – Root Locus Plot for the Agile Project System

From the previous plot, we see that a critically damped response (ξ=1) occurs after enough resource gain (knowledge) is applied to emerge from the right half plane. The intersection with the real axis defines the optimum *resonant* frequency for iterations. Increasing gain beyond this point begins to slow response until it once again arrives at marginal stability (at the origin). The leading indicator that stability is starting to be affected and departure from optimum delivery is occurring is when churn and thrashing stops. On an Agile project, this can be interpreted as when the backlog prioritization is stable for in-progress iterations. It means that tacit knowledge is emerging just-in-time within the sliding window. This is the point that delivery teams describe as "the sweet-spot" and where people describe the environment as hyper-performing, kind of an electricity in the air. This is where maximum velocity occurs, the optimum control response.

Depending on where we locate the zeros, a different amount of gain can be accommodated and therefore a greater velocity. This relates to the issue of Agility at Scale. If we move the poles further out to the left, we can accommodate more resources if the frequency increases. To accelerate velocity, either a reconfiguration of the plant is necessary to maximize cycle time, or acquisition/reuse can improve manifested gain thereby enabling a higher frequency.

3.8.3 – Frequency Domain Analysis of Stability and Performance

The Root Locus analysis and design of Control Systems entails the use of graphical plots on the complex s-plane as a result of taking Laplace Transforms. Another frequency domain technique leverages the fact that the frequency response of a system is defined as the steady-state response to a sinusoidal input signal. These techniques leverage the *Fourier Transform*, which like the Laplace Transform converts the closed-loop system into the frequency domain for analysis. But this mathematical conversion uses $j\omega$ only. Graphical stability and performance analysis methods include the *Nyquist Criterion* technique, *Nichols Plots* and *Bode Analysis* [68]. Figure 3.24 represents the frequency response form of the Open-loop Transfer Function **G**.

$$G(j\omega) = \frac{K(1+\frac{1}{z_1}j\omega)(1+\frac{1}{z_2}j\omega)}{j\omega(1-\frac{1}{a}j\omega)(1-\frac{1}{a}j\omega)}$$

Figure 3.24 – Frequency Response Transfer Function

The latter of these techniques yields an approximation or asymptotic-based resultant plot that is easily understood and analyzed. It leverages a logarithmic decomposition of the pole contributions of the plant (the Agile project), the pole and zero contributions of the controller from K_I and K_D, and the gain contribution from the proportional control term K_P. Figure 3.25 illustrates the Bode plot for our model of an Agile project.

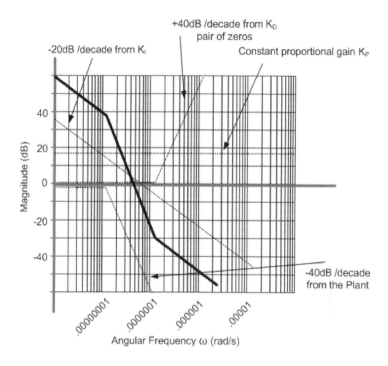

Figure 3.25 – Bode Magnitude Plot for the Agile Project System

In this Gain plot, we can see the net result of adding contributions from our system model components as per Bode construction rules [68].

Each zero, shown as a dotted line adds an increasing gain at a slope of +20 decibels per decade (listed at the bottom by the angular frequencies and shown on the logarithmic paper. Converting a gain to decibels is performed by multiplying 20 by the logarithm of the term. Each pole, also shown with dotted line decreases gain by -20 dB per octave. Each term comes into effect at the breakaway frequency, which is determined by the inverse of the coefficient of the Fourier Transform terms. Note that we have 2 concurrent poles for the plant and 2 concurrent zeros for the design we selected for the derivative controller. Lastly, we see a sample constant gain contribution corresponding to K_P, and a negatively sloping contribution of -20dB at the origin from K_I.

The second plot that we leverage as part of Bode analysis is the Phase plot. Figure 3.26 illustrates the corresponding graph to the Gain plot.

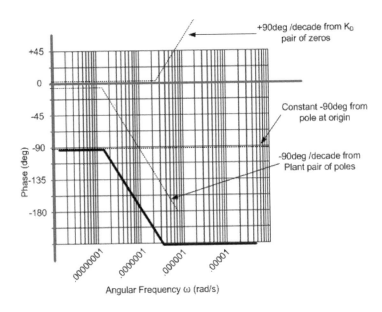

Figure 3.26 – Bode Phase Plot for the Agile Project System

In this plot, we see that each pole from the plant adds -45deg of phase (-90deg in total), and the derivative control adds +90deg in total. The contribution from the K_I component is a constant -90deg of phase, and the K_P does not affect phase. From these two plots, we can understand answers to the tacit questions asked previously in section 3.7.

For purposes of discussion, Figure 3.27 overlays the two previous plots onto one diagram.

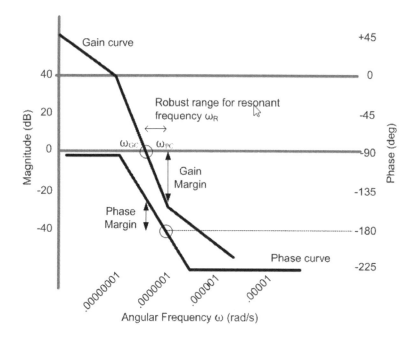

Figure 3.27 – Combined Bode Plot

From Control Theory, *Gain Margin* is the amount of gain that can be added before the system becomes unstable. From the above plot, we can see that adding too much gain (resources on the project) can result in a destabilized plant. We instinctively know this, and shows up at the point where the phase curve becomes -180deg. Also from Control Theory, *Phase Margin* is defined as the additional phase lag (the downwards asymptotic curves) that would have to be added to make the system unstable. This shows up where the gain curve crosses zero dB. This can occur if we lower the frequency too much. Note however that we can also destabilize the plant by increasing the frequency by too much, as this would eat into our gain margin. For each of these performance designations, we can now understand that for a system configuration, which results in a specific Bode plot, we only have a range of "resonant" frequencies in which to operate. We cannot arbitrarily throttle up frequency (shorten iteration duration) too far, or throttle down frequency (obviously not to zero like in the case of the waterfall) or we risk the possibility of instability and poor project performance. If we wish to push iteration lengths to the "extreme", we are forced to reconfigure the plant (which we have control over) such that the resultant pole locations shift. We can also modify the nature of our derivative control term, leveraging different practices to effect different zero locations and thereby change the shape of our control loop. But for any system configuration, there exists an optimal operational range and robust region in which stability is assured. Future work will focus on decomposing various software engineering practices in terms of Control Systems Engineering to highlight the benefits and liabilities that such tradeoffs always manifest.

The analysis performed above assumes no delays within the system. This however is rarely the case. But unnecessarily adding delay into the control loop is at the heart of the Agile Manifesto. Control Theory has a long period of study of this problem. Figure 3.28 illustrates the contribution of delay into the transfer function.

$$G(j\omega) = \frac{K(1 + \frac{1}{z_1} j\omega)(1 + \frac{1}{z_2} j\omega)}{j\omega(1 - \frac{1}{a} j\omega)(1 - \frac{1}{a} j\omega)} e^{-sT_D}$$

Figure 3.28 – Transfer Function with Delay Term

The delay term changes transfer function by adding a transcendental term with e^{-sT_D} term. This term does not add any gain to the Bode Plot, but does add negative phase. This reduces our phase margin, and therefore the robustness of our system. The implications are that the controller gain has to be reduced to maintain stability. Also, the larger the time delay inserted, the larger the gain reduction required. This can be interpreted in terms of Agile doctrine. Specifically, documentation effort that delays developer resources (proportional gain or K_P) has the effect of adding phase to our system. This has the potential to destabilize our system.

Figure 3.29 illustrates the effect of the additional phase component.

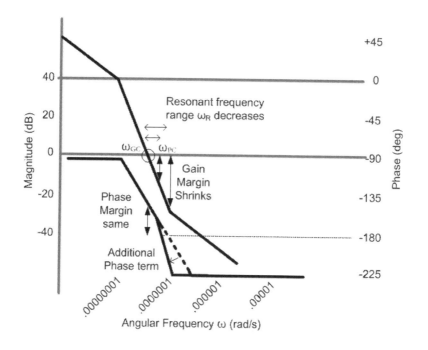

Figure 3.29 – Effect of Delay on Phase

Within the MIT System Dynamics group and Sloan School of Business, study has recently emerged related to the effects of delay on the Learning Organization [75]. This work seems to support the above reasoning from Control Theory, albeit from an Agent-based modeling and simulation basis. What is interesting from this study is the notion of un-perceived delay – delay that is inserted into the system without the organization even knowing that it exists. The research suggests that learning (and therefore organizational performance) is severely hampered if actual delay goes unnoticed.

Both results, from either Organizational System Dynamics research or more fundamentally with Control Systems Engineering are consistent. They both explain why the "Waterfall" must no longer exist. The software project delivery organization that engages in this system model is not even aware that delay is being inserted into the system. This suggests that for all but the luckiest projects, perceived delay is not the same as actual delay. Invariably, iteration will have to occur to close the gap between actual realized scope progress and the actual setpoint, but only after an extremely large delay has resulted before such a recognition occurs. In effect, Waterfall projects are an extremely low frequency accidental iterative development approach with an extremely high risk of instability due to ignorance about the real delay terms being introduced into the system transfer function. This explains a great deal indeed, and should put to bed any remaining argument.

3.9 - Future Exploration

The purpose of this chapter was if nothing else to introduce the field of control systems engineering to the community of software engineering. The hope is that the rigor within this field have an impact on the discussion related to software engineering methods. Many theories are offered as a straw-horse to initiate discovery and debate. Instead of anecdotally describing software engineering practices in absence of scientific grounding, the profession should take the next step and begin the exploration of a foundational model. It would seem reasonable that PID Control theory can serve as a starting point.

In future releases of this work, analysis using state-space matrices and Linear Algebra is available and represents modern as opposed to classical control theory. These techniques leverage simulation and time-domain analysis rather than frequency domain analysis. Also, the emerging field of *Adaptive, Non-Linear Control* deserves special attention due to our recognition of software projects as complex adaptive systems. On this latter topic, control of *Bifurcation* and *Chaotic* systems is at the cutting edge of Control Systems Theory.

Cooperative problem solving is the common theme in the System Theory subfields of social dynamics research and Learning Organizations, Game Theory and Complex Adaptive Systems. The challenge is to integrate the knowledge and results of study from these threads. Control Systems Engineering provides a concrete foundation for integrating the other branched threads with the benefit being many years of practical application and actionable results in the physical world.

Chapter 4: SDLC 3.0 – A Complex Adaptive System of Patterns

We have just explored a model and the Applied Science with respect to IT project organizational systems, what some have called *Chaordic Systems*. These dynamic systems are highly unpredictable, non-linear and complex. It is suggested that although these systems are stochastic rather than deterministic, a project organization is "controllable" such that deliveries can be influenced to converge within their inherent near optimal bounds. And it is the system of practices that comprise the plant and also implement the controller that affect system dynamics. What is needed is an understanding of the potential modern software engineering practices and how each affects the project's dynamic response. And this suite of practices should not be exclusive to those popularized within the Agile movement.

To perform the work of studying the dynamic effects of the practices, certain principles should guide the reasoning process. The next sections discuss these guiding principles for studying the meta-model of software engineering complex adaptive systems. This is followed by a circle-the-wagons view (context-diagram) of the breadth of the system of practices we need to study.

4.1 – Abstracting the Principles of SDLC 3.0

The following section describes a set the philosophies that have been leveraged in articulating SDLC 3.0. These have been garnered through many years of consulting and engagement in real IT organizations and complex projects/programs. Through the process of working in the trenches, and seeing many differing contexts and organizational challenges, this list is abstracted to help the reader identify whether they share similar experience and beliefs. If you identify with these principles/philosophies, we invite you to join us to influence the evolutionary path of the future of SDLC/ IT software project delivery through the Yahoo Group "sdlc_3".

4.1.1 – Value-focused

It is hard to argue with the notion of focusing on the customer's definition of value. But too often, an inside-out perspective as opposed to the "you attitude" ensues within IT. Assuming that IT serves and enables a business enterprise, it is business stakeholders that are the customer of IT. And so, instead of focusing on an IT'ism such as the term "Agile", a customer centric label for SDLC 3.0 might well be "more-for-less". For business customers, results are measured not only in cycle time and the associated opportunity costs when delays occur, but in costs-vs.-benefits. This overarching philosophy is a front –and-centre principle of Lean Thinking and necessarily leads to the relentless removal of waste.

4.1.2 – Pragmatic

Pragmatism comes from experience. Practitioners on the ground do not have the luxury of being pedantic or religious about methods or practices. They will leverage "whatever it takes" to achieve the results demanded by their customers. And their results do speak for themselves such that you can always spot a pragmatist – one who consistently achieves success. SDLC 3.0 intends to be experience-based. The profession does not need yet another ivory tower. And the contributions made must be adoptable and must be useful in a practical manner.

4.1.3 – Integrated

It is time to end the "iterative method wars" that SDLC 2.0 represents. Not only must we retire the notion of the over-simplistic waterfall, we within IT must stop competing with our method-wares. Instead, all experience is necessary if we are to start the road of improvement towards better business results. It is ignorant to discount things that were "not invented here". Wisdom comes from learning the lessons of the past, and the job at hand should be to harvest these lessons into a useful toolkit. In other words, leave nothing on the field. This includes not only integrating the iterative SDLC methods into a system of useful tools, but also the discipline-centric bodies-of-knowledge (i.e. PMBOK, the IEEE Software Engineering SWEBOK [76]), and the non-project delivery knowledge as well (ITIL, the Enterprise Architecture EABOK [77] & The Open Group Architecture Framework – TOGAF [78], and COBIT).

4.1.4 – Holistic

SDLC's and the projects that leverage them do not happen in a vacuum, but rather live within a larger enterprise business context. Modern IT enterprises contain many missions, including Business-IT Alignment, Resource Optimization, Enterprise Risk Management, and Service Operations. The sometimes oversimplified project-centric perspective where Agile approaches are focused are far downstream from the strategic activity that occurs in IT. That is not to say that Agile, Lean and Unified Process principles and practices should not be abstracted and applied to such things as Portfolio Management. Instead, a holistic view ensures that the stream of strategic/coarse grained demand for IT is integrated with fine-grained demand for service all the way to the production environment.

4.1.5 – Value-stream engineered

Modern IT organizations are complex. As such, the engineering tools that enable us to reason about such complexity typically involve visualization. Tools like value-stream mapping and state-space models enable us to identify waste. The world of Lean Thinking calls this approach to business *Learning to See* [79] . Just as we engineer software systems by leveraging complexity reducing tools, we should also leverage such tools to engineering the IT Business system.

4.1.6 – Component-oriented

By breaking up methods into their constituent parts or "components", one is more likely to enable reuse in a wider variety of situations. Just as we architect software using objects for information hiding, abstraction, polymorphism and the like, practice or pattern "components" enable knowledge hiding along with an understanding of the relationships among interfaces into a system of patterns. In this way we can seek to isolate practices subject to a high degree of change while preserving stability of the overall system.

4.1.7 – Compliant

SDLC 3.0 is founded on the notion of balance. The spectrum that exists between ultra-ceremony approaches and associated practices, and the ultra-low ceremony approaches has always fanned a heated and passionate debate. The degree of "ceremony" within this political spectrum typically surrounds the amount of documentation produced. But this spectrum is more about risk tolerance, and documentation is coincidental to the issue of the evidentiary requirements of compliance. While risks are not mitigated through documentation, the organizations that judge the due diligence of risk mitigation efforts can only use persisted information as forms of evidence. This should in no way imply documents, as a data-centric perspective achieves the same standard of care with documents simply being the result of running a "report". But make no mistake, the reality is that Sarbanes-Oxley (SOX) [80] and Statement of Auditing Standards- SAS-70 [81] audits are here to stay for the foreseeable future, and the implications of a failed audit are large.

4.1.8 – Actionable

Practices need to be actionable. Blindly stipulating with broad strokes that low-tech is always the answer is culturally sensitive to community norms, but ignorant. For example, always avoiding the use of tools simply because that word lives on the right-hand side of the Manifesto is unwise. Doing so leads to obvious difficulty when dealing with such issues as scale or geographical distribution when low-tech yellow sticky's are advocated for Kanban boards when workflow technology can achieve the same de facto function without the problems of form.

4.1.9 – Including

Getting beyond community jargon is essential and a key feature of SDLC 3.0. Boiling down practices to their essence fosters inclusiveness such that various communities can come together. Attempting to build a centrist movement where we can agree on synonyms and synergies should replace extremist, rigid, black and white dogma and interpretations.

4.1.10 – Evolving/Living

Once the task of integrating prior knowledge and experience available from modern software engineering approaches is complete, the job is not finished. The world of Software Engineering needs to develop a culture of Kaizen or continuous incremental improvement. While it may be argued that this has occurred to date, it should also be noted that the continuous improvement has been locally optimized to within method, discipline or organizational boundaries. Evolution of the Software Engineering state-of-the-practice requires these limits to be transcended such that optimization of the software delivery value stream as a whole can occur.

To this point, SDLC 3.0 is not intended to be an end but a beginning. The idea of integrating and baselining modern software engineering approaches should lead to continued development and future baselines, whether they result from corrective, perfective or adaptive maintenance. New versions should also reflect major new practice experience features.

To this end we have stood up a software engineering backlog for managing this continual improvement. It can be found at www.sdlc-3.com/cqweb/login use "contributor/contributor" as credentials.

4.2 – A Domain Model for Modern Software Engineering

A discussion has emerged within Agile circles asking the question -"what is next"? In one breath, Agilist's stipulate that their approach is nirvana. In the next they cite the need for continuous improvement, which results in a search of an entire new method. Or worse, they compare and contrast approaches en-masse. Take recent comparisons of Lean and Agile - which approach came first (which was Lean by the way); which is better; or how to contort one into the other. This unfortunately misses the point. Treating an approach as a prescriptive all-or-nothing proposition is definitely counter to the underpinnings of the Manifesto.

Because each of the modern software engineering approaches stems from differing experiences (contexts), it is unreasonable to assume that they will fit en-masse to every project or organization. The differing approaches need to be instantiated, which necessarily means tailoring the method to the circumstances on the ground. To tailor a method for the circumstances on the ground (the context) means to select the elements of the approach that makes sense. Historically this has meant tailoring artifact templates or selecting tasks to perform. But this approach to tailoring is misguided, as templates represent persistent stores for knowledge, and blur or hide how the work needs to occur. And tailoring tasks implies the ability to predict, especially when the tasks are overly granular. Instead, insightful tailoring of a method undertakes to select the correct practices for a situation. Modern software engineering approaches are commonly decomposed into a set of principles and practices. A practice is *"a technique effective at delivering a desired outcome"*. Controversially, a "best" practice is a technique that is believed to be more effective at delivering a particular outcome than any other technique. It just so happens that these definitions are very similar to that of a pattern. A pattern is *"a solution to a problem within a context"*. Therefore, patterns are a crisper way to describe methods due to the fact that by definition patterns are only relevant when context is considered. Such "method patterns" define the essence of the proven solutions to software delivery problems within given contexts.

When looking at all modern software engineering approaches as a set of patterns, the question naturally arises as to whether there is overlap, synonyms or redundancy. The answer to this question is that due to the branched or silo'd nature of the SDLC 2.0 generation of methodology, much commonality exists. If this commonality can be integrated among the various community-specific practice sets, a system of patterns can emerge such that unique, community specific pattern experience can be leveraged by all in context. Such an integrated modern software engineering system of patterns is the essence of SDLC 3.0, the title of this book.

When one begins to catalog the various patterns/practices, one can identify a discrete set of "why's" within the various approaches. These pattern archetypes are clustered around 10 basic value propositions. Figure 4.1 lists these practice types:

Figure 4.1 Archetypes of Modern Software Engineering Practices

Figure 4.2 that follows represents a domain model of modern software engineering practices as integrated into SDLC 3.0. Such a "visual glossary" identifies the synergies where practices are unique within their communities' stated bodies of knowledge, and where commonality and similarities exist.

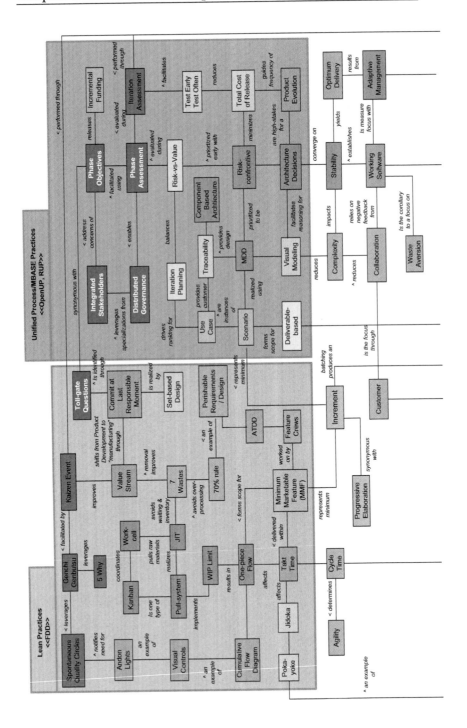

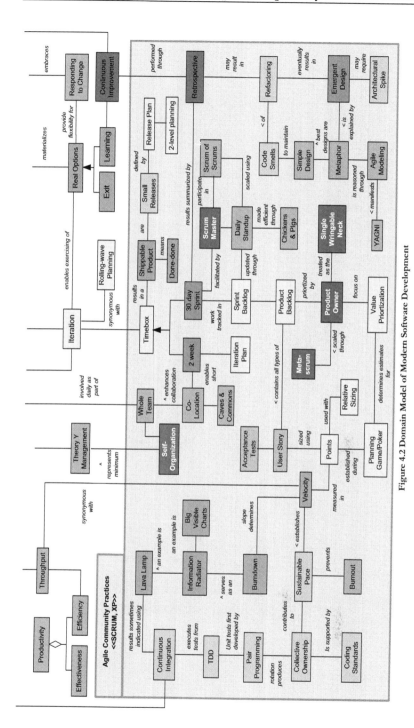

Figure 4.2 Domain Model of Modern Software Development

In the domain model, each package (large file folder box) represents an integrated set of practices independent of the method to which they are found. In this way, the practices are separated from brand loyalty and integrated into a relationship with the other practices that the community embraces. Extending this further, encapsulating the common terms that are not unique to a specific IT community enables the three modern software engineering communities that have evolved during the SDLC 2.0 era to be integrated.

When looking at the domain model, one can see linkages among each of the three community practice sets. This illustrates that contrary to the beliefs held close by the faithful, such practices are either "I say tomato, you say tomato" type differences that are trivial in nature, or are slightly differing examples of concepts that were originated from differing evolutionary paths. For example, surrounding the core philosophy of iterative development and learning through concrete forms of feedback are the practices of *Kaizen, Iteration Assessments* and *Retrospectives*. Each are differing socialized terms for the same central concept and the differences are irrelevant, at least to the point of necessitating unique differentiated methods.

Each community typically has focused their efforts looking inwards, most often gravitating to what they know. They even have had the tendency to focus on ruling out neighboring community practices, or attempting to subsume value-add practices under their brand umbrella. For example, some within the Agile community claim Lean under their brand. This is a misrepresentation, as Lean precedes Agile thinking by many decades. Figure 4.3 illustrates the long lineage of Lean leading up to its application to software development.

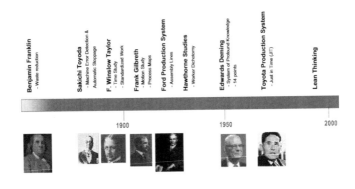

Figure 4.3 – The long lineage of Lean

A wiser approach is to explore the true essence of where process improvement ideas originated such that learning can continue beyond prima-fascia grounds. Each community has innovated practices due to unique conditions on the ground that lead to their articulation. Within a set of circumstances (the project context), the "best-of-breed" practices should be leveraged. This is opposed to the "best-of-brand" type choice that is typically made at the beginning of a project. Instead of selecting method X en masse, a more pragmatic approach is to select practice A from X, B from Y and so on. These specific practices support and integrate with the common ground practices that are the essence of modern software engineering (and are non-negotiable).

In Chapter 3 we described the system's model view in which these practices operate. Figure 4.4 illustrates a high level contextual view of the project organization.

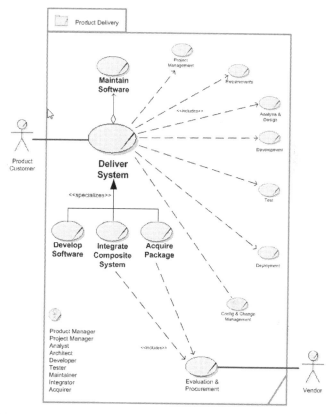

Figure 4.4 – Software Development Project Capabilities

The above picture describes the core mission of a software development project, identifies who instantiates this ecosystem (the customer), and articulates a reasonable division of capabilities discharged by various types of specialized roles. But this view only articulates the "what" – the kinds of activity that are performed, and by "whom". It does not prescribe the "how", which is left to the selection of practices that match the situation. And it does not prescribe any particular sequencing, but rather that these activities are involved in the delivery of software.

SDLC 3.0 represents a system of practices/patterns, which defines all the behavioral aspects of the software development ecosystem. It articulates the "how" we do things in the context of differing situations. These behaviors in turn imply structural aspects to our work configuration. We can select a practice from a communities' specific base of experience, but it needs to be integrated within the common ground that is the essence of modern software engineering.

The next chapter describes the common ground practices that comprise modern software engineering and the broad experience base that it represents.

Chapter 5: Common Ground in Modern Software Engineering

Contrary to the volume of the rhetoric during the "iterative method wars" period of time, commonality does exist. While terminology may differ, the management science behind the core practices is not materially different. Figure 5.1 illustrates a higher, executive-level picture of the Modern Software Engineering domain model presented in the previous chapter.

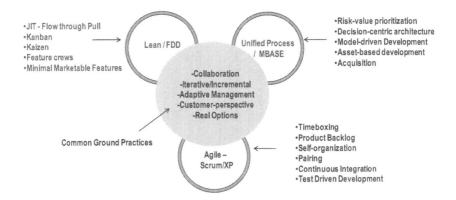

The following text labels appear in the figure:

•JIT - Flow through Pull
•Kanban
•Kaizen
•Feature crews
•Minimal Marketable Features

Lean / FDD

Unified Process / MBASE

•Risk-value prioritization
•Decision-centric architecture
•Model-driven Development
•Asset-based development
•Acquisition

-Collaboration
-Iterative/Incremental
-Adaptive Management
-Customer-perspective
-Real Options

Common Ground Practices

Agile – Scrum/XP

•Timeboxing
•Product Backlog
•Self-organization
•Pairing
•Continuous Integration
•Test Driven Development

Figure 5.1 – High-level model of SDLC 3.0

Not only does each iterative development era community share common ground, but communities that are typically associated with holding on to traditional approaches and the accidental waterfall have always articulated some of these practices in their bodies of knowledge as well. For example, the PMBOK has included Sections 1.2.3 and 6.1.2.3 since 2004, which advocates the use of Progressive Elaboration and Rolling-wave planning. Such terms are different ways of articulating incremental development and the horizon of visibility/predictability when it comes to planning, respectively. Other common ground practices have only recently been identified because the community themselves are only awakening to the nomenclature. An example of this common ground practice would be Real Options Theory [82].

5.1 – Iterative/Incremental Development

Fundamental to all modern software delivery methods is the notion of iterations or cycles. Iterations serve as a central feedback mechanism to facilitate learning from frequent demonstrations of working software (increments). The increments that result from developing iteratively serve as the true measure of progress, which implies that scope completion, not effort expenditure is what is to be monitored and controlled. Also inherent with iterative development is early testing engagement, and more frequent engagement with customers.

Iterative development has been a cornerstone practice with all successful development, even as far back as the Waterfall. The original "first generation" Waterfall method paper reflected on the experience that to be successful, "one needs to do it twice". However, in many instances that followed either misinterpretation, change resistance or other human factors resulted in less than successful application of the core tenet.

Differences with how iteration is approached exist within the three modern software development communities. Emphasis within the Agile community is on time-boxing as applied to iteration. Such a practice is intended to limit WIP, and establish a stable metric for velocity, the amount of scope delivered per fixed period of time. Even within Agile, different approaches advocate different frequencies of iteration, with XP advocating 2 week periods, and Scrum advocating 30 day periods.

The Unified Process advocates fixed nominal iteration periods per phase, with the suggestion that differing themes within the phases require different iteration durations to achieve meaningful increments of working software. Early iterations focused on Architectural risk reduction require potentially longer iterations, while Construction Phase iterations leverage smaller duration iterations. However, in contrast with Agile approaches, iterations within the Unified Process are deliverable-based as opposed to time-boxed. The emphasis is on completion of each increment of software rather than completion of the time-box.

Lean takes a similar incremental approach as the Unified Process. But to limit WIP, the contents of an increment are singular. This implies an iteration-of-one scope element – one-piece-flow. Such micro-increments do not leverage time-boxing, nor do they batch multiple "minimal marketable features"[83] together, something that could be seen as occurring with the normal concept of iterations. As such, Lean has been called "iteration-less" development.

The scientific basis for why iteration and negative feedback works was discussed in Chapter 3. Other works that explain the economic benefits of iteration have been published in recent years as well. One notable example from Hakan Erdogmus and J Favaro at the National Research Council of Canada (NRC) is to explain the value accrued from iterating through the use of Real Options analysis [84]. A Real Option is a right but not an obligation to exercise a decision at a future time. Real Options are similar to Financial Options (derivatives), but apply to business decisions in the face of uncertainty. In the NRC paper, the suggestion is that Learning, Exit and Delay/Timing options, each which hold inherent value, can only be exercised if a project organization developing software iterates. Otherwise, the ability to leverage deferred decisions would not be available, and value would be left on the table. Figure 5.2 illustrates the concept of Real Options as applied to explaining the economic value of iterative development over single-pass waterfall.

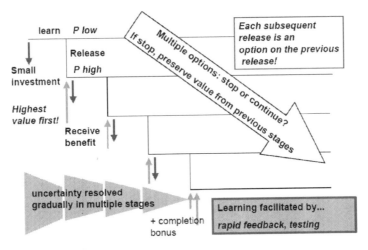

Figure 5.2 – Real Options Decision Tree [84]

The word Agility serves as the basis of the Agile Manifesto. The pace of change was the critical element or "home base" for the applicability of these methods [85]. Therefore, the emphasis within the Agile community has always been on rapid development cycles to enable reaction to change. As we saw from the above explanation related to real options theory and the value from learning and exit options, feedback is necessary to accrue this value. Although only anecdotal in nature, the advice from Agilist's has always been to increase the iteration frequency in the face of more rapid change. But this community is not the only community within modern software engineering to articulate similar ideas. Within the Unified Process community, the mantra centered around iterative development has been "test-early, test-often". And within *Lean Thinking* circles, whether it be Lean Manufacturing or *Lean Software Development*, the notion of building quality in and prevention of errors through *poka yoke* has always worked hand in hand with the principle of "fail fast".

5.2 – Focus on the Primary Artifact ...Working Software

Lean Thinking principles and Value Stream Analysis tells us that primary value-add activities should be maximized and non-value add activities should be questioned. This is so that delivery of value can occur as fast as possible and that IT can yield the highest productivity, both efficiency and effectiveness. Similarly, the Agile community has always focused on "Working Software over Comprehensive Documentation", as articulated in the Agile Manifesto. Other practices like XP's Core-team attempt to protect the constraining element within the primary value stream, namely the developers.

With the Unified Process, the architecture-centric emphasis is intended to govern that early focus is on the "right" software. Such a practice ensures late project agility by ensuring that the riskiest, hardest development occurs first. Rather than relying on Product Owners/Customers to drive development and potentially avoid the necessary but often invisible aspects of the software, the Unified Process ensures that last minute gotcha's do not occur. Also, effective visualization and abstraction are seen as a way to minimize the amount of development that actually has to occur. In essence, this practice is intended to alleviate the core constraint of software delivery (developers) by developing less stuff. Unfortunately, due to the immaturity of apprentices of the practice, all too often modeling becomes a primary form of waste.

Focus on the primary work product is identifiable to the business stakeholders to which software development serves. Michael Porter's book "Competitive Strategy" introduced the concept of the value chain to the world in 1985 [86]. In this work, he articulated what is core value within an enterprise and what is secondary value in deriving margins for a firm. What was most important from this observation is how it plays into competitive strategy or in general the efficiency and effectiveness of the firm. By focusing improvement efforts on the primary value chain, competitive advantage is most likely to occur. This is the basis for the focus on the developer within Agile circles, as it is only code that is of primary value to customers, so getting better at turning out code (as opposed to documents) is of the most importance. Figure 5.3 illustrates Porters value chain.

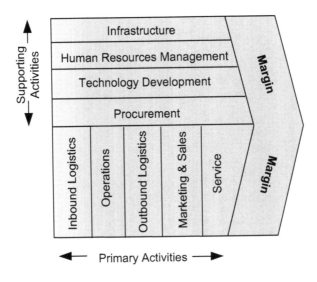

Figure 5.3 – Michael Porter's Value Chain

5.3 – Waste Aversion

The corollary to the focus on primary value is the relentless elimination of waste. Waste results from any activity that adds cost without adding value. Toyota's Taiichi Ohno identified the primary sources of waste, which he called *"The Seven Deadly Wastes"* [13]. These are as follows:

Table 5.1 – Taiichi Ohno's 7 Types of Waste

Waste Type	Description
1. Overproduction	Producing more than is needed for immediate use.
2. Delay/Waiting	Any delay between the end of one process and the start of the next activity.
3. Transportation/ Conveyance	Unnecessary movement of products, materials or information.
4. Motion	Unnecessary movement of people, such as walking, reaching and stretching.

5. Inventory	Any raw material, work-in-process, or finished goods that exceed what is required to meet customer needs just in time and to maintain process stability.
6. Over-processing	Using more energy or activity than is needed to produce a product – or adding more value than the agreed standard.
7. Defects/Correction	Any production that results in rework or scrap.

The Agile community has long held a waste-adverse perspective. Terms like *"YAGNI – you ain't gonna need it"* [87] are intended to instill a philosophy around waste removal. However, Agile limits the treatment of waste with the assumption that everything is waste that can be immediately removed, regardless of whether it is Type-1 (un-necessary) or Type-2 (necessary) waste. Specific practices within the Agile community focused on waste reduction include Daily Stand-ups from Scrum and Sustainable Pace from XP. This latter practice relates to the 8th deadly waste identified later by Ohno, namely *"Employee Burnout"* [88].

The Unified Process approach has always embraced the idea of working software as the primary source of value and the elimination of waste. Unfortunately, due to the largest manifestation of this process meta-model being the Rational Unified Process, the Unified Process has largely been deemed to be wasteful due to its document centric perception. With almost 100 artifacts/deliverables articulated in the tailor-down framework commercial product, it is easy to see how this perception was created. But even though the large number of documents was a result of taking an object-orientation concept for building robustness into the framework, the Unified Process through the guidance of instantiating only what makes sense for a given context has always been waste adverse.

When it comes to leveraging the waste articulation from Taiichi Ohno, various authors have attempted to extrapolate the waste categorization to software development. Table 5.2 illustrates this in the case of Lean Software Development book:

Table 5.2 – 7 Types of Waste from Lean Software Development

Waste Type	Lean Software Extrapolation
1. Overproduction	Extra features
2. Delay/Waiting	Waiting
3. Transportation	Task switching
4. Motion	Motion
5. Inventory	Partially done work
6. Over-processing	Excess processes
7. Defects/Correction	Defects

Expanding upon this work, the following serves as an attempt at continuing to extrapolate the seven types of waste. It is intended to stimulate exploratory discussion and is subject to improvement. In the first table, we take the interpretation of *Overproduction* to be producing stuff (in advance) that is not asked for by the customer.

Table 5.3 – Stopping Overproduction

Producing Artifacts, Just-in-Case:

Production of non-value added work products should only occur for specific reasons. Typically this amounts to necessary waste, waste that would not be required and could be eliminated if work were performed in a different manner. Producing large requirements documents (sometimes retroactively) "just in case" because they might be needed in the future to understand why the system was built, and what it is supposed to do represents overproduction. This is sometimes cited in compliance regimes as a necessary control objective to mitigate knowledge loss risks. These costly work products are perishable, and the knowledge management objectives cited above can be better served by artifacts that are of use to the customer like User Guides and Training materials. And design documentation nowadays can always be reverse engineered through the use of automation. If other forms of waste are to be prevented through the use of Asset Based Development, design documentation is likely to be the result of prior reuse opportunity identification, and its creation serves a higher strategic delivery objective. But not all design fits into this category, so just producing reams of documentation "just because" is wasteful.

Demand Management:

Ensuring that all production traces back to customer orders is a fundamental principle of Lean. Implementing fine-grained demand management (also synonymous with the Scrum Product Backlog) ensures that resource expenditure is focused on bona-fide customer need. This means no more extra technology "features" for the sake of IT. In this way, customer orders "pull" IT supply through the use of a constantly prioritized queuing mechanism.

In the second table, we interpret the *Delay* waste type as that related to the effects of underutilization due to work configuration. This includes delays in making the decisions about the approach and work breakdown structure for a project.

Table 5.4 – Avoiding Delay / Waiting

Impedance Mismatches among the role centric BOK's:

Differing philosophies on what needs to be done by different specialized disciplines on a project typically leads to unnecessary delay. Too often, work is performed as per an upstream BOK. This is instead of producing work output for the downstream consumers who should define what they need so that they can perform their work.

Pedantic debates about approach/methodology:

Get on with it already. The huge amount of delay incurred by philosophical or pedantic debates and personal preference still result in today's IT enterprises. And how many times have you seen the hitting of the reset button because of a changing of the guard. Modern software engineering should be stable and mature enough to limit these discussions to one of practice fit, not wholesale method fit.

Lack of Parallel Development Support:

Delaying the delivery of value due to the serialization of internal work breakdown structures is extremely wasteful. Always batching demand into a serial train of projects is too often the norm, rather than thinking in terms of parallel product generations and performing maintenance iterations in parallel with new development.

In the third table, the interpretation of *Transportation* waste is focused on document movement that is shuttled about projects and organizations. It is most commonly associated with functional-oriented as opposed to value-stream oriented organizations.

Table 5.5 – Reducing Transportation

Documents thrown over the wall:

Reducing the "document-centric" culture prevalent in traditional/legacy software engineering approaches is an opportunity related to Transportation/Conveyance waste. Serialized, non-collaborative or silo'd work approaches which rely on persistent stores of information (documents) to be "thrown over the wall" are instances of this type of waste. Techniques such as Joint-Requirements-Development, team-co-location, pair-programming, and multi-hat wearing address this type of waste. And when necessary due to geographical and temporal constraints, trends in Application Lifecycle Management – ALM [89] facilitate increased collaboration and reduced document-centricity.

In the fourth table, *Motion* waste within software engineering is found in the physical movement of people. This typically takes the form of meetings. Studies show the effect that meetings have on organizational productivity. The time spent in the meeting is not the only work time lost due to the meeting, but also the distraction of an impending meeting as well as the re-establishment of the original train of thought from the dropped task all surround the meeting timeslot. And if you look at some calendars of project resources in some enterprises, it is as if some feel that the fuller their calendar, the more productive they are.

Table 5.6 – Reducing Motion

Physical Meetings in Leau of True Collaboration:

Scrum Daily Stand-ups are a way to cut down on inefficiencies related to a "culture of meetings". This Agile community practice limits the amount of less-than-ideal engineering hours. Taking this strategy even further with Lean and enabling a larger scaling of the practice. Recent trends have emerged to achieve the same "what was done yesterday, what was done today and what is blocking you" type of collaborative information sharing through the virtualization of the practice related to ALM collaboration technologies. The need for face-to-face communications can be more efficiently "pulled" in a real-time, continuous and automated way. A *"virtual, real-time standup"* realizes the same openness, better efficiency than that of physical "stand-ups", and results in continuous visibility without the physical movement of people.

Inventory is one of the key wastes within Lean Thinking and is at the heart of key Lean practices. Historically, inventory waste was very toxic within Japanese manufacturing circles due to the limited real estate of companies. But the queuing theory concepts targeting this type of waste in manufacturing can be extrapolated to knowledge work. Identifying inventory of various forms such that it can be removed creates overall flow and work evenness. As will be discussed in Chapter 6, this is shown to maximize throughput/productivity.

Table 5.7 – Limiting Inventory

Batch Planning Inventory:

The continual avoidance of rolling-wave planning guidance from the PMBOK typically leads to large up-front critical-path-method efforts that hold up utilization by core value-stream members – the developers. Batched planning efforts for projects or even iterations represents inventory waste. Instead, the planning of work breakdown should be performed just-in-time for individually prioritized scope as queuing theory suggests. The planning of work should occur once a Request is transitioned into the In-Progress state by a self organizing team, not in advance by a centralized planner. One piece workflow also avoids spikes in resource needs associated with the batching of work which can lead to the bad resource utilization technique of multi-tasking. This practice leads to very costly "context" switching of resources, which is known to cause a loss of productivity on the order of 20% time per concurrent task [90].

Requirements Inventory - BRUF:

Producing stockpiles of un-developed, un-tested requirements represents inventory waste. Regardless of whether requirements are document-centric or not, they should be viewed as "perishable goods". Elements of elaborated scope should flow to the next downstream effort (realization) as fast as possible, as they add no intrinsic value by themselves.

Design Inventory – BDUF:

Producing stockpiles of un-developed, un-tested design artifacts represents inventory waste. Regardless of whether the practice of model-driven development is performed, design should be viewed as a tool to get to the next best effort – development.

Integration & Test Execution Inventory:

Leaving software un-integrated and un-tested is an extremely costly form of inventory. Inserting delay in the feedback loop of the project system can not only have a destabilizing effect, but the cost of delay curves related to late discovery of defects suggests that 11th hour testing and late integration must be avoided. This is commonly associated at the extreme with the waterfall level of batching. The Agile community practice Continuous or near-continuous integration should be leveraged to their fullest extent to avoid this type of waste.

Risk Inventory:

Letting risks pile up in an unmitigated, un-avoided or un-accepted state represents inventory. A risk confrontive strategy focuses on removing uncertainty inventory for the IT investment. The Unified Process forces risk management early through risk-then-value prioritization. As such, there should be no more "hall pass" for doing risky stuff last.

Decision Inventory:

Decisions should be delayed for as long as possible so as to enable the real options value to accrue. But the batching of decision governance unnecessarily can let decisions pile up as inventory. This can result in the passing of the "last responsible moment", where the ability to make a decision becomes too late.

Overprocessing is the addition of more energy/effort than that needed to meet customer demand. It manifests itself in many differing ways.

Table 5.8 – Over-processing

Building the perfect mousetrap:

It would appear that recent discussion related to treating software engineering as a "craft" might be tantamount to developers wanting to build the perfect mousetrap when one is not requested. Craft automobiles are sold at a premium and target a niche market. Considering all business environments as being the consumers of "luxury market software" would seem unreasonable. A self-serving interpretation of this pride in workmanship movement could amount to building Porche's when an economy car will suffice. Similarly, attempting to localize all possible changes through design robustness techniques such that the software can "withstand the 100 year storm" might be total waste when the software's lifespan is only a few years.

Breaking the 70% Rule:

Having downstream work-centers pull work products from their upstream counterparts ensures that over-processing waste does not occur. Instead of specialized resources focusing on local optimization of their output, a shift towards optimizing the time-to-value occurs. Practices like whole-team iteration time-boxing and the US Marine-Corps 70% rule [91] are similar manifestations that focus on ensuring that outputs within the value stream are "just barely good enough".

Modeling for the sake of modeling:

Closely related to the previous waste, analysis paralysis or boil the ocean reasoning efforts amount to substantial over-processing waste. Problem solvers can sometimes fall into the abyss when dealing with high complexity, and a fear of failure can lead to second guessing and over-processing in the areas on modeling or the amount of analysis undertaken.

Manual metrics collection:

Attempting to provide meaningful visibility into IT investment health is a reasonable governance goal. Accepting outcomes only at project completion represents a lack of due diligence. But too often, manual data collection attempts to provide this insight which results in a lot of busy work. This is due to a lack of data that should naturally be available from the normal course of doing work. This type of waste can be avoided through modern workflow and process-centric configuration management infrastructure.

Pet technology insertion:

Limiting technology choices as a strategy through usage of Asset-based Development is focused on eliminating this type of waste. Mandated acquisition-orientation and technology-stack reasoning tools that facilitate quick matching of problem to reasonable solution can have very large order payoff. This approach also limits the waste from selfish technologists trying to keep pace with technology on the customers' nickel.

Always doing "Architecture":

Because of the multitude and ambiguous definitions of architecture, teams often spend many cycles "doing architecture" when none is required. For example, attempting to do formal Viewpoint/View reasoning as described in IEEE 1471 [92] when a simple decision-rationale approach will capture the necessary reasoning is an example of over-processing waste. For example, many typical J2EE projects probably don't have much risk as the "operating parameters" of the typical technologies are well known and documented.

The final category of waste from Taiichi Ohno is that of *Defects*. Obviously, defects occur in software engineering. But certain issues can materially lead to the probability of defects, so eliminating these "root causes" leads to a reduction of defect waste.

Table 5.9 – Defects

Eliminate context switching:
Increasing work focus by reducing the context switching associated with batching reduces defect and rework waste. Also, the simplicity of a pull-system oriented process reduces process complexity which can lead to the possibility of defects. A move towards continuous integration of smaller, more atomic product requests/orders leads to less drift within a code-line. Leveraging automated builds through integration with configuration management infrastructure leads to a more even flow and enables more real-time visibility into potential problems. Stopping defects early before they can collect in batch avoids disruptions that can occur due to "line-stoppage".
Embrace Asset-based Development:
Build less stuff and you necessarily will have less defects. Instead of just diving into the coding effort, taking a step back and leveraging assets in the form of packages, cloud services and developing composite systems can have a drastic effect on defect reduction.
Estimation without Integral and Derivative Data:
Any estimates on effort given without looking at current project state velocity or historical averages are worthless. And worse, it is probably the single most reason for the Standish Chaos results to date. Estimates based on patterns of demand with a historical context that can be used for calibration over time is the only form of estimation that should be considered for effort. All other estimates should be given in relative sizing terms only.
Two pairs of eyes:
Two pairs of eyes are better than one. Specialized pairs of eyes are more effective at spotting problems than that of generalists. This implies that single Product Owner-only governance is inefficient and ineffective. Let alone costly, as the amount of knowledge and experience that would be required for single person, effective governance would require very expensive resources. And even if a firm could afford them it is doubtful that such resources exist in large numbers.

5.4 – Adaptive Management

There is a recent movement within PMI circles to establish Agile Project Management as a portion of the PMBOK. While it is understandable that the PMI wishes to include the Agile brand in their literature, a more fundamental term should be applied to the project management approach of modern software engineering – that of *Adaptive Project Management*. Such a label is related to Systems Theory and articulates the "steering" of complex software project environments.

To explain adaptive as opposed predictive management, a metaphor is instructive. This metaphor is that of sailing. The project manager can be seen as being the captain with certain levers at their disposal such that they can discharge the duty bestowed upon them by a project sponsor to steer the project safely and successfully to its goal. This is consistent with most if not all management structures in corporate IT, and yet embraces the fundamental tenet of "embracing change" that is central to Agile. To explore the metaphor, the Figure 5.4 illustrates one "project type", namely crossing the Gulf Stream from Florida to the island of Bimini in the Bahamas.

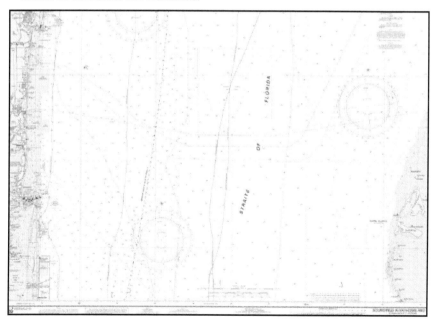

Figure 5.4 – Nautical Chart of the Straits of Florida

The reader may take objection to this analogy at the outset as it relates to Software Development. IT rarely has the convenience of "fixed land masses" to move towards. While it is true that the scope/goals of a software project are much more unknown than the position of Bimini on a longstanding nautical chart, so too can it be said that entirely unprecedented projects are becoming more or less rare. Whether a project manager/leader has the convenience of a simple chart to understand the environment in which he/she must "set sail" related to changing technologies and business conditions is debatable, but such information is typically available for most IT endeavors in some form, somewhere. Payroll systems have been built for a long time, as have accounting systems and the like. When it comes to scope and customer goals, they are not as stochastic as one might think. What is far more variable is the interacting agents (the people) and the errors that occur within their interactions and knowledge transfer. This is akin to the high degree of variability of the water above the chart in the previous picture. In the chart, water depths are plotted in relation to the relative stable tectonic plate below. But what changes and materially affects the instance of crossing the stream is the nature of the currents that change due to variable water temperature, and the variability of the winds that affect the rate by which the vessel will be impacted by the gulf stream current.

To run this project - one of successfully crossing the stream in such a manner that arrival in Bimini occurs at all, and at such a time as anchoring/docking can occur with the benefit of daylight - two different approaches can be taken; one that leverages feedback to adapt to changing conditions of the weather, the sea and the performance of the vessel; and one without, based on (at best) historical intuition (i.e. educated guess) as to how to point the vessel into the stream, or (at worst) wishful thinking.

An inexperienced captain / project manager might see the simplicity of taking a best guess at hitting the goal of Bimini. The thinking might be something like just get over there close to the island, and then finish off the final leg with a late-stage correction when within sight of land. But what appears to be a reasonable and elegant solution turns out to be very risky, inefficient and historically dangerous or at the very least unpleasant. In this situation the captain is forced to weather out the night at sea until daylight returns so that anchoring or docking and clearing customs can occur. Figure 5.5 illustrates the lack of leveraging feedback known as waterfall in software engineering and Dead Reckoning in sailing.

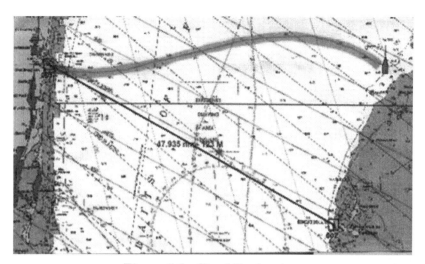

Figure 5.5 – Dead Reckoning

Note the final location in the worst case scenario when a totally uneducated guess was made as to the heading to proceed upon. In this case, the vessel ends up at Great Isaac lighthouse, fraught with hidden perils and rocks from the Great Bahamian bank which has claimed so many ships (i.e. the Bermuda Triangle). What is illustrative here is the totally unpredictable amount of being set-down by the Gulf Stream current. This current varies at different points during the crossing, ranging from 0 knots to almost 2.5 knots in the middle, and is always changing throughout the year. A better educated guess could be made as to the heading to follow – say 150 degrees Magnetic; but it would still amount to a stab in the dark as to where one would end up almost no ability to recognize location visually from the landmasses (if you are lucky to even get such a point of reference at sea).

In the second example and one that illustrates Adaptive Project Management. In this approach, the recognition of the high degree of change is enacted within the management plan. At a reasonable frequency the captain starts by looking at historical advice as to a reasonable early crossing heading, which takes into account the integral of all prior learning. But once underway and with the actual instance of the voyage taking place with the particular vessel and crew in question, frequent observations are taken (the feedback) as to the GPS (Global Positioning System) position such that a track can be plotted. If the Rhumb-line (the direct and shortest distance between the start and end points) is strayed from, the captain can make adjustments in the heading to accommodate for the track error (at that point in time). The cycle repeats. The frequency of plotting waypoints determines the amount of cumulative error that will ensue. This is important because the resources that are available are not unlimited – whether it be fuel or daylight – similar to a software project and the expectations of the paying stakeholders. Figure 5.6 illustrates the metaphor for the Adaptive Project Management approach which is common in all modern software engineering methods.

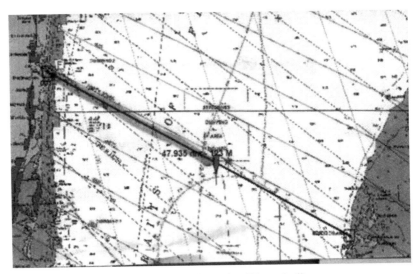

Figure 5.6 – Sailing the Rhumb-line

These two approaches relate to software engineering in that the requirements that collectively form the "heading" for the project are likely to be flawed and are subject to change. All Standish Chaos reports suggest this. So if the software development heading is likely to be flawed, waypoints need to be leveraged to "steer" the project along the optimum course in terms of resource utilization. And the customer (acting as the GPS) needs to take a reading for the project as to the actual versus apparent position on the way towards the goal.

5.5 – Customer Collaboration

A central philosophy related to achieving an understanding of what needs to be built within modern software engineering is the concept of the "you-attitude". This means that one should not assume that they know the customers reality, and one should attempt to seek to understand these wants and needs. This is the essence of Requirements Engineering. But within modern software engineering, one should not think of achieving this understanding solely through a medium of documentation. For reasons discussed earlier related to the nature of tacit knowledge, collaboration first and foremost is required to achieve convergence of the actual need or want. This is the essence of *"Customer collaboration over contract negotiation"* and relates to the required high trust environment needed to elicit tacit knowledge as mentioned in Chapter 1. Both forms of relationship (collaboration and contracts) are approaches to build trust. Collaboration by definition from Webster's dictionary is *"to work jointly with others or together especially in an intellectual endeavor"*. Contracts are sometimes referred to as *"formalized relationships of trust"* in legal circles. But one could argue that to achieve all the six elements of contract requires prediction. Hence the former approach to building the requisite trust relationship is preferred due to the difficulties related to prediction.

Any and all tools should be leveraged if they are effective at achieving an understanding of customer goals efficiently. Note however, that experience has shown that the best feedback medium is through working software due to the rich communication that ensues through demonstration. But "requirements" in the written form do serve a need in projects. Requirements elicitation techniques serve as thinking tools when a software need is complex. And requirements documentation (in whatever form) serves the purpose of persistence related to establishing placeholders for scope in a Product Backlog. Also, requirements serve as a medium for portable review by stakeholders when physical co-location or real-time review and collaboration are not possible.

If one agrees that well formed requirements are 1) Understandable, 2) Unambiguous, 3) Precise, 4) Concise and 5) Testable [93], then scenario based approaches to requirements engineering are another common thread of agreement within modern software practices. This practice has origins that are very prevalent within operational planning enterprises like the US DOD. A scenario describes one possible time-ordered sequence of events. Scenarios represent a simple, natural and semantically relevant approach to capturing a customer's perspective on what is needed within the software product. Scenarios have long been leveraged within the Unified Process community, where they serve as the actionable unit of scope.

Use Case requirements engineering techniques are an example of what could be termed generically "scenario-based practices". Scenarios are "instances" of Use Case "types". In other words, scenarios are the objects formed out of the Use Case class which bundles all the possible run-time variances of behavior. The Use Case type is an important, customer-centric abstraction of desired observable behavior which yields a valuable result in their eyes. As such they can be thought of as an interface to the system to be developed. It hides the complexity of all the permutations and combinations of potential behavior which must be considered and is of interest to the internal development team. Figure 5.7 illustrates the relationships between Use Cases and their scenarios.

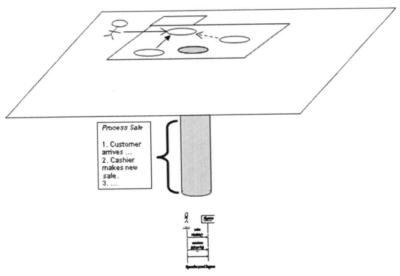

Figure 5.7 – Use Case breadth versus depth

It should be noted that scenarios are also applied to other forms of requirements like quality attributes / non-functional requirements. In this case they are known as *quality scenarios*.

Within the Agile community, user needs are commonly captured through "User Stories". Originating from the Extreme Programming body of knowledge, User Stories are described as:

> *"a software system requirement as one or two sentences in the everyday or business language of the user. Every user story must at some point have one or more acceptance tests attached, allowing the developer to test when the user story is done and also allowing the customer to verify it. Without a precise formulation of the requirements, prolonged non-constructive arguments may arise when the product is to be delivered. They are similar to usage scenarios, except that they are not limited to describing a user interface".*

> XP goes on to say… *"when the time comes to implement the story, developers will go to the customer and receive a detailed description of the requirements face to face."*

www.extremeprogramming.org

When looking for parallels between the two communities, basic definitions are instructive. From Wikipedia, a story is defined as *"a description of a sequence of events"*; and from Webster, *"an account of incidents or events "*. Contrast this to scenario, which from Wikipedia gives us *"a synthetic description of an event or series of actions and events"*; and from Webster, *"a sequence of events especially when imagined; and especially- an account or synopsis of a possible course of action or events"*. From these public definitions the similarity is obvious. So why then do the communities hold such strong-felt views as to the differences between Scenarios/Use Cases and User Stories?

One reason might be from a common misconception Use Cases are heavyweight and wasteful. This is probably due to the examples of "documentation for the sake of documentation" that have occurred from time to time, which is symptomatic of deeper problems like a lack of appreciation of iterative development practice. But when the User Story is complete, it should contain a very similar amount of ceremony/documentation. The view that stories are lighter weight is probably due to a lack of accounting for the acceptance test suite that is required for completeness. So when just looking at the stack of stories in the low-tech format of index cards as the degree of requirements documentation, it is easy to take a stance that Use Cases are bloated. But if you consider that the high-level placeholders for Use Cases are usually in the form of a Use Case Survey (albeit listed in a document and not as index card "records"), and that when proper are only supposed to be brief one or two sentence summaries, then an appropriate apples to apples comparison can be made.

The fundamental difference between the two communities' articulation of the same concept is the degree of reliance on real-time communication, and who extracts the need from customers. The Unified Process advocates that Analysts who understand the problem domain explicitly elaborate the scenarios, whereas the Agile community relies on real-time definition of the scenarios by solution domain Developers in conversation with a customer, not an Analyst. And whereas Analyst's act as facilitators to document the requirements in the Unified Process, the Agile camp outsources the placeholder definition to the customer. Also, the scenarios/stories explicitly serve the dual purpose of test artifacts, so Developers also define functional acceptance tests. This is not to say that having requirements artifacts serve dual duty is a bad idea, as Use Case scenarios and functional test cases are only separated by tracking state changes with instance data.

From the above discussion, we can see that the implications of the choice of User Stories versus Scenarios are more about division of labor than the essence of the requirements work product. The form chosen ultimately needs to serve the same function. But selecting the right practice for a project is more about understanding the context and its constraints. When co-location and real-time feedback becomes challenging, the persistence of more specific details is typically seen as the approach for scale, and typically specificity arrives at something closer to the Unified Processes Use Case approach. A pragmatic middle ground might be to treat the scenarios as tests first and foremost, with Analyst's serving double duty as testers to remove the serialization that occurs from overspecialization of roles.

One area of contention and misperception among the approaches is the commonly articulated anti-pattern *"Big Requirements Up Front - BRUF"*[94]. The Agile community assumes that due to the Unified Process phases, focus is on elaborating all requirements up front, and in great detail. This only occurs with teams that do not understand the innate progressive elaboration aspect of the approach. Both communities actually embrace the notion that the written word, whether in document or other form, is likely to be flawed with respect to the key attributes of requirements and therefore the paraphrasing of stakeholder need is better facilitated through feedback from working software demonstration. Lean embraces either scenario concept for requirements engineering, or the use of the higher-level, business identifiable "Feature" as a way to articulate customer need. But the principles of Lean suggest that first and foremost, the strategy should be to constrain the atomic unit of scope to be what is minimal – the notion of a *Minimal-Marketable-Feature - MMF*. This is due to the strategy of one-piece flow and the limiting of WIP to optimize throughput and minimize cycle time.

5.6 – Openness, Visibility and Learning

Learning is a common theme of all modern software engineering communities. Whether under the name *"Kaizen"* or *"Kaikaku"* from the Lean community, or *"Iteration Assessments"* from the Unified Process community, or *"Retrospectives"* within the Agile community, learning from the feedback of tested and demonstrated working software is universal. It is a core value element provided by the practice of iteration. But the philosophy of continual improvement is not only practiced within these communities. It is embraced within both the PMBOK and ITIL communities as well. However, as previously stated, the key to enabling effective learning is the knowledge accrued from the growth of the primary value-stream element – working software. This sometimes serves as a basis of tension between traditionalists/waterfall advocates and iterative development advocates. With traditional approaches, learning is effectively only achievable reactively through the use of "project retrospectives" or lessons learned. These are performed at the end of projects for the benefit of future projects.

To enable learning, visibility is required such that the concrete results of the tested working software can be analyzed and root causes can be determined. Lean advocates *Visual Controls, Kanban* boards and *Genshi Genbutsu* (go and see), while the Unified Process advocates measurement to enable learning. This latter practice is controversial within Agile circles, as it can lead to either a document-centricity, or a reliance on tools to yield the necessary data. Instead, within the Agile community, the supportive practices of open workspaces, pairing, big visible charts and establishing a high-trust culture between customer and delivery team are the favored philosophies.

In all three communities, a results-oriented or "market" culture/sub-culture [95] is the goal focused on the open delivery of business value first and foremost. Customer visibility is a key tenet of all modern approaches, as opposed to the stealthy tactics of the past practiced by some dysfunctional teams. The concept of dysfunctional teams was articulated by Patrick Lencioni in 2002 [96]. In this work, a model of five dysfunctions is articulated with the first level being absence of trust.

This leads to a progression starting with fear of conflict, lack of commitment and avoidance of accountability. Finally, it is suggested that the paramount dysfunction is inattention to results. All these dysfunctions are targeted by this common ground practices related to openness, visibility and learning.

5.7 – Reduction of Complexity

Complexity has long been seen as one of the leading cost drivers in software economics [49]. Software is increasingly complex and research into how humans deal with complexity is longstanding. Examples include simple paradoxical references like psychologist George Miller's 1956 statement *"An individual can process seven give-or-take two items of information in their correct serial order in his or her short term (15-30 seconds) of working memory"* [97]. Going back further, "Factor Analysis" from Charles Spearman in 1906 states that *"multi-dimensional systems thinking requires holistic multi-factor thinking, multi-future thinking combined with causal feedback thinking. A crucial link between practical consulting, applied cognitive science and applied system science is the use of visual facilitation which increasingly makes use of the power of interactive visual representations of mental models behind decisions."* [98]. Figure 5.8 illustrates the representation of "how we think" as described in Cognitive Sciences.

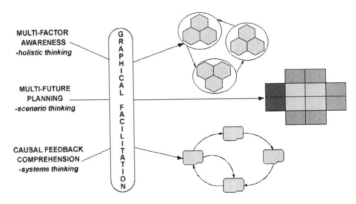

Figure 5.8 – Essence of Visualization

Indeed Visual Modeling is an area shared among modern software engineering approaches, which through the inclusion of various practices, attempt to reduce both essential (related to the problem itself) and accidental (through the way work is done) complexity. The Unified Process lineage has long held visualization as a key practice for reducing complexity. Modeling what we don't quite understand aids not only in cognitive reasoning through abstraction, but also facilitates outgrowth practices like Model-driven Development (MDD), where the objective is the reduction of process friction between Requirements elicitation, Analysis and Design. However, the MDD practice resulting from the object-orientation/component-orientation and service orientation evolution of development technology has sometimes resulted in some anti-patterns which were presumably at the heart of the Agile Manifesto's first element *"Individuals and Interactions over Processes and Tools"*. The common articulation of this anti-pattern is "modeling for the sake of modeling", which is the over-reliance on heavyweight CASE (Computer Assisted Software Engineering) tools and round-trip engineering. Some in the Agile community use these anti-patterns to seed their arguments that <u>all</u> modeling is bad, and that simple metaphors are sufficient to understand the solution. XP refactoring and the notion of *emergent design* seek to avoid visualization altogether, and instead rely on the lower levels of abstraction that exists within code. But these anti-modeling factions seem to lack the understanding of how complex problems tackled, and that code is not always the best tool to reason about all problems. Or perhaps they have not been faced yet with the type of problems that get value out of this practice. *Agile Modeling* seeks to embrace visualization as a tool to be used under the right circumstances and context. Such a practice seeks to leverage the valuable aspects of Visual Modeling in an effort to enhance cycle-time, without the over-reliance of vendor-driven tools. The use of low-tech white-boarding and persistence through photographs is the norm with this practice, with modeling performed collectively, just-in-time through *model storming*.

The Lean Software Development community and its outgrowth from FDD have long advocated modeling through the practice of Domain Driven Development – DDD. This practice seeks to understand object relationships that are necessary to support the realization of Features. This practice traces back to the origins of FDD and the Object Technology methodologists Peter Coad and Rebecca Wirfs-Brock. Within Lean Thinking circles and Lean Product Development, visualization has long been held as an important practice to deal with the complexity of the "fuzzy front end"[99], and is seen as an opportunity for strategic leverage over the outcome of the project.

Chapter 6: Unique Contributions of Lean, Agile and the Unified Process

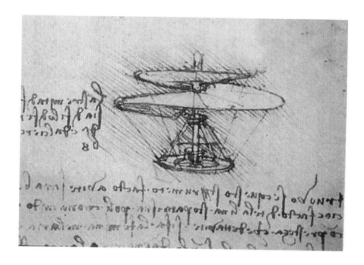

It is reasonable to assume that just as all practices are not likely to fit all situations in Enterprise IT, so too does this uniqueness lead to innovation and advancement from time to time. *Necessity is the mother of invention* as the saying goes. Each of the modern software engineering communities can claim unique contributions based on the proven experiences that serve as their origins. But just because the contribution was "not invented here" should not mean that it should be ignored, lost in time or labeled as not being part of the doctrine of the "true believers".

6.1 – Agile

Innovations resulting from the "internet time" pace of the dot-com boom resulted in new and unique practices for use in software product development [100]. The venture capital funded products that were being incubated in the rush to stake a claim dominated the project landscape. This environment demanded very rapid delivery of features and functionality as startups competed for funding. The time to market pressures meant that weeks or even days could make or break an innovative e-Business site. With this backdrop in mind, the following practices can be claimed under the Agile community umbrella. While the ideas for their instantiation had simmered for some time preceding the articulation in present form, it was the Agile movement that lead to widespread adoption.

6.1.1 – Time-boxing

The practice of time-boxing creates a project environment that strives for creating a natural rhythm for delivery of value through the tension and pressure that time-boxes provide. As Parkinson's law stipulates, *"Work expands so as to fill the time available for its completion"* [101]. So in an era where fast delivery is potentially more critical than quality (including architectural qualities / qualities of service), time-boxes made a lot of sense. Instead of letting the work taken on by a team run to completion, forcing a cadence of date specific iterative deliveries is preferable. Differing philosophies were presented within the Agile community related to the duration of time-boxes – from 2-week iterations in XP to 30-day *"sprints"* in Scrum, a name given to accentuate the notion that speed is of the utmost importance and the cost of delay great.

The mechanics of running a time-boxed iteration are shown in Figure 6.1.

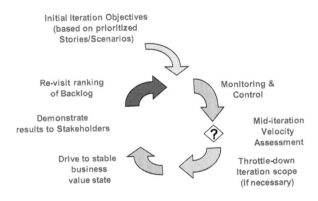

Figure 6.1 – Time-boxing mechanics

The iteration starts out with the team planning how much scope to tackle. Various names have been given to this first step within a iteration, with Agile practices like *"The Planning Game"* and *"Planning Poker"* being typical. Once scope has been decided (and taking into account other factors that will be discussed shortly) the work begins. At mid-iteration a decision is made based on the trends of work completion and whether the team will be able to make the commitment of *"done-done"*, which is working, tested and potentially shippable software. The key aspect of running a time-boxed iteration is that it is scope that is scaled back at the midpoint so that meaningful value can be delivered. This is instead of allowing the scheduled release date to slip. For most traditional project managers, this has proven counter-intuitive and controversial, but goes hand in hand with the nature of expectations setting and customer collaboration within Agile projects.

6.1.2 – Product Backlog

A very simple concept based on queuing, a *Product Backlog* is simply a constantly re-prioritized mechanism for collecting and managing product requests. It serves as the interface to the customer and represents all demand for IT service for a particular product. There can be many physical forms of a Product Backlog, from low-tech yellow Post-it notes on a whiteboard (the usual Agile practice), a stack of 4-by-6 index cards in queued stacks, or electronic versions from various vendors. One key concept of the Product Backlog is that it is the Customer or *Product Owner* who is responsible for managing the backlog – including submission, prioritization and obsolescence of items. This effectively removes the need for a Change Control Board (CCB). This fundamental paradigm shift related to scope management favors embracing the reality of changing scope rather than trying to control it. Also, this has caused perception that Analysts are not longer required, as the team now can go directly to the source for demand requests. This is easing somewhat with the recognition that business stakeholders may not be able to articulate what they need. Or that "Analysts" are relevant through the realization that backlog items eventually require a more elaborate form such that acceptance testing can occur. Figure 6.2 illustrates the simple Product Backlog. Product requests are collected, prioritized and allocated into time-boxed iterations for completion. A similar mechanism called a *Sprint Backlog* is also used for managing the work breakdown for the iteration – the tasks/work items necessary to fulfill the demand. This backlog is used internally by the team for coordination, for management purposes and mid-iteration assessments.

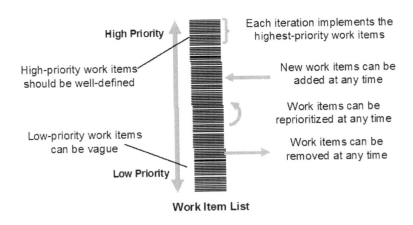

Figure 6.2 – Product Backlog Queue Prioritization [102]

The key idea introduced with Backlogs is that the team is forced to "put first things first" and work the highest priority items first. And instead of leveraging an overly detailed and potentially prescriptive task sequencing found in command-and-control style schedules based on CPM, the backlog mechanics reflect a belief that far more fluidity exists in modern software engineering. Note that the Product Backlog is never likely to be complete or empty until a product is retired. As such it reflects a Product Management versus a Project Management perspective.

6.1.3 – Burn-down & Velocity

A contribution definitely stemming from the Agile community is the use of the first derivative of scope to determine progress. The rate of change of remaining scope per unit time is termed *Velocity* to instill the notion of how much ground or distance is being travelled. The central idea is that we drive the Product Backlog down to zero, and use the measure of velocity to enable an extrapolation of the trend (the slope) to assess when we will likely complete the effort.

Figure 6.3 illustrates the concept of a Product Backlog and the trends of cumulative scope, scope remaining and estimate to complete (also called a *glide-path*).

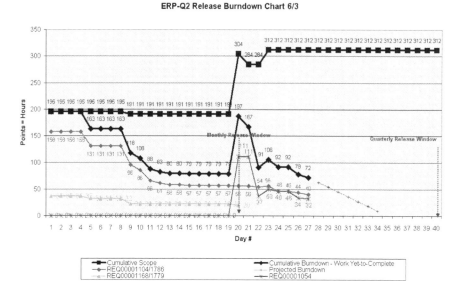

Figure 6.3 – Burn-down Charts

Note that the fundamental difference from traditional progress measurement is that delivered scope is what is measured, not work effort. This is because work effort has a complex relationship to scope, and just because you are doing work doesn't necessarily tell you what your progress is at a point in time. As an analogy, work reflects the fuel that is being expended. You could be full-throttle with a sailing vessel pointed up the Savanna River and still be going backwards in the current.

Note that because the trending of burn-down is performed, the rate of change of velocity (the second derivative) can be taken to understand whether the team is accelerating or decelerating. Appropriate actions are taken based on this information, and this is tantamount to "Derivative Control", as discussed in Chapter 3. With respect to assessment of velocity for a team considering scope for a next time-boxed iteration, typically an averaging is performed to achieve a stable indicator of the achievable pace per time-box. This practice is tantamount to "Integral Control" as described in Chapter 3.

6.1.4 – Co-location

Co-location is a practice that sometimes is most controversial in adopting organizations. The logistical difficulty with moving members across geographies typically brings resistance. And this practice is often cited as one of the largest factors for the often claimed lack of scalability with Agile. However, when one looks at the root of the science behind the practice, on can agree that it makes a lot of sense. Beyond some of the cultural overtones of this practice, enabling the richest collaboration and communication environment is the objective. Table 6.1 below illustrates the percentage of communication that is achieved through the various mediums.

Table 6.1 – Statistics regarding communication effectiveness [103]

Communication Component	Percentage
Words	7%
Voice (pitch, speed, volume, tone)	38%
Visual (eye contact, body language)	55%

In its typical form, the practice is described as *"caves and commons"*. Everyone is collocated in a common project or "war room" for the majority of project work. Separate offices or cubicles (the caves) serve as environments where team members can go so as to not disrupt the team with telephone calls, or so as to be able to get some quiet time to think alone. This practice realizes the notion of *Whole Team*, in which customer/business representatives are involved daily in the project.

The challenge with co-location is typically rooted in the realities of the businesses in which IT is embedded. And as IT serves the business and stakeholders, influencing a decision towards this practice is sometimes difficult – at least in the context of including "whole team". For example, requiring the head of Equity Trading (the Product Owner), who works on the trading floor in midtown Manhattan, to collocate with a single IT project in Jersey City on the other side of the Hudson River is not very practical. Some sort of compromise is typically achieved, but defeats the core principle of the practice, especially as related to the optimal communication strategy to extract the tacit knowledge from the business customer.

The key point to take away from this challenge is that form follows function, and if the nirvana scenario of communication is not possible with respect to co-location, it doesn't mean that an organization "can't do Agile". It just means that pragmatism must be inserted such that less than perfect strategies for achieving similar results can take place. Instead of tying the head of Equity Trading to a desk, constantly being distracted in his trades by IT folks interrupting him/her for clarifications on User Stories (that somehow he/she had time to develop after the trading day), Collaboration Technologies seek to fill this void. These technologies, discussed in Chapter 9, are intended to enable effective collaboration when faced with the above unfeasible scenario, or scenarios where geographical distribution is required like with follow-the-sun or offshore strategies.

6.1.5 – Self Organizing Teams

Related to the beliefs of the fallacy of prediction and "command-and-control" plan driven development is the practice of *Self-organizing teams*. This practice manifests itself in Agile most noticeably with the absence of a "Project Manager". Instead, for example, the closest role articulation in Scrum is the *ScrumMaster*. This person is responsible ironically for the "process" (whereas the Product Owner is responsible for the "product"). The nature of this role is more about facilitation when it comes to Sprint Planning, coordination, issue or "block" resolution when it comes to execution of a Sprint , and interfacing with management for reporting (if required from the process perspective).

This practice has sometimes been associated with the concept of "Theory Y Management" [104]. This style of management, articulated through research at MIT Sloan School of Management, states that management assumes employees *may be* ambitious and self-motivated and exercise self-control. This is the opposite of "Theory X Management" (which many traditional managers practice) in which management *assumes* employees are inherently lazy and will avoid work if they can, needing to be told what to do. These contrasting philosophies surround the issue of workforce motivation and self actualization, and suggest that a trusting management environment must exist for the phenomenon of highly performing software delivery teams to occur.

This software engineering practice was not invented by Agile, but has definitely been popularized through the movement. The United States Marine Corps have practiced this for over 200 years at the unit level.

This does not mean that there are no "managers" in the "Corps Business" [105]. It is just that at the operational levels of the organization, this style of organization has proven the most effective for the swift and complex problem solving environments that it finds itself engaged. Delegated authority is given to these units because the teams on the front lines have the most real-time information with which to make decisions. Management focus changes to be that of an escalation path for exceptional conditions where the team does not have the necessary visibility into the right course of action. For example, the decision to be made might require situational awareness of other teams on the ground, or more long standing strategic objectives that are not known to tactical units.

A study of this style of governance typically leads to discussions around the meaning of leaders, leadership and management. They are fundamentally different things. To understand the fundamental difference between the two, it is instructive to look at the definitions for both:

To Manage – to handle or direct with a degree of skill: as to exercise executive, administrative, and supervisor direction

To Lead – to guide on a way, especially by going in advance; the process of social influence in which one person can enlist the aid and support of others in the accomplishment of a common task

Webster's Dictionary

Agile from the beginning has sought to apply the lessons of leadership learned from organizations like the USMC. The USMC needs to know a little something about leading high performance teams. Getting human beings to willfully face death in the face of their "jobs" is no easy task, and forcing one into combat has proven to be ineffective.

Discussion seems to surface every so often between the faithful of the PMBOK (sometimes called the traditionalists), and Agile (sometimes called the progressives) in which claims of obsolescence of the Project Manager role are made. On one end of the argument, Project Management Professionals (PMPs) point out that they have very differing skill-sets then typical developers. On the other, ScrumMaster's emerge from development ranks (which is encouraged) who act more as coordinators and without the benefits of management training. The middle ground in the above is that Project Managers with their soft skills and experience within traditional Management circles should adapt to embrace the USMC management style. Sometimes called *Servant Leadership* [106], it is grounded on the inherent uncertainty of rapidly changing environments and problems. And it is consistent with studies related to human motivation [107]. In effect, existing Managers need to become Leaders, leveraging all the skills they have accrued over the years, shelving what does not reflect reality in modern software engineering, independent of any one method's branding. Make no mistake, management of large scale investments will still be the norm within business circles for some time to come with all the compliance and fiduciary duty legal issues. But if common ground exists to help better articulate the real value proposition Managers can provide to IT Delivery teams, it is that of Leadership.

6.1.6 – Continuous Integration & Release

Continuous Integration (CI) is a practice originating out of the XP community that is commonly mentioned in conjunction with Agile. It could be argued that it was popularized and made practical by Martin Fowler from ThoughtWorks through the contribution of an open source tool called *Cruise-Control* [108]. This practice is now a hallmark of the typical custom development project that is deemed Agile, with most if not all Configuration Management (CM) vendors claiming CI capability. The key concept is to integrate and test early and often (common with all modern software engineering). But CI takes this concept to the extreme, with a per check-in build being triggered if configured in this default way, with at least daily check-in advised. Issues typically arise when builds do not have time to finish for extremely large developments, or with product-line and multi-generational product management, so various strategies exist to support almost continuous integration, with staged builds and variations in build scope. With more robust parallel development strategies and their use of branches, integration build and test triggers occur on a per-demand element (feature, story, scenario, activity), so "effective" integration from the isolation occurring due to branching occurs at a less frequent pace. But this is supplemented with the typical daily check-ins and local developer builds and test execution, along with potentially daily resynchronization enforcement with the mainline.

Along with the build trigger mechanism that ties CM infrastructure with build servers, unit test jobs are also triggered at a near continuous frequency with the key goal to prevent defects from "breaking the build", thereby ensuring project health. Visual mechanisms are commonly leveraged like the always popular *lava-lamp*; specifically, it changes colors when a build is broken, and adds bubbles the longer builds remain broken. This is a common culturally admired mechanism to immediately show the outcome of the build triggered by a check-in on the mainline code branch.

This practice is effectively equivalent to the Lean concept of *poka yoke*, which means "mistake proofing" of which two types exist - preventative and detective. CI is arguably an example of both. And if one performs the ideal of one-piece flow increments, you typically arrive at the same practice, just under another name and maybe not so elegantly automated with tools.

Continuous/near continuous release is a little more contentious of a practice it turns out when dealing with most complex IT organizations. With the Agile practice of *Shippable Product*, the intent is to have a complete increment of a product ready for a customer. That means *done-done* within the Scrum community. But if you read the practice, it doesn't necessarily mean that a release will occur, contrary to what some Agilist perspectives might say. The key issue is the ability for the business customer to consume a release. More often than not, the frequency by which demand is realized and is shippable is higher than the frequency of release cycles. This is due to the inherent risks associated with change, and leads naturally to the discovery of a frequency that matches the nature of the demand and the nature of the risks.

At whatever frequency realized demand can be "pulled" by the customer, any deployment must be automated and scripted for repeatability and avoidance of human errors, and integrate with Release Management orchestration. This will be discussed in more detail in Chapter 8.

6.1.7 – Pairing

Pairing is a practice that was popularized by Extreme Programming. Its origins however evolved from references such as "dynamic duo" by Larry Constantine [109]. *Pair programming* is when two developers sit at the same terminal and take turns developing software. The one typing the code is called the driver, and the other is called the reviewer who performs real-time code reviews. This practice is typically linked to another Agile practice, *shared code ownership*, where pairs rotate among teams such that a shared, collective understanding of the entire codebase is achieved. Several benefits have been cited with this approach, including knowledge loss risk mitigation, increased discipline and time management, and the concept of having two pairs of eyes rather than one to solve complex problems.

Noting the origins of this practice one wonders why it is limited to homogenous disciplines like developers. It would seem that the practice attempts to locally optimize developer activity which after all is the primary value-add activity in software development. But many of the problems associated with the necessary overhead of software development due to division of labor considerations and the requirement for cross-functional skill-sets in modern software engineering might be alleviated through the concept of pairing along differing lines. This concept is arguably behind the Microsoft practice of *"Feature Crews"* [110].

A feature crew is a small, self organizing team made up of a problem domain resource (an Analyst) and a solution domain resource (a Developer). As will be discussed, this configuration is also known as a Lean work-cell. The key skill-sets of the Analyst are brought to bear to facilitate an understanding of demand through their knowledge of the problem space, and the soft skills necessary to elicit the tacit knowledge associated with the demand. The Developer is responsible for leveraging their problem solving skills (design) in concert and concurrently with realizing a solution based on current technologies and technology constraints. The key benefit of pairing along this way is that the team evolves through the *Forming, Storming, Norming, Performing and Adjourning* team lifecycle [111]. They learn how to interact with each other in a non-silo'd way such that their slice of the software delivery value stream is efficient and effective.

6.1.8 – Test Driven Development (TDD)

Another example of *poka yoke* that emerged from the Agile community is known as *Test Driven Development*. The precedent for this practices stems from the XP community and Kent Beck. Test-driven development is realized through the idea of having developers design unit tests (as opposed to functional or acceptance tests) before writing code. These tests are typically developed using unit test harness tools like *JUnit, FitNesse*, etc. These unit tests are integrated with Continuous Integration infrastructure such that they are executed every time code is checked in to a common source code repository. The practice can therefore be described as a preventative *poka yoke* mechanism.

Similar pre-cursors to this practice have existed in relation to certain object-oriented languages. One such language is Eiffel, invented by

Bertrand Meyer [112]. The practice that attempts to achieve a similar thing through using *ensure:* and *assert:* invariant pre-conditions and post-conditions within class operations is referred to as *"Design by Contract"*. The differences are that the "test" execution in the Eiffel approach is performed at run-time within the code – sometimes thought of a self-testing code, and a common concept in exception handler design. This contrasts the *Test-Driven Development* approach that focuses on tests that are externalized from the code, executed while performing implementation (i.e. at design time), and which leverage discrete instances rather than boundary conditions and ranges.

Both of these approaches exist at the code level. In the TDD case, the practice of emergent design is favored over visual modeling, and reliance on the code-level of abstraction is the norm. However, another manifestation of guiding developers to think about failure conditions before writing algorithms (thereby abstracting interfaces, either type-based towards the specific, or instance-based towards the generalized specification) is *Operational Contracts* from Desmond D'Souza [41]. This practice attempts the same preventative objectives as TDD, but at a design level.. In this practice, pre-conditions and post-conditions are specified for a class as invariants – the operational contracts.

6.2 – Unified Process

The UP grew out of the risk-adverse environments of aeronautics and defense, and problems of extreme complexity and scale. Typically the cost of failure within these environments is measured in hundreds of millions to billions of dollars or worse, human lives. It is therefore natural to see that the concept of risk is front and center within this community. All the unique practices from this community can be thought of as delivery risk mitigation measures in some manner. And the nature of these projects is still widespread in industry today, so it would be reasonable to assume that there is value in integrating these practices. While Agile doctrine is almost silent on the topic of risk, the Lean community embraces this concept in the practices centering around Real Options.

6.2.1 – Risk-Value Prioritization

All modern engineering schools teach engineering ethics, which focuses on establishing a social consciousness among soon-to-be practitioners of engineering in the world. This includes software engineering. The typical example given is the collapse of the Tacoma Narrows Bridge.

More recent examples are the Citicorp tower crisis [113], Chernobyl [114], Ocean Ranger [115] and the Space Shuttle Challenger [116]. The point is that risks left un-mitigated can lead to large scale problems or even catastrophes.

Figure 6.4 – Engineering ethics and loss of life [117]

Bad things happen when we just let solutions "emerge" magically. While this is all fine and good for the arts, it means a lack of due diligence when it comes to engineering. Professional engineers exist because they exercise a fiduciary duty (a higher standard), and failure to faithfully exercise this duty can lead to material loss and death. More and more, software is an integral part of the engineered world we live in, and therefore the approaches that are leveraged for bringing software intensive system products to market need to acknowledge the business, political, sociological and legal environment in which they must coexist.

This is the essence of the *risk-value prioritization* practice within the UP community. Failure is forced early such that risks can be mitigated before they can disrupt the outcome of an investment due to late materialization. Figure 6.5 is the common visual articulation of this practice.

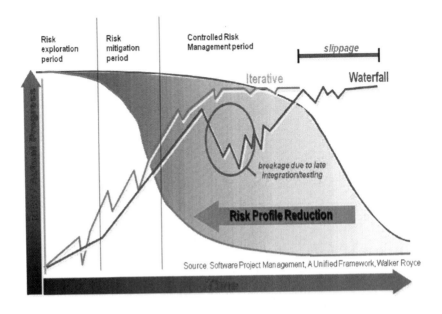

Figure 6.5 – Risk-value prioritization shift [118]

In this picture, which is also used to articulate why "Waterfall" leads to the kinds of results to which it can be attributed. Due to late integration and testing, large scale breakage happens late in the project with respect to stakeholder delivery expectations. Occurring so late, no ability to recover exists and large scale slippage occurs. Not so obvious in this picture, however is the implications of "doing the tough stuff first". There is a governed period of time early on in the lifecycle, after risks to delivery have been identified, where active mitigation of these risks must occur. Failure to prove risks to solution feasibility have been mitigated, the project can be re-constituted or shut-down due to lack of investment viability. The Unified Process within this practice also advocates that this proof must come in the form of tested, working software, albeit in incomplete form (stubbing of non-essential interfaces and the like). This working software is termed the "executable architecture", as it represents the essential or "high-stakes" portions of the software only (the architecture) in executable form.

The key requirement for this practice to add value is that risks must be identified early on – within 6-weeks typically (Iteration 0) – the Inception Phase. Not all projects will identify risks to feasibility, whether it be due to reuse or lack of complexity. If this is the case, which arguably is the case with most commodity technology stacks for CRUD (Create-Read-Update-Delete) applications, then this risk mitigation period can be drastically shortened, and the customer value perspective can be emphasized. This is probably the root cause for the Agile communities aversion to the UP's Elaboration Phase. Although this community very loosely acknowledges this *kentou* period of time (Japanese word for study), the projects that are the "sweet spot" for Agile perhaps are not doing Architecture in the truest sense. Or at the very least, they are not risky, where now most of these projects are about fine-grained design built around known technology components with known qualities of service.

One challenge the Agile community has faced is the perception of a lack of applicability to large-scale endeavors, or mission-critical programs. This is probably due to the perception of a lack of rigor and explicit risk mitigation and knowledge capture in these methods. Large scale, mission critical systems that are unprecedented require a little more rigour than emergent design – meaning that when peoples lives are at stake, it is highly unlikely that "trust me" will suffice. But methods like Scrum have always had albeit a vague placeholder for this practice:

Visualize a large pressure cooker. Scrum development work is done in it. Gauges sticking out of the pressure cooker provide detailed information on the inner workings, including backlog, risks, problems, changes, and issues. The pressure cooker is where Scrum Sprint cycles occur, iteratively producing incrementally more functional product. The Planning and System Architecture phases prepare the input that is placed in the pressure cooker. The input consists of ingredients (backlog, objects, packets, problems, issues), recipe (system architecture, design, and prototypes), and cooking sequence (infrastructure, top priority functions, next priority...). [31]

What we are seeing now within the Agile community is a discussion around the concept of "technical debt". This can be described as being the result of doing the easy things first – typically due to the inability to negotiate early technical exploratory iterations in leau of value delivery.

By ignoring these early iterations, value to the stakeholders is lost due to the inability to cancel the project (exercising exit options). No reasonable visibility into late project failure due to unmitigated risk is possible without early risk-confrontive testing of architecture.

The analogy is like that of engineering integrated circuits and the silicon substrate from which they are made. Testing of a seed crystal must be performed, through various techniques such that it is reasonable to assume that yield and semiconductor properties will match the intended purpose. Once this has been determined – up front – the seed crystal is drawn out of the molten silicon to form a silicon ingot, where wafers are then cut and polished. If the up front analysis proves wrong, the crystal growth from the extraction process will fail, resulting in great cost and delay.

6.2.2 – Decision-centric Software Architecture

The Unified Process has long been described as *"Use Case Driven, Architecture-centric, Iterative and Incremental."* Yet the definition of software architecture historically has been highly variable and poorly understood. Emphasis within the IT community has been related to Viewpoints, Views, and Perspectives [119]. However, recent observations in industry suggest that software architecture is more about mitigating the risks surrounding "significant" IT investment decisions than with the approach to communicate and capture the knowledge within a solution. A software architecture can be viewed as a solution "decision-set". The architectural reasoning process can be viewed as analogous to Investment Portfolio Management with the Architect being more like an Investment Manager. A system's software architecture evolves as and is synonymous to a set of significant design decisions that address stakeholder concerns about the qualities of service of a solution. Such decisions materially affect the success of the technology investment.

Decision-centric reasoning techniques address a multivariate problem, because the architecting process must deal with multiple concurrent concerns. A decision-centric approach is an evolution from the viewpoint-centric approaches of the past decade which emphasizes visual modeling and blueprinting to describe design decisions. However, architecting is much more than the techniques used to reduce complexity and communicate precisely. Architecting is about balancing competing interests from multiple communities of stakeholders, and about being able to support those decisions on the basis of cost, benefit and risk – the overall "goodness" of the solution in terms that are concrete. Figure 6.6 illustrates the spiral nature of the decision-making process.

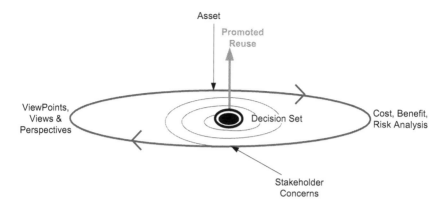

Figure 6.6 – Decision-centric Architecture

Many terms relate to the IEEE 1471 (Recommended Practice for Software Architecture Description) concept of "Stakeholder Concerns". Some of these related terms coming from other bodies of knowledge include Quality Attributes (SEI) [120], Qualities of Service (real-time space), Non-functional/Supplemental/Supporting (RUP, OpenUP), and "URPS+" or "ilities" (Booch). It is this type of requirement/statement of need that serves as the architectural drivers of a solution. An architectural driver (also known as a Sensitivity Point) is a force that shapes the ultimate solution tactics and decisions. Although a broad array of solutions may "work", there exists an optimum solution that achieves balance among competing stakeholders. It is architectural drivers that assist the architect in arriving at the optimum solution in the most efficient manner, and it is architectural drivers, that if ignored, lead to "spectacular failures".

Reasoning about the trade space of stakeholder concerns is performed both visually through blueprints, and through the use of well known decision tools. Applying the pairwise comparison technique within the Analytical Hierarchy Process (AHP) [121] enables the unbiased and efficient ranking of stakeholder perspectives. Figure 6.7 shows the basic linear algebraic form of AHP. In modified forms of this approach, application of the first-level of analysis only occurs as specified within the AHP process in a facilitated group forum to achieve group consensus as to the matrix cell scoring. Techniques implicit within the method and based on Linear Algebra identify bias and assist the Architect in facilitating negotiations related to priority.

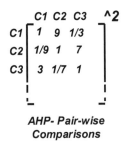

AHP- Pair-wise
Comparisons

Figure 6.7 – Analytical Hierarchy Process-AHP

From the prioritized stakeholder concerns, groupings that correlate to common "Quality Attributes" which can be arranged into a Utility Tree, with the cumulative rankings per Quality node arising from the related concerns. The resultant Utility Tree in Figure 6.8 represents the Architectural Utility as viewed and negotiated with and between stakeholders, which is leveraged within the alternatives and tradeoff reasoning process.

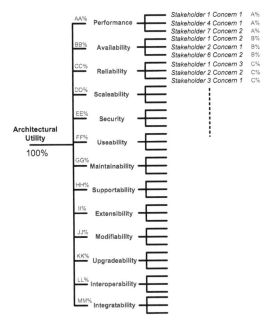

Figure 6.8 – Multi-attribute Utility Tree (MAUT) [122]

Quality Attributes of concern represent various *Aspects* of quality of service of the software architecture. Therefore, defining which concrete functionality is to achieve various qualities (or scales of service quality in the case of degraded service modes) is essential to ensure that the quality investment in the solution is focused and optimized. Identification of the functional context for reasoning about the highest ranked Quality Attribute/Concern is achieved by selecting the indicative Use Case scenario realizations (also known as architecturally significant Use Cases). Each Concern should leverage one Use Case scenario realization for further exploration. Such Use Case realizations also form the basis of defining associated Quality Scenarios (a.k.a. Quality Test Cases), which are required to facilitate exercising the evolving executable architecture to provide concrete evidence of solution merit to architectural governance bodies and interested stakeholder communities. Figure 6.9 illustrates the use of extension Use Cases as *Aspects* to frame Quality Scenarios in the proper context.

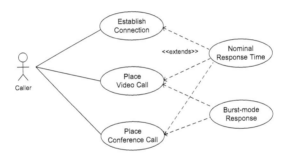

Figure 6.9 – Using Aspects as context for Qualities-of-Service [123]

During the process of architecting a solution, the above "test harness" will serves as a quantitative basis for reasoning about the overall solution. A reference catalog of proven patterns/tactics that have been leveraged within specific prior efforts is consulted. Synonymous with the term tactic, a pattern is a solution to a problem within a context. This level of reuse is logical (sometimes referred to as "derivative" reuse) but guides the architect towards physical implementations and aids awareness and identification of various sources of manifestation of the tactic. Figure 6.10 illustrates the relationship between a quality attribute and the various tactics that can be taken.

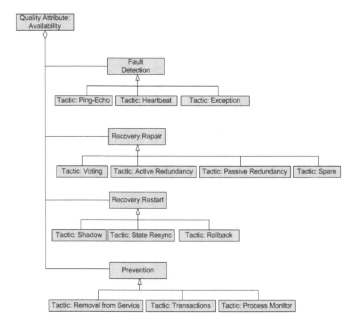

Figure 6.10 – Quality Attributes and Tactics/Patterns [124]

The objective of recognizing a reusable pattern is to "seed" a necessary decision related to addressing a concern by leveraging a candidate approach. These proven tactics represent prior successful decisions, typically showing repeated successful deployment on at least 3 prior developments. Such tactics serve as candidate decisions, because reasoning is required to determine applicability with the project's context.

Reasoning about a candidate decision occurs in two ways. The first is the historically common approach – visualization. For the Use Case Realizations selected to reason about Quality Attribute implications and possible tactics, relevant Viewpoints and Views are prepared for the comparison of alternatives, and later communicate choices. This elaboration includes structural elements from either logical and/or physical views. Figure 6.11 illustrates the nature of Viewpoints and Views as articulated in IEEE 1471.

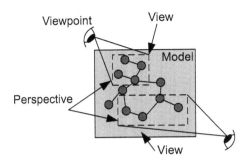

Figure 6.11 – Viewpoints and Views

Perspectives and their related collection of views are leveraged to perform the same function for cross-cutting concerns.

Visual Modeling supports the decision reasoning process in that it reduces complexity. It is just one tool leveraged by the Architect to understand the various aspects of the required solution, and serves the additional purpose of communicating such reasoning in an un-ambiguous and precise way.

Concrete assets that can be leveraged in realizing the structural elements required by the realized scenarios become apparent through the visualization. Typically these are known as mechanisms, or more generically, building blocks which imply a scale of physical implementations from design class clusters -> frameworks -> components/services -> packages. Acquisition of tangible assets, rather than custom development yields lower risk for fulfillment. The quickest way to accelerate development and reduce uncertainty about outcomes is to "build less stuff". The challenge with acquisition-orientation as a strategy for development is getting visibility into the degree of fitness-for-purpose of the building block(s). Visual Models from prior efforts can facilitate gap analysis; this is because visual models help us understand, and we need to understand the element of reuse under consideration. Use Case Scenario realizations enable an efficient and unambiguous approach to gap analysis. Scenarios represent stimulus by which Quality attributes can be exercised (a.k.a Quality Scenarios).

The other tool available for reasoning about the fitness for purpose is through investment analysis. Bringing a decision "all-to-dollars" [125] through the quantification of benefits, costs and risks of the fulfillment decision enables an actionable way to successfully add more decision elements to the set. Portfolio analysis as the decision set grows and tradeoffs are identified enables "what-if" reasoning to occur. Thinking of an architecture as a decision-set is akin to treating it like an investment portfolio – like a stock portfolio Performing similar analytics on the decision-set portfolio enables identification of the optimum decision-set, such that the latest incremental candidate decisions can be recommended to the stakeholders of the architecture. Inevitably, various tradeoff points exist between concerns and their associated quality attributes. Such tradeoffs require the negotiation and facilitation skills of the architect to stress the overall "goodness" of the holistic solution. Key in successful ratification of candidate decisions is to mitigate the tendency by stakeholders to locally optimize individual concerns and ensure a focus on the overall mission of the system.

With each successive decision taken on how to address each ranked stakeholder concern, the goal is to converge the potential solutions available, such that each successive alternatives analysis and its respective tradeoff space becomes smaller. This is enabled through the weighting of the concerns at the onset of architectural reasoning, and because the concerns are elaborated and negotiated on a weighted order, the probability of converging in an efficient and stable manner is high.

Finally, after it is determined that a solution (entire decision-set, aka architectural stack), or portion of the solution (individual decisions) are value-add, such decisions need to be identified as candidates for other project contexts. Central enterprise repositories typically facilitate architectural Asset Management and can facilitate visibility into opportunities that exist to future project architects. Such mechanisms are part of a broader knowledge management effort relating to IT Delivery lessons learned.

6.2.3 – Model-Driven Development (MDD)

Due to the fact that the Unified Process grew up through the efforts of one of the world's largest CASE-tool vendors, it isn't surprising that Model-driven Development is a central practice within the method. But it is not a required practice. The goal of the practice was to enable a higher-level of abstraction (think 5GL – fifth generation language) above and beyond the use of 3GL programming constructs, and has been the holy grail of software development for decades. Putting aside emotional attachment to op-codes, this is no different than the prior evolutions from machine language to assembly and finally high-level languages. The next logical step is to enable "visual programming" such that humans can contemplate and solve more and more complex problems. Not only does this idea enable rapid assembly of reusable components, but easy identification of such opportunities.

Figure 6.12 illustrates one approach for the systematic development of systems through visual models. It represents a derivative of the 4+1 Views of Architecture ideas contained within the Unified Process.

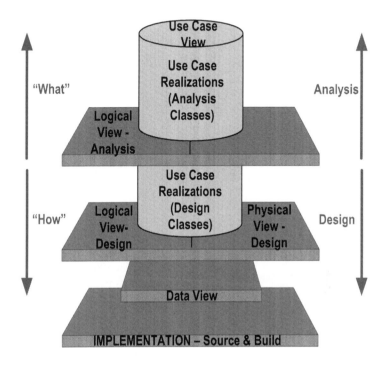

Figure 6.12 – 3+1 Views of Architecture [126]

Figure 6.13 illustrates details the relationships between the stakeholders, their typical concerns, and the diagrams that are useful in addressing these concerns. It also shows the correlation among the views and the UML diagram types that are typically leveraged.

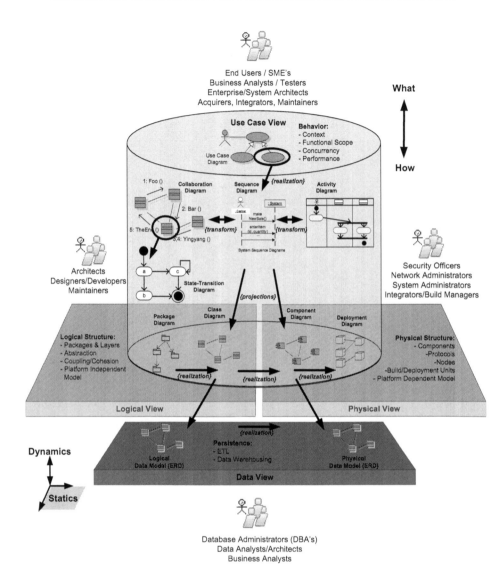

Figure 6.13 – 3+1 Views of Architecture [126]

In the above figures, a model driven development iteration starts with identification and communication of system value propositions are captured for a system under consideration. Typically performed graphically through what is known as a Use Case Diagram, this Viewpoint is focused on breadth and establishes context through the identification of interrelated systems and what is out through "actors". Textually this same information has historically been captured in a Use Case Model Survey, which is supposed to be minimalist, and akin to a Product Backlog but without the queuing overtone. Iterations are planned by selecting instances of Use Cases to realize or build (not entire Use Cases). These instances are scenarios, and are equivalent to User Stories with fully elaborated acceptance tests. Scenarios are dynamic, and therefore are orthogonal to the static type oriented Use Case Diagram. Through first identifying analysis or "what" abstractions that make up the scenario the logical structure of the system can systematically be discovered as represented as "what" classes – technology neutral abstractions. This is followed by deeper realizations of the scenarios, where lifelines in the scenario visualizations (sequence diagrams) are "pulled apart" using design patterns such that design or "how" classes emerge. These design classes are then realized within components behind interfaces based on analysis of coupling, cohesion and likelihood of change in the Physical View.

Model-driven development arose out of the Object Oriented Analysis & Design approaches of the 1990's. Differing techniques for synthesizing systems were codified into tools such that generation of code could occur into languages such as C++ and Java. Reverse engineering capabilities leveraging the same parser engines of the development environments enabled what was known as round-trip engineering. This requirement to commit designs into code, where drift could occur when the "filling in the blanks" occurred is the main reason for why model-driven development has received a bad name. And it is arguably these CASE tools that are the target in the first Agile Manifesto value *"Individuals and Interactions over Processes and Tools"*. But the systematic problem solving techniques, when taken away from the tool burden does seem to achieve broader acceptance, even within Agile circles. Some day the last mile may be achieved such that the higher abstractions of classes and patterns can be leveraged to completely manifest a system. Today, the practice's primary utility should be seen in being a problem solving technique, where it makes sense, typically in safety critical systems engineering.

6.3 – Lean

In explaining why Lean practices yield such significant results related to its application to a process, a simple simulation is usually illustrative. Assume a coin represents a typical fine-grained request for maintenance change of a software intensive system. Assume that you have a single "work-cell" unit, which comprises an Analyst, a Designer/Developer, and a person playing the role of Tester. To execute the simulation, have each player line-up in order and flip 15 coins and then hand them off to the next person in line. Each player must flip 15 successful "heads" before passing (ie. pushing) the entire batch to the next in line. The next role then has to do the same thing, and so on. Once the entire batch is pushed across the "release" finish line, this time is measured from when the simulation began. Note that the requirement to hit "heads" a number of times accounts for the more random nature of software development, which is different than repetitive tasks like mass production manufacturing. For the second execution of the simulation, once a coin is successfully flipped to heads, it is placed on the table, and the next player in line can begin flipping. Again, measure the time it takes for all the coins to be "released" to market. What you observe, is that the time to delivery is significantly shorter when we have a batch size of one.

6.3.1 – JIT & Queuing Theory

The above phenomenon, which has its roots in queuing theory, is the basis for what is termed as the Lean / "Just-in-Time" (JIT) philosophy [127]. It is an established body of science, with early origins of study originating in what is commonly known as Little's Law [128], named after John Little from the University of Rochester in 1961. This theorem states the following in relation to Throughput:

$$Average\ Completion\ Rate = \frac{WIP}{CycleTime}$$

$$= Throughput$$

From the above, Throughput is maximized by decreasing cycle time. To improve cycle time there are two options; reduce the number of things in process or improve the average completion rate. Of the two, reducing the number of things in progress is easily actionable. This relation holds true once the latent capacity of the queue has been reached. This effect has been applied to such studies as packet-based communications and channel capacity, or in traffic flow theory and optimum density per lane. Figure 6.14 illustrates the relationship of cycle time to WIP as described in Little's Law:

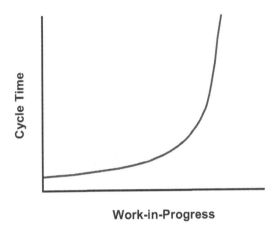

Work-in-Progress

Figure 6.14 – Cycle time vs WIP

This idea has also been written by others not within the Lean Thinking space. Drawing on direct observation of what happens when workers are over-utilized, this anecdotal reference states that as more multi-tasking occurs, less and less productivity results. Even this anecdotal work supports the counter-intuitive notion that management should not be trying to fill every hour in a knowledge workers day through tactics like the matrixing of resources into multiple projects/maintenance efforts. . Table 6.2 illustrates what typically happens through multitasking, with hits of 20% in productivity occurring for each additional concurrent tasks. The root cause is suggested as being the loss of focus and requirement to "context switch" between tasks, something in computing that is known to cause a hit in performance.

Table 6.2 – Effects of context switching [90]

Number of tasks	% available time on each task
1	100%
2	40%
3	20%
4	10%
5	5%
> 5	Random

6.3.2 – Kanban

In a Lean just-in-time system, limiting WIP enables the objective of decreasing cycle times by avoiding the productivity hits of context switching. A JIT "pull" production control system uses signals to control the movement of materials between work centers. JIT also controls the replenishment of materials when they are consumed for manufacturing and move downstream to the next work center. A *Kanban* system is referred to as a *pull system*, because the *Kanban* is used to pull parts to the next production stage only when they are needed. Material movement occurs only when the work station needing more material asks for it to be sent. Basically, the just-in-time inventory system is all about having "the right material, at the right time, at the right place, and in the exact amount", without the safety net of inventory or having materials "just-in-case".

Kanban is a Japanese term that literally means "visual card" and is one of the primary tools of a JIT (just-in-time) pull system. *Kanban's* establish a cycle of replenishment for production and materials. Note that the strict interpretation of *Kanban* being "cards" is un-necessary, and as will be discussed in Chapter 7, Toyota itself no longer does *Kanban* this way. In using a *Kanban* system, we attempt to reduce this number to 1 for any given set of resources (work-team).

Note that the guidance from this body of management science would suggest that the focus should be on micro-increments, not iterations during the more deterministic stage of an IT delivery. This is in contrast to Agile approaches like Scrum, which attempts to limit WIP using time-boxed iterations. Leveraging Lean Software Engineering refers to leveraging pull-systems through mechanisms like *Kanban* to realize the benefits modeled through Little's Law and observable through one-piece flow.

Currently, achieving the maximum throughput by identifying the point where cycle-time begins to increase (also known as Critical WIP) is performed by trial and error. However, recent exploration most notably in application to control systems have leveraged more robust mathematical tools to model the dynamics of the queue for purposes of predicting Critical WIP [129].

Figure 6.15 illustrates a Lean Software Product delivery value stream.

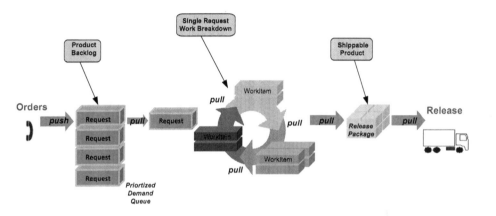

Figure 6.15 – Pull delivery of value

The first value activity within this process is the collection, prioritization and queuing of fine-grained customer demand (i.e. Product Requests). A Product Request can be seen to be equivalent to the Production *Kanban*. This element is implemented with the Scrum Product Backlog Management practice (equivalent to the Lean Kanban approach). Both advocate a customer push of demand rather than traditional requirements-driven pull-oriented approach. Having stakeholder needs pushed rather than Analyst elicitation of demand prevents delay in seeding the backlog with demand due to "analysis paralysis" or locally-optimized requirements engineering silos.

In the next activity within the value stream, the leadership of a Software delivery team pulls a prioritized request from the Product Backlog based on team availability, just-in-time. Only at this point is the work breakdown structure planned in detail. This differs from traditional plan oriented approaches, in that Lean does not "batch" the planning effort or attempt to plan far into the future. In that sense, it represents rolling wave planning.

Once the work breakdown structure of tasks/work-items is established, this list of work is effectively a queue for the realization of the Request. Tasks should not be prescriptively and overly sequenced, nor should they be associated with highly-suspect bottom-up estimates. If possible, leveraging a historical basis for estimation is much more efficient, and yields higher credibility over time as default task estimates are continually re-calibrated based on similar demand realization.

With Task / Work-item Pull, the downstream work-cell "pulls" the upstream output when ready. Instead of an Analyst pushing a "spec" (i.e. throwing it over the wall), designer/developers pull the spec once they are ready. A small amount of lead-time is required to seed just enough requirements capture to enable the downstream effort to commence. This enforces the "70%" rule such that over-processing does not occur. This concept has also articulated as "perfect is the enemy of good enough" [130], or within software engineering circles as "work for the next best effort".

The final stage within the value chain is the batching of completed requests within the payload of a Release. Batching at this stage in the value chain is preferred, as change risks require regression mitigation which requires economy of scale considerations for efficient execution of large test suites. The frequency and capacity of the Release change event pulls the right amount of realized demand, just-in-time. Establishing the amount of change that can be released during a change event is defined by the customer based on risk tolerance and a balance with time-to-value considerations.

6.3.3 – Cellular Development & Theory of Constraints

One of the fundamental transformations that occur when applying Lean is that of organizational structure. With Lean, organization revolves around the horizontal value-stream rather than vertical functional hierarchies. Emphasis on team and synergies and flattened management structures replace the multi-level, top-down management structures, and performance measures are focused on team-based value delivery rather than locally optimized results. The implications related to the pull of resources to fulfill WIP limited Product Requests are that matrixing strategies are altered. Specifically, this implies that resources are not assigned as individuals. Rather, whole teams are matrixed against the demand, where teams rather than individuals pull the queued demand into their "work-cell" as they are freed up. This basic matrixing work-unit is called a "Lean Work-cell" and the overall organizational structure is referred to as a Lean Team-based Organization.

The following are attributes of a Lean Work-cell:

- Team is cross functional with meaningful skill-set overlaps
- Request realization work-breakdown is integrated/concurrent
- Size of work tasks are small, not batched
- Focus per role/task is on quality, not task progress
- Teamwork is present all the time
- Optimizing takes place for the whole, the Request fulfillment value-chain, not the individual tasks

Figure 6.16 illustrates the Lean team-based matrixing approach:

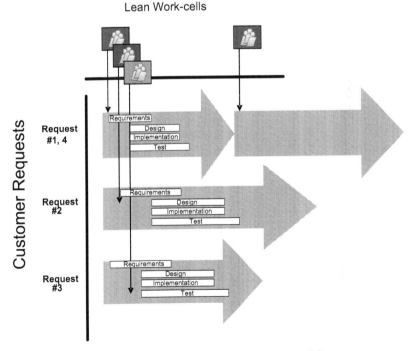

Figure 6.16 – Lean Work-cell Organizational Structure

Lean Work-Teams yield serialized Requests in-progress per team, with highly concurrent and collaborative realization tasks. This direct application of Goldratt's Theory of Constraints aims at alleviating the critical bottlenecks that serialized work can produce. While similar to the resource strategy of Agile approaches like Scrum and XP, the Lean approach can be described as the matrixing of high-performing teams into Requests as opposed to individuals into batched time-box iterations.

With Lean Work-teams, labor constraints still exist, and therefore the need for division of labor is still present. Meaningful specializations of a reduced number are typical with Lean Work Teams, with enough overlap such that other team members can pitch-in if necessary. This is in contrast with some over-simplified Agile advocacy of usage of near identical generalists centered around developer skill-sets, which due to labor pool constraints leads to supply difficulties and the expensive and unlikely proposition of finding robust analytical and quality assurance skills within developer pools.

One of the "Features" related to this approach to organization, in conjunction with limiting WIP and one-piece flow is related to the process improvement analogy articulated by Taiichi Ohno. He used the analogy of lowering the level of water in a river in order to expose rocks and obstacles to explain how removing inventory showed where flow of production was interrupted. Once the barriers were exposed, they could be removed. This forced each shop to improve its own quality or cause a holdup in the next downstream area. Applying this notion to Software Product Development, Lean organizational structures naturally lead to visibility into performance, where process problems become immediately evident. Different teams are directly comparable such that learning can occur as to why results are different. This is different than serialized, role-based matrixing, where it is often unclear as to the root cause of process failures and where local-optimization is typically at fault. And team-based matrixing affords direct observation of the progression of the team lifecycle [111], and the ability to reward and protect high-performing teams while enabling re-structuring of teams that are struggling.

Similar to Agile, with a Lean Organizational structure, the opportunity exists to leverage the proven U.S. Marine Corps practice of self-organization [105]. This shifts the focus of management towards a Kaizen culture and on studying process improvement rather than work allocation and scheduling. Each empowered team establishes mutual commitment and responsibility (initially at a single-batch work-in-progress level). Note that early studies into worker productivity motivation factors are consistent with what has been practiced by the USMC, where it was found that the primary motivator in workers is not compensation, but rather management style and social norms [107].

6.3.4 – Application of Real Options Theory

Architectural decisions are typically the ones that are above the organizations risk tolerance and therefore require a degree of rigor to ensure that bad decisions are not taken. Such "high-stakes" decisions, as they are described within the Lean community, are suggested to be taken as late as possible. The practice of "commit at the last responsible moment" seeks to avoid wrong decisions which are quite costly to undo later. Contrary to popular belief, there are three, not two possibilities related to the outcome of a decision – a right decision, a wrong decision, or "no decision". This practice, studied as part of the Toyota Product Development System, suggests there is value in leveraging this last case. The concept seeks to defer decisions until the maximum amount of information is available such that the probability of a correct decision is likely. The body of knowledge is commonly applied in financial and investment services under the name Options Thinking. When dealing with investment, the right but not the obligation to exercise a decision or choice is called a derivative instrument. In physical forms of decisions, the term "real options" was coined by professor Stewart Myers at MIT's Sloan School of Management in 1977 to capture the same essence as that found in financial capital markets.

*A **real option** itself, is the right — but not the obligation — to undertake some business decision; typically the option to make, abandon, expand, or shrink a capital investment decisions.*

Wikipedia

A "sweet-spot" exists when it comes to the timing of design decisions. This is where solution delivery delays incur more risk to the project than the decision-risk mitigation efforts yield. Figure 6.17 illustrates the notion of balancing the risk of a bad decision with the risk of delaying a decision.

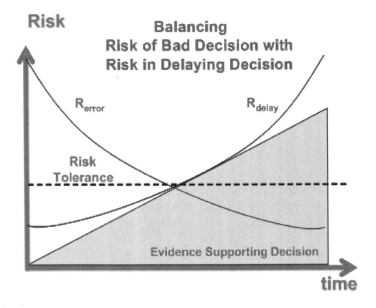

Figure 6.17 – Balancing late and bad decisions

In software development projects, determining when an option "vests" and retires has proven difficult. Recent study suggests that marking the point in time where a Real Option vests actionable is by monitoring risks. Specifically, the point when a Real Option taken out on a high-stakes decision should be exercised is when the risk of error is equal to the risk of delay. A formal body of knowledge had emerged to enable this concept. It is used in the valuation of Real Options for making technology investment decisions. Pioneered at Boeing, it is called the Datar-Matthews approach [131, 132], and drastically simplifies the Black-Scholes approach for options valuation. This approach leverages fuzzy mathematics to simplify the decision tree analysis that "unfolds the future" with respect to valuating potential investment outcome probabilities in present day terms as the investment lifecycle evolves. This enables reasonable questions to be answered like:

- *Why, by how much and in what should I be investing today?*

- *Are these investments increasing my return opportunities?*

- *What are the risks and how am I hedged?*

- *How does this investment optimize my portfolio holdings risk-return?*

6.3.5 – Set based, Concurrent Engineering

Many who first hear of Lean in the context of Software Development are skeptical. Typically, the argument is made that Lean is based on the Toyota Production System – TPS, and this is only applicable to manufacturing. While Lean did originate from TPS, it is not only applicable to manufacturing. And Lean did not solely originate from TPS. Another system of practices leveraged by the likes of Toyota also contribute to the Lean body of knowledge as applicable to software engineering. This body of knowledge is known as the Toyota Product Development System (TPDS) and has only recently become popularized through exploratory study.

One practice that hails from this system is *Set-based, Concurrent Engineering*. This practice, directly related to the concept of deciding as late as possible as just discussed in the previous section, is born of necessity to ensure that timeliness to market is not sacrificed through the risk mitigation practices of delay. By concurrently developing many options to the solution of a problem, the likelihood of having the "right" choice available increases as knowledge becomes available and the *Chief Engineers'* understanding becomes clearer. Multiple approaches are explored in parallel, and the options space is narrowed as other degrees-of-freedom are reduced through the manifestation of decisions in other areas. Eventually, convergence on the best possible option emerges. This practice has resulted in impressive product development success within Toyota, with 10 of 15 JD Powers and Associates first place awards ensuing [133]. These results are relevant, as it is reasonable to assume that this product development complexity is at least on par with software development. Figure 6.18 illustrates the idea of set-based, concurrent engineering.

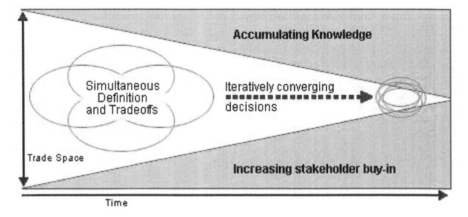

Figure 6.18 – Set-based, Concurrent Engineering[134]

It should be noted that the idea of set-based concurrent engineering does have precedent within software practice in other communities. The Unified Process community has long leveraged this approach within the approach to acquisition called "Evolutionary Process for Integrating COTS". In this modification to custom software development, the idea of having differing spheres of influence on the decision making process coincides with the advice to not prematurely rule-out options due to overly rigid constraints [134].

6.3.6 – Product-line practices

There seems to be renewed interest in the concept of Product Lines [135], not only within the Agile community, but in the broader software engineering community. But Product-lines are a key practice leveraged in successful automotive product development organizations like Toyota. Within the TPDS is an acknowledgement that the "fuzzy front end of product development" can lead to impressive returns later in a products lifecycle. As such, Toyota invests heavily in building robust "platforms" upon which to base their product development strategy. They attempt to standardize on a few core foundational lines which have robustness engineered in such that variability can emerge over time off of these standardized structures. What we see as Camray's, Sienna's and Avalon's actually leverage the same power-train and chassis. Obviously the engineering that goes into this approach is more expensive than the one-off design, but if these costs are shared over many products, there comes a point when a pay-off point is reached.

Other industries do the same thing – take wireless phones; the radio technology components are standard platforms in which variability in look and feel, controls and marketing features can sit. The field of software engineering has long sought to apply similar practices through the ideas of frameworks, stacks and high-order reuse packages. But renewed interest is now being enabled through such technologies as SEAP – Software Engineering as a Platform and Cloud computing. The market is racing to finally realize the promise of the commoditization of commercially available standardized parts.

Figure 6.19 illustrates the economics of Product Line practices.

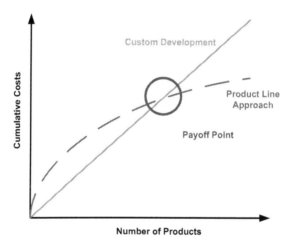

Figure 6.19 – Product Line Practice Payoff

In the above figure we can see that it is more costly during the early design stages of a product line than with custom development. And this gap widens as more products are contemplated in the product line. But there reaches a point when the economics start to favor the product line approach. The early investment of establishing a reusable platform starts to result in lower costs overall for the suite of products. Some have suggested that reuse of high-order like product lines sees that payoff around three. Meaning that for product lines which number more than 3, this approach while looking more costly on the outset and for a single product starts to look attractive.

Chapter 7: Towards Agility at Scale

A common concern related to the application of Agile approaches is related to scale. Various authors have identified the sweet spot for these methods to be team sizes of 40 or less [85]. Similar criticisms exist in how Agile projects integrate into the broader IT Enterprise. Response to these criticisms has lead to attempts to extend the original practices in light of such realizations, some examples being *Scrum-of-scrums*, and *Meta-scrum*. But some fundamental issues remain related to the assumptions and choices made by Agile approaches, with some still believing that they are universally applicable unaltered in all circumstances. Some of the purists within the Agile community have even labeled such pragmatic extensions with labels like *"Scrum-butt"* or *"Faux-Agile"* whenever teams waiver from doctrine. The reality however, is that bona-fide issues exist when it comes to scale. These issues include practical division of labor, effects of scale on delivery dynamics and response, organizational structure for Agility at scale and implications of "The Mythical Man-month", and some of the realities related to acquisition reform strategy. This latter concern is very real since the passage of the Federal Acquisition Reform Act of 1996 (also known as Clinger-Cohen) [17].

To yield insights into pragmatic solutions to these very real Enterprise IT issues, SDLC 3.0 focuses on leaving nothing on the field so to speak. Meaning that the challenges Agile naturally finds itself confronted with have either been solved before within other communities (which historically have had to deal with the issue of scale) or can provide potential areas of exploration when combined with Agile. Leveraging the entire field of modern software engineering practices from within the Unified Process, Agile and Lean communities is the answer. The combination of all modern software engineering practices – Lean, UP and Agile has yet to be leveraged.

7.1 – 30 Day vs. 2 Week Iterations (vs. no Iterations)

When looking at the nature of Dynamic Systems, one can identify two distinct periods of time in the system's response pattern. These periods of time are when the system is in a transient state, where the transitioning of the system towards the new setpoint occurs; and the steady-state period of time, where the system reacts and corrects itself from perturbations and disturbances. It would seem reasonable that because the system behaves differently during these two distinctly different states, the control effects that influence the system should be different. And indeed this is the case when you look at Control Theory. In the case of the transient period of time, the influence we apply to the plant during t_{rise} is different than when we are near steady state. For example, Proportional Control and the stabilizing anticipatory Derivative Control influence heavily how fast we converge on the setpoint, whereas Integral Control influences the amount of steady state error (SSE).

Leveraging this metaphorically, we can view the early period of time as focused on closing the gap between apparent and actual scope quickly. The earlier period of a product development, where "architecture" is performed and sometimes referred to as "the fuzzy front end" is where the system (the project organization) is transient. The goal is to achieve t_{rise} in as short a period as possible such that (for reasons of investment valuation from Real Options theory) investment feasibility can be determined as related to the perceived scope setpoint of the endeavor. During the steady-state period of time, the control strategy shifts to one of stabilization. In software product delivery, this could be characterized as the period from t_{rise} to $t_{settling}$ and beyond which is sometime referred to as the build-out and the maintenance for the software product.

The concept of Risk fits nicely into this model when it comes to the convergence of Perceived vs. Actual scope, as well as accommodating error due to imperfect knowledge – solution feasibility, solution execution defects, etc. The transient period of time can therefore be seen as synonymous with the risk mitigation stage, where we are focused on reduction of uncertainty of all kinds – including the uncertainty of scope. It just so happens that this is the essence of the Unified Process, which is firmly grounded in risk management practice due to its Spiral Model and MBASE influences. The Risk-Value practice has always leveraged two distinct stages – that of "Engineering" and that of "Manufacturing". In the former, the risk profile is transient where risks are identified and then active risk mitigation is the focus. The latter is typified by risk maintenance. All follow-on development effort of the product post project is still in the risk maintenance mode unless the risk profile changes.

The question naturally arises then, what is different between these two stages. Does a different dynamic for each not make sense? It would seem reasonable that the answer is yes. We know from queuing theory that micro-increments and one-piece flow is more efficient than the batching of iterations. So when we are focused on trying to maximize efficiency in the steady-state period of a product delivery, it would seem reasonable that the use of iteration-less development and Digital Kanban makes sense. This is due to the ability to scale up far more linearly than with the iteration-based team structure. Within the Unified Process, the post Lifecycle Architecture (LCA) point in time is where commitment to scaling up investment and resources is achieved.

This leaves the "engineering" stage of the product lifecycle. Given the smaller team size due to the desire to accrue exit real options value if the investment is unattractive, the Lean/Kanban approach does not appear to add much value. Instead, it would seem that we are not looking for maximum throughput, but rather maximum closure on uncertainty. Because uncertainty is typically broad, this implies that a broad and shallow treatment of scope is necessary to achieve risk mitigation and drive concurrence on actual scope and architectural qualities. Focus in this stage is on proving out high-stakes decisions among a small team, not on delivering immediate customer value for unprecedented problems. Therefore, it would seem reasonable that iterations are the best work breakdown structure for providing the negative feedback necessary to influence/control the plant. The question is then what is the "best" or "proper" duration for iterations. This directly translates to what is the optimal frequency choice in Control Theory parlance. We know that timeboxing represents a WIP limiting mechanism which impacts productivity, so this leaves us with a choice of 30 day sprints from Scrum or 2-week iterations from XP (obviously other frequencies are available, but these are what is currently socialized within the Agile community).

We know from our discussion of the analysis techniques within Classical Control Systems Theory that higher frequency leads to better transient performance. We also know that too high a frequency for a given gain (number of resources applied during the engineering stage) leads to instability. Indeed, authors have written about iterations being too short during the early stages of a project as hazardous [136]. From this, it would appear that the longer iteration duration would seem to be less risky in terms of phase margin (stability measure from our discussion of Bode plots) for problems of scale or high complexity. Figure 7.1 illustrates the concept of inserting "robustness" into the "fuzzy front end" stage of development.

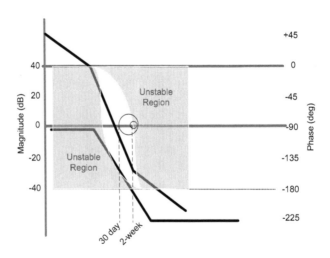

Figure 7.1 – Stability margin with 2-week vs 30day iterations

While it may not be optimal in terms of delivery response, the practice as implemented through the lower frequency can be seen as being more "robust" from a control systems perspective. This means that the project system has some "padding" between the selected operating range and the instability point. For projects that are not as complex or do not have the same component scale, a higher frequency is possible like with XP.

Figure 7.2 illustrates the strategy of applying different "control" strategies depending on the different product delivery stages.

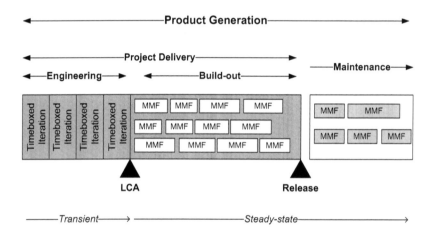

Figure 7.2 – Product Delivery Stages - Transient vs. Steady-state

The figure above shows that timeboxed iterations as a strategy for implementing negative feedback gives way to micro-increments and Digital Kanban development post-architecture. This represents a hybrid of Lean, Agile and Unified Process temporal dimension strategies for product delivery work breakdown. Instead of picking one of the three IID strategies that exist within modern software engineering, the key point is that all actually play a role in mature product development.

7.2 – Complexity and Technical Debt

Not all projects are created equal. If we assume that all projects are technically complex then we necessarily insert waste into our process. Equally, when we ignore complexity and assume that the correct solution approach will magically emerge, we can incur large amounts of waste. The key is understanding the nature of the demand before us and making a conscious decision as to whether we need to bring complexity-reducing tools to bear. This implies that we think before we act – an old engineering adage.

Kentou is a Japanese term meaning "study". It is commonly known in Lean Thinking circles as being associated with the Toyota Product Development System – TPDS. This is not to be confused with the Toyota Production System – TPS, the focus of most Lean Software Development reflection in recent years. TPDS leverages many of the core concepts of TPS from queuing theory – like JIT (creating flow through pull), *Jidoka*, *Heijunka*, waste reduction, and *Kaizen*. But the practice of "Front-end loading the Design Factory" is different, and executed during the *Kentou* period of time. Now hard-core Agilists would chalk this up to "Big Design Up Front – BDUF", but it should not be so easily discounted as pure *muda* just because of the practice name. Toyota's results in terms of product development as reflected in JD Powers & Associates rankings would historically suggest a second look. Modern automobiles are extremely complex, with arguably as fast paced a business environment as IT. And the systems and software that are <u>engineered</u> into current car models I would argue are at least as complex as that faced by an open source J2EE stack project.

It just so happens that software engineering has acknowledged the *Kentou* period of time historically. And even Agile supports this notion. The problem is that, probably for political reasons, this explicit period of time where investment feasibility is proven before committal has been buried. If you read *"Controlled Chaos-Living on the Edge"*, the seminal paper on Scrum from Pattern Languages of Program Design (PLoP), you will find reference to *"during the design and system architecture phase of Scrum, the designers and architects divide the project into packets. Packets are assigned to teams based on priority and scheduling constraints. Based on the degree of coupling between packets, groups of up to six teams are organized into a management control cluster. This continues upwards until a top level cluster has been created."* So although significant design/architecture is nowadays discouraged in favour of emergent design and refactoring at the lowest levels of abstraction within the Agile community, Scrum always had it albeit in implicit/tacit form. Obviously the Unified Process/MBASE has always had the Elaboration Phase, which is focused on experimentation and accruing learning real-options to mitigate the risks surrounding investment feasibility through significant design decisions (software architecture).

So one naturally wonders what the right answer is to the question: *Is Kentou Muda?* As expected – it depends. Practices, even from the TPDS are contextual. If you study Toyota's product development strategy, you will find that they engage in four different types of product development effort – from white sheet to product platform line to product line to in-between model programs/projects. Toyota typically does a lot of the second and third types of product development, so engaging in the rigor of *Kentou* would be muda for type 4 efforts, and might be scaled back for type 3.

I would suggest that most if not all sweet-spot agile projects are the third and fourth types of product development. Meaning not much architecture is actually going on at all. No wonder hard-core agilists say Architecture is YAGNI. And they are right. Architecture is about significant design decisions, not the blueprints which have unfortunately been a misunderstanding within the IT industry. Architectural description should be focused on the knowledge management of assets within a larger product management strategy, rather than how it is typically applied on a per project basis, where it is quickly perishable. Blueprinting should be left mostly to the second and third types of product development (and obviously the first) where we are developing the assets in the first place; that is not to say that modeling as a tool to combat complexity can not be used, just in a pragmatic way with an understanding of "why".

So going back to the Agile J2EE/.NET stack sweet-spot, *Kentou* happened over many years within the entire open source world to produce the components/services/frameworks that are now so prevalent. But all software engineering projects are not J2EE stack projects, so painting with a broad brush is also not reasonable. You need to know what type of demand you are faced with to understand whether *Kentou*/Elaboration is of value.

This leads us to the latest term for a problem of scale/complexity as seen in the Agile world – technical debt. The key with this is to know when you are borrowing. Unfortunately, when Kentou is ignored and teams "just get coding", the likelihood for un-intended technical debt is higher. With technical debt, the assumption that we can just refactor ourselves out of any difficulty leads to bankruptcy. Take the analogy of building a bridge. If we were to start with minimal lightweight requirements and make assumptions as to the load support needed and the width of the surface, we might be able to start "developing" the bridge so as to be able to establish velocity and show the customer progress in the project. Now aside from the more deterministic nature of bridge building and the hard lessons that have been learned on prior evolutions (like Tacoma Narrows), what type of bridge did we set out to build. Tweaking that bridge so we can add bike lanes on the outside can surely be "refactored" into the design along the way. And as long as we got all of the high stakes requirements, this might be true. We may not have that unprecedented of a problem space after all. But we get to the last mile of the bridge and we discover that an aircraft carrier needs to be able to cross under our bridge to get into Vancouver Harbour, and at low tide we are 15 feet too short. Oops, we just ran into technical bankruptcy. This was because we built a floating bridge, not a suspension bridge and ignored uncertain future events to establish the style of bridge. Technical debt is like that – if we forgo any assessment of risk and uncertainty so as to just get on with it, our fitness for purpose could very likely fail. And our late project velocity will obviously suffer tremendously. Toyota and their Japanese product development philosophy embrace the "fuzzy front end" to the fullest extent to achieve Agility at scale. But they also understand when their product scope is fuzzy and when it is not.

Somehow in the Agile world, the focus on leveraging high-order reuse has been lost. And the reality is that acquisition orientation is emerging as a force within the IT industry, whether as a result of Clinger-Cohen, or due to the emerging maturity of SOA, Cloud and SEAP. Focus in most of IT will soon be on leveraging assets – asset based development, not creating new assets from scratch. The *Kentou* period of time will re-emerge as being valuable all of the time in a different form-factor of software product development – one that tries to acquire rather than require and code. Composite system development/COTS are much different than green-field developments. The early stages of product development afford the highest degree of leverage where the trade-space is the largest, and cost of exploration (through working software) is the lowest. And it represents a period of time when technical deposits can be made as opposed to technical debt.

7.3 – Pragmatic Division of Labor

One key issue at scale is the question of division of labor and the delegation responsibility by the business. In current Agile approaches, the strategy is to collapse the value-stream by having business representatives provide demand directly to software product development teams. In the true role of Product Owner, a business process owner is responsible for submitting demand in the form of light weight User Stories. But the reality in most large scale businesses is that identifying demand that aligns with business processes, or provides new and innovative business opportunities is complex. And the skills required to seed the Product Backlogs for project teams necessarily requires the decomposition of business complexity (take Corporate Actions for example), but also require an understanding of technology. In most large scale IT organizations, this "bridging capability" is fulfilled through the outsourcing of this function to Enterprise IT by the business side. As an analogy, it can be thought of as something akin to investment advisors. Instead of researching everything possible regarding a company such that an investment opportunity can be reasoned about, efficient investors favor leveraging the special skills of Investment Management firms who maintain in-house analysts, securities data feeds, portfolio analytics and Straight-Through-Processing (STP) trade execution.

With SDLC 3.0, the analogy described above is embraced as reality in all but the most trivial enterprises. SDLC practices and role articulations must reflect the realities of the business, not the IT-centric wishes for offloading critical value propositions back on the customer. Instead of leveraging Product Owner's as de facto Enterprise Architects and push Business IT Alignment responsibility back inside the business, it is more practical for Product Customers to collaborate with a Lean EA function to leverage a meaningful division of labor. This view conflicts with an oversimplified one-size fits all approach to IT Investment Management. It disputes the Agile simplifications that suggest that no value is delivered through alignment reasoning. Demand arising solely from a business Product Owner implies that they are the most efficient resource to understand the complexity of the existing automation beyond their business process line responsibilities. Even if Agile Product Owners did possess this generalist knowledge consistently, they would be a very expensive resource. At scale, this level of competence does not exist, so division of labor in the form of T-shaped people or Specialized-Generalists [137] is a more economically viable model for delivering alignment and investment feasibility value. The oversimplified Agile argument has shown itself to be problematic in highly unprecedented and large-scale transformation system delivery projects and has lead to a perception of a lack of applicability of Agile at scale. Note that this is not to say that the anti-pattern of performing big-bang, radical redesign or boil-the-ocean type Enterprise Architecture efforts should occur. This portion of the value stream must also be Lean and focused on flow such that cycle time for delivery can be minimized.

The former division of labor choice and where to draw the IT Project context boundary also has implications for the governance of the IT investment. To illustrate the scale issues related to selection of governance practice, take the following two examples – Distributed Specialized Stakeholders engaged through discrete toll-gates, and the single Product Owner stakeholder approach. If the business is under the mandate to prevent (at least attempt to prevent) problems with the production IT environment and the associated negative effects on business operations, then certain concerns need to be addressed before changes are introduced into production. We know from experience that this preparation should happen early and often. In the first approach, concerns are addressed by specialized resources that can make informed decisions about readiness related to their area of expertise. For example, concerns about leveraging virtualization or data security issues can be addressed early on, and it is unreasonable to assume that everyone is an expert in such issues. Instead of waiting to assess these issues until right before release, the distributed stakeholder approach as seen in the Unified Process leverages incremental and just-in-time collaboration with the most qualified resources for the governance task. Contrast this with Scrum/XP, which assumes that a Product Owner on the business side can discharge this responsibility. And because Scrum/XP advocates releasing realized functionality immediately in an incremental fashion, all governance concerns must be addressed in a very quick timeframe so as to enable the monthly or weekly frequency. In large scale efforts this is not realistic. So where it appears that governance is lighter in the latter case, it could easily be argued that this approach is at best risky and at worst ineffective. Instead, focusing governance efforts within just-in-time themed periods of time effectively means that the governance approach can be thought of as a pull-system. With large-scale IT enterprises which have various governance specializations, this is the only approach that scales. Figure 7.3 illustrates this contrast.

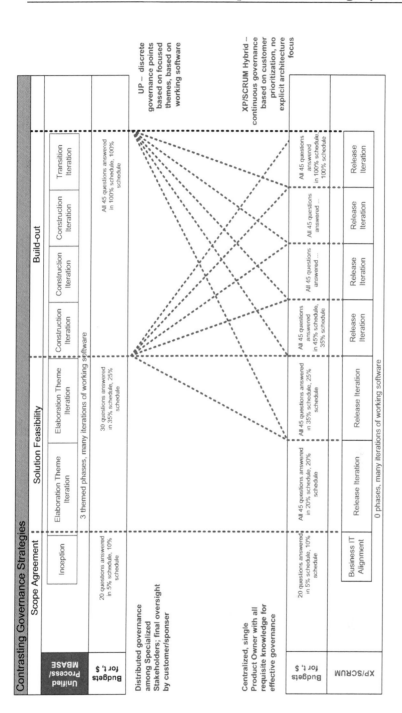

Figure 7.3 – Discrete and Specialized/Distributed vs Continuous and Generalist/Centralized Governance

The timing of when governance concerns are addressed is not the only issue related to single governance oversight. If a single Product Owner could somehow manage to address all of the concerns leading up to production changes on a frequency advocated with Scrum/XP for large scale and complex efforts, the question that naturally arises is how expensive and mature would such a resource have to be. This resource would not only have to be able to translate business change requirements into technology strategy and IT demand(Business-IT Alignment), but would also have to understand current strategic technology plans based upon industry trends. If they could fulfill this function which necessarily requires business domain knowledge, they would also have to know current norms with SAS-70 compliance standards of care. They would have to have detailed knowledge of data security and risk based portfolio management options valuation techniques. They would have to be able to assess technical quality scenario test results, provide feedback on scenario/User Story details due to tacit knowledge reasons, and have a detailed understanding of production control procedures and data center operations. The point – this would be a very expensive resource indeed. And in a large IT Enterprise which typically engages in hundreds and even thousands of IT investment projects, it is arguable whether such a pool of resources would even be available for even that one firm. In short, a single super-governor strategy does not scale.

7.4 – Organizational Structure for Scale - Lean

Beyond the identification of the issue of scale when it comes to demand generation and IT investment governance, the issue of how to structure the internal delivery organization naturally arises. When the mainstream Agile approaches were articulated, the assumption and indeed the advice was to keep teams small. This ignored a large spectrum of problems and has the potential to limit the applicability of Agile. Various approaches were "invented" somewhat after the fact in an effort to head off the critics. The interesting thing is that the answer to scale has been around for quite some time. Agility at scale is possible and requires adaptation of the purist interpretation of the mainstream Agile approaches.

Certain pragmatic practitioners have done just this, and ironically they stem from an organization which has been dealing with large scale software developments within ruthless product market cycle times for many years. This company is Microsoft and the practice applied to deal with Agility at Scale has been leveraged for many of the large scale products that are market-share leaders in industry. The practice that Microsoft employs is known as "feature-crews" [110]. In essence, the consistent approach to issues of scale and the need for Agility is to break down the scope as viewed by the customer. Once a core team has determined the architecture (the engineering stage), this team is then available to "pair" or partner with a series of small teams, each who is responsible for delivering customer identifiable capability in the product. The concepts behind this practice, however, were not invented by Microsoft but rather are a key element of Lean. Toyota and other manufacturers have employed the concept of the cross-functional and semi-autonomous Lean "work-cell" for quite some time. In essence, issues of concurrency and the requirement for speed produced from one-piece flow and JIT led to this configuration.

To illustrate the challenges that vanilla Agile approaches run into, let us first explore the typical scaling strategy employed in Scrum. In Scrum, the advice is for the creation of teams focused on "packets", and each of these teams report in a management control cluster of a size of no larger than six. This arrangement continues up hierarchically to the top most cluster. The limit of 6 necessarily leads to the hierarchy. Each team must operate within a timeboxed iteration, and iterations must integrate during this timebox such that the complete system of value can be delivered at the end of each sprint. Coordination among teams is effected through the practice *scrum-of-scrums* which adds incrementally the daily-standup overhead the higher up in the hierarchy the participant reaches. For example, assuming each daily standup takes the 15 minutes as they should, with a modest project size of ~180 team members arranged in a hierarchical scrum-of-scrums pattern, daily standups would be occurring all day. This is because the usual advice is to stagger the meetings rather than have them concurrent such that flexible coordination is still possible, and "chickens" can still attend. With a team size any larger, you run out of hours in the day so the practice becomes impacted. Also note that certain members may be required to attend multiple meetings which also defeats the efficiency gain objectives of the practice through the limiting of meetings.

Figure 7.4 first illustrates the coordination and issue reporting strategy taken by the Scrum Agile approach.

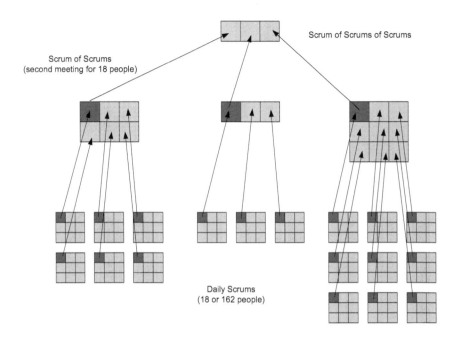

Scrum of Scrums of Scrums

Scrum of Scrums
(second meeting for 18 people)

Daily Scrums
(18 or 162 people)

7.4 – Typical Agile Scaling approach ,

The timeboxing requirement in Scrum suggests that each iteration must result in shippable product. And so if any one of the parallel teams misses a sprint, this tenet of Agile fails, as the Product Owner/Customers expectations are that this will occur. The work configuration is risky because planning overhead, retrospective overhead, and daily standup overhead increases in a non-linear fashion. The more layers that exist means that more front-end compression occurs. Eventually as the number of levels increases, the communication overhead non-linearity's cause the timebox to be useless with nothing of value possible at the end because the iteration is taken up with coordination. It is at this point that our chosen iteration duration becomes unstable.

The typical reactive strategy to deal with this is to relax the constraint for coherent iteration boundaries where they become staggered, and everything becomes out of sync and truly isolated. Integration, planning, retrospectives and Product Owner engagement all become challenged.

Figure 7.5 illustrates the effects of scaling using the Scrums-of-scrums approach.

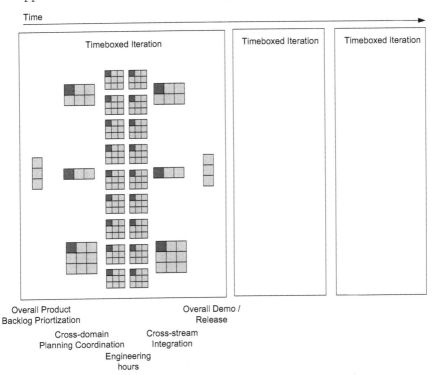

7.5 – Timing considerations with Scrum

In contrast, the Lean approach abandons iterations altogether, but rather focuses on micro-increments. Each micro-increment is a minimal-marketable-feature and can be released independently of all other features. Instead of performing all of the delicate planning for a batch of features such that the coordinated sprints will result in a coherent output, features are assigned to crews that can be planned out just-in-time in such a fashion to be decoupled from any of the other planning by other crews. The feature-crew approach leverages a common specialist service layer which is shared among feature crews. No division occurs in the upper layers, and the developer-analyst pairs should be specialist generalist in nature such that they can deliver the feature fully as a pair. Instead of the layer or component based decomposition based on specialization, the self organizing teams are small and self sufficient to be able to deliver the value independently. The definition of what is a shared service team and what is not should be made on the basis of maturity of the technology and cost of finding the scalable resource pool with this skill. As few specialist service provider pools as possible should be favored, as they can become a bottleneck.

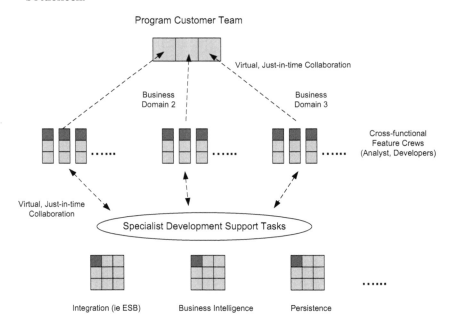

Program Customer Team

Virtual, Just-in-time Collaboration

Business Domain 2

Business Domain 3

Cross-functional Feature Crews (Analyst, Developers)

Virtual, Just-in-time Collaboration

Specialist Development Support Tasks

Integration (ie ESB)   Business Intelligence   Persistence

Shared Technical Services Pool Teams

7.6 – Lean Feature-crew Matrixing Structure

Note that in the early period of the development project, a small core team is leveraged focused on getting the architecture right. Once this toll-gate is passed, these members seed the shared resource pools and also help coach the additional Feature-crews that are applied such that scale can occur to accelerate progress.

By focusing on the micro-increment, the Lean approach not only provides the visible progress and feedback that is a core tenet of Agile, but also alleviates the coordination overhead due to the fact that the scope taken on by a team at any point in time is minimal. The sync points approach a continuous nature rather than the discretization that occurs through the fixed timebox cadence.

Next, Figure 7.7 illustrates how the concept of "feature-crews" works from a timing perspective.

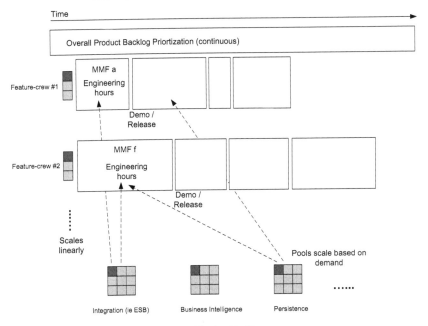

7.7 – Lean Feature-crew Workflow

One of the key differences in the approaches is the degree of isolation of independent, self organizing teams. These teams are cross-functional, with problem domain and solution domain representation. They act like a mini-business venture, responsible atomically for all aspects of meeting customer demand. Instead of being part of a larger and larger composite, they act similar to USMC units with autonomous authority. And because they are freed from temporally more sensitive fixed cadences, they can focus on the actual realization rather than coordination overhead. They also survive from product assignment to product assignment. This means that once the team has "normed" and is performing well, every attempt is made to maintain this emergent behavior. Teams evolve an understanding of the participants within their ranks, the personalities involved, the key strengths and weaknesses. Instead of ripping them apart immediately after they have gone through the team lifecycle, the team is preserved. This implies a matrixing strategy at the team level as opposed to the individual level, a fundamental shift for most organizations.

The reasoning of why this approach scales better is due to the impact of communication non-linearity as team size grows. If instead of growing a single team we add more granular teams, the scaling effect becomes more linear. Figure 7.8 presents the formulae that govern the effort related to cooperative problem solving and often associated with "Brooks Law" [138].

$$TeamEffort = \sum Effort_{person} + \left(\# Pairs \times Effort_{pair} \right)$$

where

$$\# Pairs = \frac{N^2 - N}{2}$$

and

$$N = number\ of\ team\ members$$

7.8 – Mitigating the non-linearity of Team size

What is obvious from this relation is that as team size grows, the potential number of communication links grows exponentially (non-linearily). This tells us that it is desirable to encapsulate communications within small teams so as to reduce the amount of communication overhead. If we keep teams small and have external communication links kept to a constant number which is also small, the resulting effort expenditure profile related to the effects of communication and collaboration becomes linear. A linear relation is far more likely to scale to the kinds of projects that Agile has shown to have difficulty with. Figure 7.9 shows the difference.

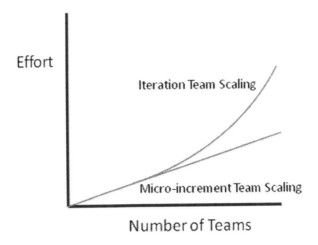

7.9 – Linearizing the Complex Adaptive System

7.5 – Distributed Collaboration

We have already established that collaboration is important. This is due to the tacit nature of knowledge. Documents are a poor form of communication and information sharing because they must be persisted which represents only the explicit knowledge capture possible at a point of time. And this is a moving target or perishable as some have articulated. The preferable approach is more frequent engagement leveraging all forms of communication in a high trust environment to drive an understanding of what to build or how to build it among the practitioners on the project.

The reality in most IT Enterprises and large scale projects is that distribution of the software development personnel and stakeholders is likely. Yet Agile approaches not only advise co-location at whatever the cost, they revel in the notion of co-location in somewhat of a cultural bias. Aside from this philosophical underpinning, nothing states that co-location cannot be virtual. The Agile Manifesto was articulated at a time when many challenges still existed related to distance. They year 2001 was still the early years of the internet, and globally distributed intranets were still expensive. I recall looking into Virtual Private Intranet costs for a project in 2001 in which almost 1000 developers in Chennai and Beijing had to collaborate with 100 analysts in Tokyo and an architecture team in San Jose California. The costs were quite prohibitive. Yet this program managed through some innovative software repatriation techniques and heavy use of multi-site video conferencing. The program was capable of being "Agile" even though one of the revered practices was not possible. Recent advice from others within the Agile community that have attempted this type of offshore configuration is to not do it [139]. The author respectfully disagrees.

In the year 2009 however, this is not a challenge technically speaking. And the costs have plummeted. For example, simple instant messaging, either standalone tools like *Jabber* or *Lotus Sametime* are available for IT Enterprises; similarily web-based services like *Yahoo*, *Dimdim* and *Skype* offer free video and text conferencing to enable effective collaboration. Depending on the culture of the organization or the project, the video can be quite important, as body language and tone are leveraged heavily in "high-context" cultures [140].

Recent trends in SDLC infrastructure are focused on "collaboration in context"[141]. The above communication tools are integrated into process-centric configuration management infrastructure such that contextual information related to task, feature or work product can quickly be associated for purposes of discussion. A recent emergence in the softening of the "no tools" mantra from the Agile community is occurring with the rise of Application Lifecycle Management (ALM) [89] technologies and SDLC collaboration tools, centered around workflow. Process enactment infrastructure like IBM's Jazz [142] platform is seen as the upcoming approach to enable Agile to scale beyond small projects (see Gartner Hype Cycle). Virtual collaboration technology is being seen as a way to embrace the essence of the practice and yield unprecedented real-time openness and business visibility without the legacy tool anti-patterns.

7.6 – Digital Kanban

In a previous section we discussed how Lean and one-piece flow of micro-increments is the key to Agility at scale. To implement JIT one-piece flow and achieve the benefits that derive from queuing theory, a WIP limiting Kanban system is typically leveraged. While popularized through the invention of the modern Toyota Production System, physical Kanban has much earlier origins. Figure 7.10a illustrates application of Just-in-Time signaling and pull-production control at a blacksmith shop as far back as 1911. It just so happens that this implementation was a result of a "Scientific Management" engagement by Frederick Winslow Taylor. The metal pockets (empty or occupied) serve as visual controls and a form of an early Kanban board. The system limits the queued work at each machine.

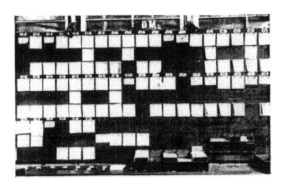

7.10a – Early Kanban – The System Company, circa 1911 [142]

Attached to the board were rudimentary Kanban's that controlled production flow. Figure 7.10b illustrates these early signal cards.

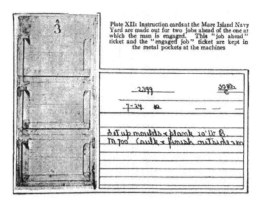

7.10b – Early Kanban – The System Company, circa 1911

Physical Kanban boards have been leveraged in Japan for implementing JIT since they were popularized by the Toyota Production System. Figure 7.11 illustrates a typical Kanban board in use in manufacturing.

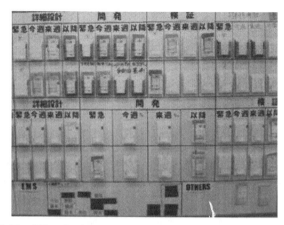

7.11 – Physical application of Kanban in Japan [143]

Recent interest has emerged related to the application of Kanban to Just-in-Time/Lean Software Development. However, the trend of direct and literal replication of the earlier works (usually only going as far back as Toyota's application of the practice) continues within the Agile software development community. Social norms within this community are to favor a low-technology, physical and manual approaches for achieving the visual controls practice. Figure 7.12 illustrates an example of the physical application of Kanban boards for the Just-in-Time pull-oriented control of software demand realization.

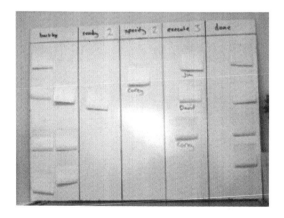

7.12 – Physical Low Tech Form of Kanban in
Software Development [143]

Many modern manufacturers (Toyota included) are now implementing electronic forms of Kanban. The objectives of leveraging automation for implementing pull-system control are to avoid common problems like the loss of physical cards. Integrating electronic Kanban with ERP allows real-time demand signaling across the supply chain and improved visibility. This data can be leveraged to optimize inventory levels and provide better tracking of supplier lead times for replenishment. Yet even with this trend from Manufacturing, Kanban continues to be implemented within the Agile Software Development community as physical "cards". Typical with literal interpretation, form supersedes function, and the objective of control visualization is lost in the mechanics and procedures. To enable Agility at scale, electronic forms of Kanban must be leveraged to not only enable the approach for scaling through Lean, but also to facilitate distributed collaboration. Kanban serves as the lynchpin to enable scale on multiple fronts.

When one looks at these physical mechanisms, one can identify a number of abstractions and patterns. Specifically, the vertical columns represent enumerated states of individual pieces within the flow, albeit the state variable is reflected spatially. This state-pattern is typical of what is manifested within digital workflow automation. *Digital Kanban* is an improvement because actual cards are not used, but instead workflow oriented or "stateful" records are leveraged in their place. And where limits are imposed on manual Kanban based on the spaces of the board, business rules and dynamic parameterization can occur in Digital Kanban related to WIP limits. The only element that remains is "visibility", or more accurately, the signal or notification that an action has to occur related to supply replenishment and pull-oriented processing. Workflow notification is a direct parallel to the physical signaling mechanism, whether event broadcast- based (syndication feeds), or rules-based messages (email notifications). Integration of the pull system with enterprise Resource Management modules within typical Project Portfolio Management products yields similar supply chain inventory capabilities to that of manufacturing. Obviously, graphical user interface visualization is possible through mash-ups and basic reporting technology.

Within the Software Engineering community, this stateful workflow pattern is typical within recent trends in industry, specifically known as process enactment or Application Lifecycle Management. In looking at the detailed design of Digital Kanban, three key "Kanban's" are necessary to fully implement the necessary pull-system from product demand recognition to product release. These relationships are illustrated in Figure 7.13.

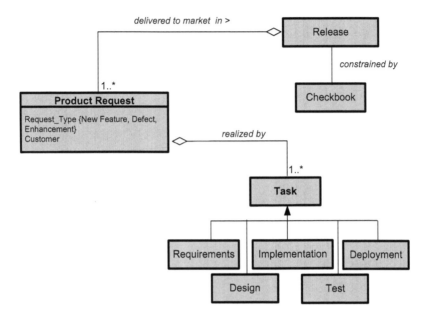

7.13 – 3 distinctive Record Types make up Digital Kanban

Product Requests are the equivalent of *Production Kanban's*. This record type represents a customer "order". Nothing gets produced unless an order is received. These orders are collected with this queue being synonymous with a Product Backlog in Scrum. The queue is constantly prioritized and re-priortized, just as with Scrum. This digital record type is typically known as a Product Request, Change Request, Enhancement Request, User Story placeholders, Minimal-Marketable Features or high-level Use Cases (sometimes called essential Use Cases[144]). Customer demand is captured in their words from their business perspective. Typical collaborative analysis of the Requests occurs just like typical change-control approaches that have been around for some time. But with Digital Kanban and Lean, it is the customer that controls the Product Backlog, not a Project Manager. There is no such thing as scope creep in the Agile philosophy. The customer can groom or change or add to the Product Backlog at will but once a Product Request becomes work in progress, this is discouraged for that Request.   Figure 7.14 illustrate the typical workflow pattern using a state transition diagram.

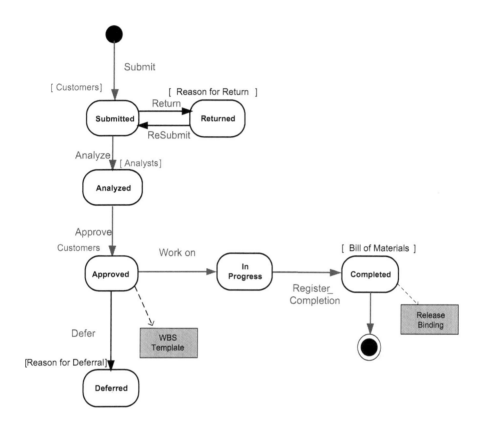

7.14 – Product Request State Machine for Digital Kanban

Tasks represent the "raw material" or effort necessary to realize a Product Request, and can be seen as *Withdrawal Kanban*. As such, the decomposition of a Product Request into a work breakdown structure occurs just-in-time and only for a single Request by a self organizing Feature-crew. As such the Tasks are children to the parent Product Request.   The state-space of the children Tasks must roll-up and correlate to the parents' state. Once all the tasks are delivered, the parent Product Request can automatically change state to the completed state. Also, real-time updates from the Task work-in-progress can be published back to the parent so that Product Request level reporting and visibility can easily be achieved. Figure 7.15 illustrates the effect of the correlated state machines.

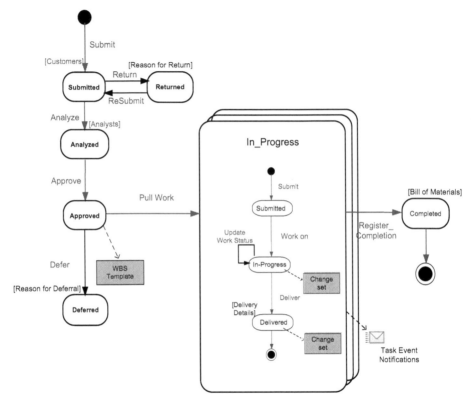

7.15 – Request-Task correlated State Machine

It should be noted that the linkage with the practice of process-centric configuration management occurs through the integration of the Task workflow with configuration management tooling. Each Task delivers a set of versioned elements such that together they represent the change-set of artifacts that must be delivered to the integration stream or branch within the context of the customer meaningful Product Request.

The third Kanban, not commonly articulated within the TPS is the Release record type, which represents a pull-oriented extension beyond the factory and downstream within the value stream. Figure 7.16 below shows the typical state patterns applied to the Release workflow abstraction.

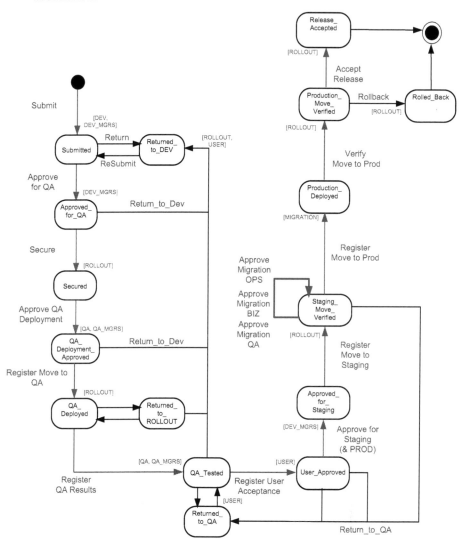

7.16 – Release record type for Digital Kanban

The Release record can be thought of as a Kanban because a scheduled Release must be available for the realized scope to be pulled into production. In this way, fulfilled demand is not pushed on production control and the business operations environment in an uncontrolled manner. Rather, change events are scheduled based on the risk tolerance of the organization and the frequency of change that the business can accommodate or desires. The Release Kanban associates payload Product Requests in a late binding rather than a predictive manner. Only the realized requests that can make the release window are eligible for being bound to the Release workflow.

Chapter 8: SDLC 3.0 within the broader Lean Enterprise

Lean provides a paradigm for enabling discontinuous gains in efficiency and effectiveness at an enterprise scale. It has a longer history than both the Unified Process and Agile. It represents a fundamentally new way of thinking in addition to the practices that have evolved over the last century or more. And it is more identifiable to business stakeholders as a basis of structuring IT. Yet the process features of both the Unified Process and Agile play a key role in an integrated system of practices. The architecture and risk management features of UP serve as the key governance structure in the overall product lifecycle, including the phase extensions of the EUP. Agile plays a vital role with various practices being applicable across the lifecycle.

Software development doesn't occur in a silo. Upstream activity leads to the identification of IT investment opportunities, and downstream activities related to the operations and sustainment of the IT investment occur as a result of the deployed software asset. Key in achieving the ideals and expected results from Lean is an understanding that SDLC participates in a broader value stream and is not the beginning or the end of the chain. Therefore integration of SDLC organizational structure, dynamics and practices must be coherent within the holistic IT value stream. Attempting to force SDLC practice constraints up or downstream is contrary to customer-centric thinking. Figure 8.1 illustrates the timing of SDLC 3.0 practices within a holistic IT value stream.

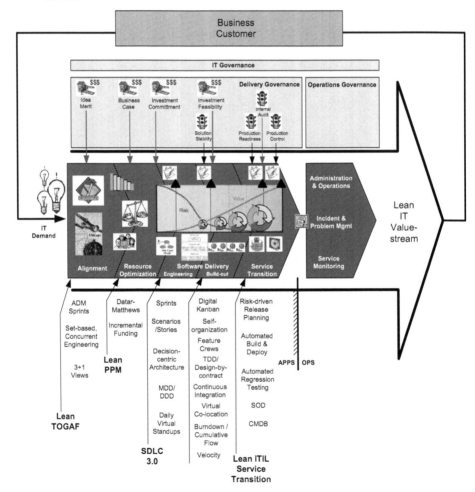

Figure 8.1 – IT Product Investment Lifecycle

This chapter discusses the integration of modern software engineering within Enterprise IT, and provides a means to reason about the entire IT Value Stream.

8.1 – Blueprints of the "IT Business"

Enterprise IT is no different than any other business or service provider. The "IT Business" has a value stream and supply chain like any other Lean enterprise. As such, the primary focus in articulation of a software delivery approach should be grounded as a demand fulfillment value-stream and should leverage the principles and practices of Lean Thinking as primary guidance at an enterprise scale. Common organizational units within IT each should be engineered with their value proposition in mind, and each "mission" should be articulated in such a way as making sense to the customer – the business that receives value from IT.

Business Ideation and the reasoning focused on Business-IT Alignment and transformation road-mapping initiates the Systems Delivery value-stream. The Enterprise Architecture function results in the identification of coarse-grained IT Demand which leads to a portfolio of IT Investment Projects. Because the complexity and cost of such transformative reasoning is high, focus should be on making investment decisions based on the total cost-of-ownership in relation to the expected business improvement benefits and productivity that the technology can accrue. Meaning, an elaborate feasibility study is not warranted for each and every change to an IT investment. Performing such a rigorous analysis on minor incremental enhancements would represent a form of over-processing waste. As such, IT Systems delivery should be treated as products with an investment lifecycle that ends in retirement.

Figure 8.2 that follows illustrates a high level context diagram for a holistic Product-oriented IT Enterprise. It captures the core business missions of a typical organizational structure, and the supporting disciplines or capabilities that support these missions. This context diagram of an IT Enterprise is leveraged to understand who the customers are for IT services, and to reason about the cohesion and coupling that should or should not exist between various functional organizations.

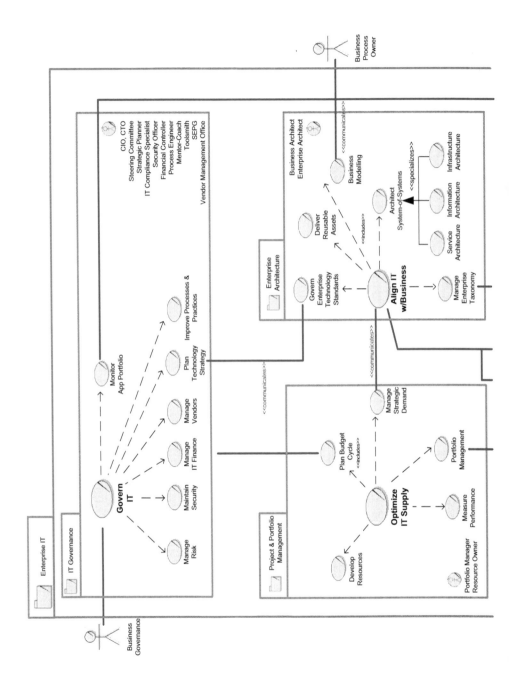

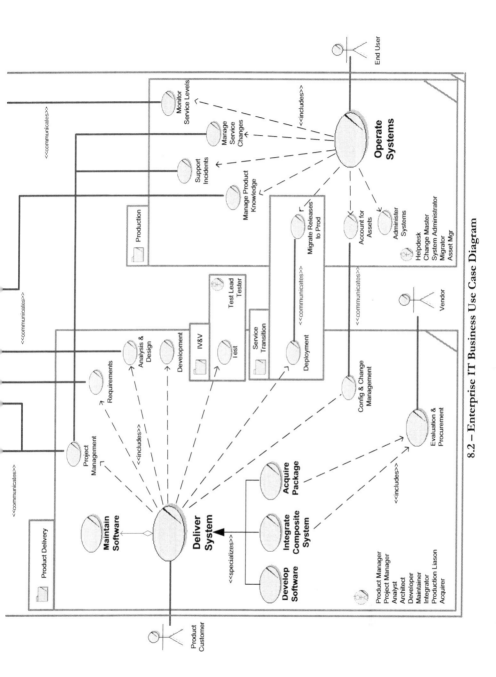

8.2 – Enterprise IT Business Use Case Diagram

The core missions that operationally deliver value to the business are Business-IT Alignment, IT Supply Optimization, System Delivery and System Operations. Each of these concrete *Business Use Cases* form the core in which all other activity and capability provides service. Disciplines like Project Management, Service Transition or Business Modeling do not directly provide value, but instead support the core mission of the various groups that the business depend upon to carry out specific functions. IT Governance provides strategic value to a different stakeholder/business actor. It provides investment governance such that the firms' board of directors can exercise due diligence and achieve their fiduciary duty.

Integrating this picture with a dynamic view of the IT Value Chain, we can further explore the best way to execute the overall IT function. Value-stream Maps (VSM) from Lean Thinking serve to enable visibility of various forms of waste including delay and waiting, inventory and over-processing. Figure 8.3 illustrates the entire Enterprise IT VSM from demand identification to product release and operations.

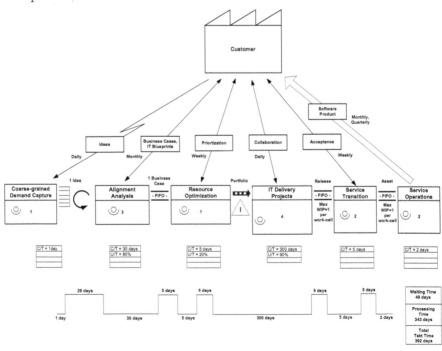

Figure 8.3 – Enterprise IT Value-stream Map

From the previous illustration, one can see that the beginning of value creation occurs much earlier than the launch of a project. This early demand generation activity marks the beginning of the engagement with the customer and the start of the clock related to time-to-value expectations. From Lean Thinking and JIT, we know that fast delivery enables the highest productivity and flexibility/agility. Therefore, the above value stream articulates pull-orientation with WIP limits all the way to the recognition of the demand for IT services. Large inventories of Business-IT Alignment output should be discouraged in favor of frequent release of the coarse grained delivery demand (Projects) and fine-grained sustainment demand (Maintenance).

Isolated study of the various complexities associated with the different elements of the value stream has resulted in separate bodies of knowledge from differing vantage-points or perspectives. This results in the potential for friction between these various process silos. The dominant BOK-based communities are Enterprise Architecture, who typically embraces TOGAF; the PMBOK; the IEEE standardization efforts and the SWEBOK; the Capability Maturity Model Integrated (CMMI) [145] suite of process improvement yardstick practices from the Software Engineering Institute at Carnegie Mellon University; and the Service Management community and the operations aspects of ITIL from the Government of the United Kingdom.

When coupling the above diversity with the broad set of SDLC practices from the three modern software engineering method communities as described in Sections 4, 5 & 6, you can understand the frustration of business organizations that pay for the development and sustainment of technology. IT processes and approaches require business participation to achieve success. But with all this terminology overload and IT jargon (and Agile is no different.) no wonder a lack of cooperation and trust often results.

8. 2 – Product versus Project Lifecycle

A single product lifecycle that includes *Investment Initiation, Investment Feasibility Risk Mitigation, Investment Build-out, and Investment Sustainment/Maintenance* serves as a non-jargon set of phases or periods of time which focus on distinctly different investment management strategies.

The key idea with phases is that focus shifts over time. This is not to be confused with equating such phases to a focus on a single work product type with an absence of delivery feedback. Instead, the theme of activity should be focused on the objectives of managing the IT investment during a distinctly different period of time in the investments lifecycle. The differing themes of activity are intended to maximize the potential for value to be realized. This occurs in various forms, with the early theme focused on Effectiveness – that is building the right things, followed by real-options value in the form of risk mitigation, unlocking learning and exit options. Finally, efficiency is the theme for the latter phases of the investment lifecycle when it is proven to be feasible and uncertainty has been reduced.

Precedent does exist for the notion of a holistic product as opposed to project-oriented SDLC. Not only does the SWEBOK standard IEEE 12207 [146a] articulate this notion, this is consistent with the definition of a project from the PMBOK, which clearly articulates that ongoing operations and maintenance is distinctly different than project work. Figure 8.4 illustrates the PMI view on the difference between Products and Projects.

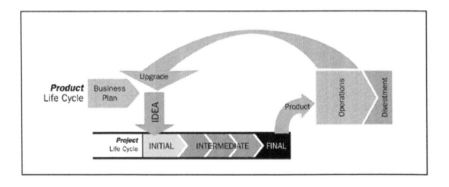

Figure 8.4 – Projects vs. Products from PMBOK

Similar observations have resulted in extension of the temporal phase structure of the Unified Process to integrate it within the broader enterprise environment. While only a first attempt at realizing a product management lifecycle, it did introduce the notion of phases with distinctively different process themes. The Enterprise Unified Process[147] adds several enterprise disciplines as well as two additional phases – Operations and Retirement. It is very similar to the IEEE standard on Software Maintenance – IEEE/ISO 14764 [146b]. The difference lies in the name of the ongoing phase that occurs after the completion of a project. Figure 8.5 below illustrates an adaptation of the Enterprise Unified Process phase structure to accommodate the notion of a software products maintenance period of time. This replaces operations which is a differing IT business mission than software delivery and is segregated from delivery through Service Transition.

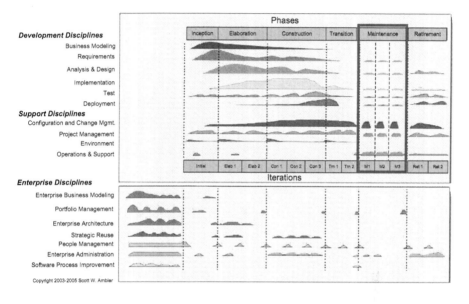

Figure 8.5 – Adapting the Enterprise Unified Process [147]

A holistic product-oriented approach contradicts a convenient over-simplification of IT delivery where everything is treated as a project. Such an approach is not Lean, in that treating all demand (coarse/strategic demand the same as fine-grained IT demand) amounts to batching, which creates inventory, waiting and potentially over-processing types of waste. When a project ends, the system development doesn't end with it but lives on through the continual burn-down of remaining and new items in the Product Backlog. Through a total-cost-of-ownership perspective, anticipation of operating costs and optimal structure for the care and feeding of the system starts way up front when the system investment idea is contemplated. Therefore viewing systems development as a Product requiring servicing after "sales" is essential, and SDLC should be structured with this in mind. Fine-grained demand can be delivered optimally through a different dynamic focused on maximizing throughput, which from Lean we know is achieved through reducing WIP and creating flow through pull.

Products exist in a potentially one-to-many relationship with projects. Projects are the investment governance vehicle, leading to ongoing operations and maintenance (OAM) of the asset or product. But for a specific product, several generations can be developed, with each generation materially enhancing capability or adapting to changing business circumstances in which the IT product is leveraged. Each product generation project typically results in a major release, also known as a X.0 release. The implication of this product management strategy is that parallel development capability and facilities are necessary to enable new generations of a product to be developed in advance of their deployment. This is because an existing, soon to be legacy generation must continue to be sustained while in production. Figure 8.6 illustrates the branching strategy that supports multiple parallel lines of development.

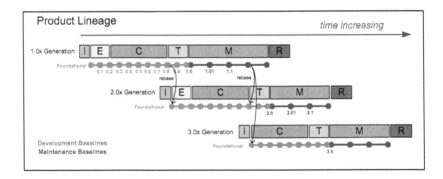

Figure 8.6 – Parallel Development

This is not to say that this implies that all demand should preclude the work breakdown and investment governance of a project. When risk and uncertainty are present with ongoing demand, like in the case of architectural changes and related high-stake decisions, batching demand into a project for governance reasons makes sense. And when new demand (even fine-grained demand) arrives in a product's Backlog, determination must occur as to whether it warrants a new generation of the product based on changing business conditions or IT technology evolution. A decision tree can be leveraged to determine if a product request should qualify for maintenance, or requires project facilities.

8.3 – Lean Business-IT Alignment

The first activity identified in Section 8.1 that is part of the core value-stream is that of Business-IT Alignment. This mission serves to identify demand for IT service changes and development that will support reconfigured and improved business processes. This value-stream element is typically fulfilled by organizational units termed Enterprise Architecture (EA). EA organizations support this core mission through developing specialized-generalist capability around business architecture (business modeling, business process improvement, business process "whatever"), and around application and infrastructure architecture. The scope of EA is broader than that of single system architecture (sometimes called Technical Architecture) due to the fact that alignment to business processes usually crosses business organizations (or companies) and involves the integration of sometimes many business systems. As such EA deals with the alignment of business process change as realized by *systems-of-systems*.

While some Agilist's view the EA function as waste, it does serve a useful purpose in that business process opportunities are identified in what could be termed a complex business system. The controversy typically hinges around immature EA organizations that launch into "boil-the-ocean" modeling exercises. The rationale usually given for these grandiose visions is that the business needs "blueprints". But this usually evolves to include the assertion that the business also needs detailed system-of-system blueprints at fine-grained levels of detail, just-in-case. This latter point, "just-in-case" is the key to resolving the tension between the perspectives of value-add vs. total muda. The answer regarding the differing views on the subject of EA is that they are both right. The business is willing to pay for innovative business process ideas that are identified through reasoning and approaches to reduce complexity. Achieving innovations result in direct value in terms of efficiency and effectiveness, customer satisfaction or increased market share. As such, it fits within the definition of value-add as required by Lean Thinking. But the fact that Business-IT Alignment deserves a place in the IT Value-Stream does not mean that it should be performed in a manner contrary to the ideals or lessons of Lean. Performing big-bang alignment activities that cause delay in the downstream realization work/projects is waste. Batching architectural statements of work produces inventory, one of the seven deadly wastes. Instead, Lean Enterprise Architecture focuses on creating flow through pull by limiting the alignment work-in-progress.

The Open Group Architecture Framework – TOGAF [148] is arguably the most common EA body of knowledge that exists in industry. But unfortunately, it has grown into somewhat of a bloated piece of process-ware. Figure 8.7 illustrates the breadth of the TOGAF body of knowledge.

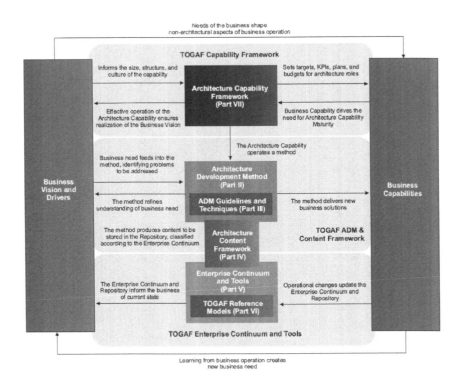

Figure 8.7 – TOGAF Scope[148]

Figure 8.8 illustrates a TOGAF Architecture Development Method (ADM) Iteration at a high level.

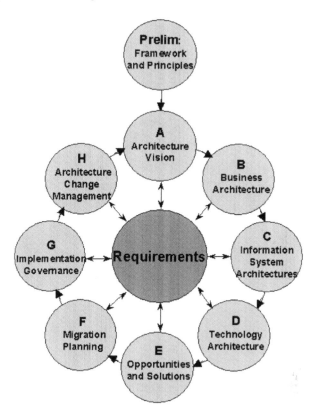

Figure 8.8 – TOGAF Architecture Development Method (ADM)

The core idea and high-level abstractions of work to be accomplished serve a purpose in circling the wagons for the structuring of EA work. This is simple and straightforward as shown in the above picture, which visually articulates iterative and incremental "business system" development. Yet all too often it is interpreted as prescriptive irrespective of context, although TOGAF v9 is attempting to correct this problem through additional guidance.

Figure 8.9 illustrates a distillation of the workflow model as articulated within the ADM.

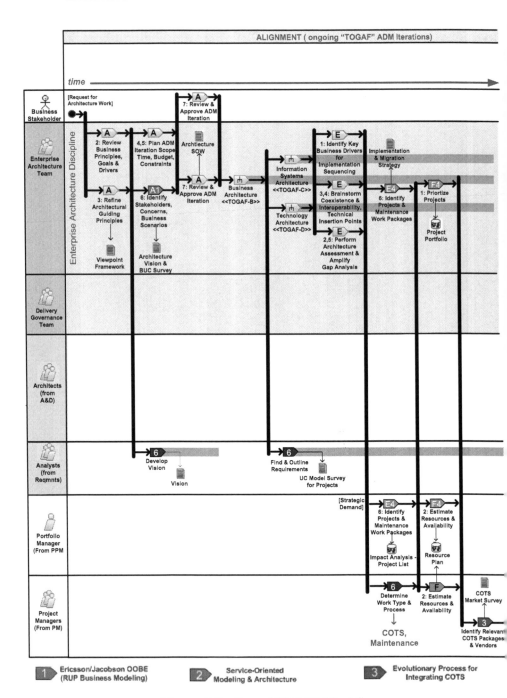

Figure 8.9 – Lean TOGAF Workflow

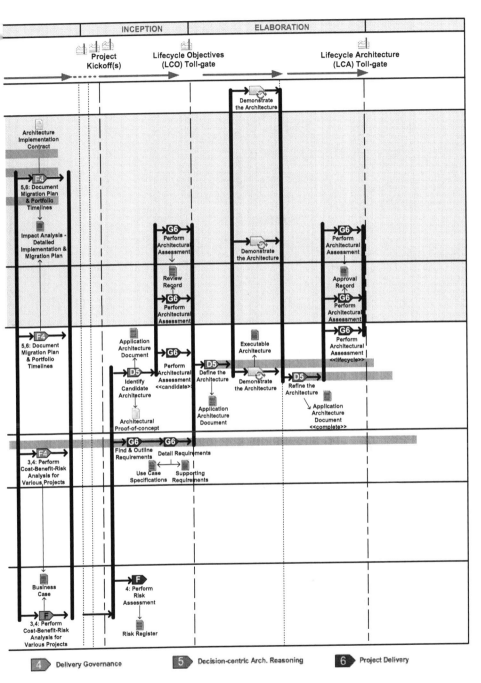

Figure 8.9 – Lean TOGAF Workflow

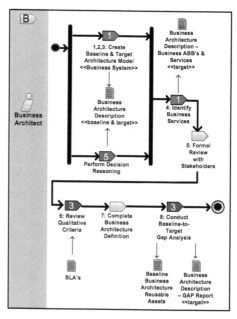

Figure 8.9a – TOGAF-B Workflow Detail

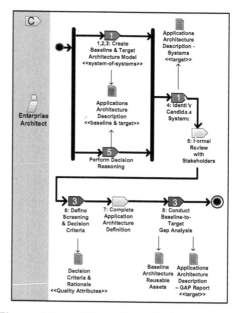

Figure 8.9b – TOGAF-C Workflow Detail

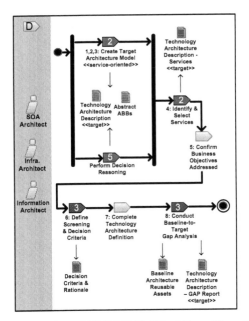

Figure 8.9c – TOGAF-D Workflow Detail

One area within the TOGAF that requires some Lean Thinking treatment is in the area of associated Viewpoint frameworks that supports the ADM and defines the recommended work products to be produced. While TOGAF defines a generic Viewpoint framework within it's almost 800 pages, the common Viewpoint framework chosen with EA circles is the Zachman framework [149]. One of the reasons for the perspective within Agile circles that EA is wasteful is probably due to this framework. Whether you agree with the "scientific basis" for the meta-model or not, it is kind of hard to disagree with the perspective that 30 Views and diagrams is a little over done. The framework is good in that it articulates the notion of levels of abstraction, such that reasoning can progress towards more detail. The problem is that there is not guidance as to how to navigate the cells, or the semantic relationships between the views. This is important because it is this navigation process that reflects the ADM. Also, one would be hard pressed to establish a system's theory basis for the choice of "what, how, when, who, where and why" as the aspectual decomposition of the views. Noting that this framework originated in 1987, Figure 8.10 illustrates John Zachman's framework.

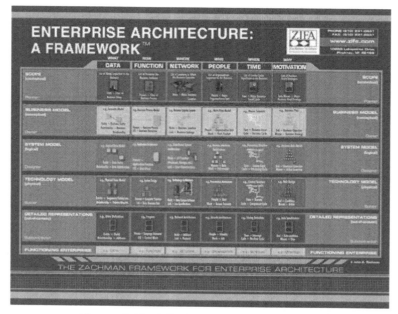

Figure 8.10 – The Zachman Framework [149]

One could easily argue that this framework represents the kind of "just-in-case" philosophy everyone has lived through in their past companies or engagements. And because of the scale and complexity of the *system-of-systems* under study when dealing with any non-trivial business, it is no wonder that numerous "boil-the-ocean" scenarios have unfolded. Requiring that all 30 views be produced in the odd chance that some stakeholder somewhere may consume the work product to address some lingering concern represents not only over-processing waste, but inventory waste.

One Viewpoint framework that reduces waste and represents a systematic ADM is the 3+1 Views Viewpoint framework. This amplification and simplification of the 4+1 Views of Architecture approach [150] advocated within UP projects reduces the number of necessary Views/Viewpoints to only eight. It is minimalistic and sufficient to address all concerns that stakeholders may have, and provides a systematic model-driven development approach for business-IT alignment, including Service-Oriented Architecture (SOA) reasoning and service identification. Figure 8.11 illustrates the EA extensions within the 3+1 Views approach.

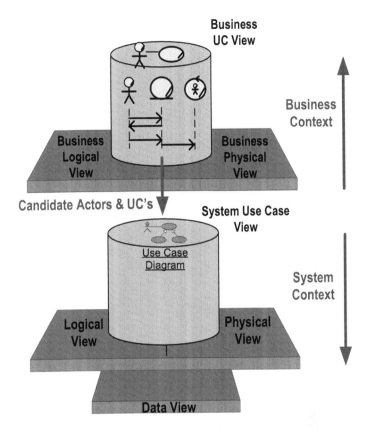

Figure8.11 – "3+1 Views" EA Framework

In this picture, a model-driven approach for the realization of business processes starts with understanding the context of the business and its core business processes. The Business Use Case View captures this context and identifies who the customers are through the use of business actors. Business-IT alignment activity continues through the reasoning of the realizing business processes. These Business Use Case Realizations articulate the business worker roles, business entities and business system services that will make the operational value propositions within the business context come to life. It is from these process models that identification of required services, systems and interfaces is achieved. Without such a reasoning technique, it would be left to the business to attempt to articulate IT need.

Once required system interfaces are identified, these become candidate system Use Cases, each potentially requiring realization modeling in the event that they are complex or cannot be acquired and must be built from scratch. This system level of model driven development is what is commonly associated with the CASE tool era mentioned earlier.

As we see in Figures 8.2 and 8.9, there is a tight interplay between the value-stream activities of business-IT alignment and resource optimization. Therefore, Lean Enterprise Architecture is the beginning of creating flow through the use of pull-systems. The next section will discuss the implications of extending a pull-orientation further into the supply chain as implemented within the Project & Portfolio Management function.

8.4 – Lean IT Supply/Resource Optimization

We discussed earlier the differences between leadership and management when it comes to *Theory Y Management* and *Self-Organization*. As such, if we agree that management offers a different value proposition than "command-and-control", the question is what is this value proposition? Some Agilist's argue that Project Managers are obsolete and no longer necessary. This appears attractive on the surface when one views Project Management as merely insurance or "scaffolding" for a project. But Project Management skills are different than the skills of the solution domain resources that deliver IT investments. The answer lies in the naming of the business mission that Portfolio and Project Management (PPM) organizations fulfill within the value stream. IT Supply or Resource Optimization is all about ensuring that an expensive resource is leveraged in as optimal way as possible. This means that although the Enterprise Architecture function identifies IT Investment opportunities based on alignment reasoning, PPM capability should be brought to bear to match supply with demand. And the management and investment analysis skills that are common within Project Management circles should be leveraged to their fullest extent such that the identified demand is realized in a value-centric prioritization. That is, the first value proposition of Project Management is in determining through cost-benefit analysis what investment returns should be expected. From this assessment of "the biggest bang for the buck", the PPM organization then matches demand with available IT supply. This resource optimization adds value by pulling IT supply to realize the demand based on problem domain, required solution domain skill-sets and resource availability.

From the TOGAF workflows one can see a close connection between PPM activity and EA activity. But the joint result from these two organizations delivering value from two distinctly different business missions is that of demand generation, typically coarse-grained or strategic demand (projects), but sometimes tactical or fine-grained demand (maintenance requests).

Figure 8.12 illustrates the result of the up-front demand identification activities within the IT value stream. The picture represents an adaptation of the extension ideas of the EUP.

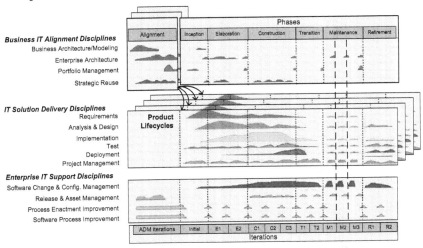

Figure 8.12 – EA Iterations and Resulting Product Lifecycles

Once demand has been discovered for IT Delivery services, one or more Product Backlogs are established, or in the case of sustainment demand, existing Product Backlogs are updated. The natural question to ask is how much demand is generated from the up-front alignment and resource optimization effort. From Lean Thinking, we know that the highest productivity is established by reducing cycle times. To do this we leverage pull-systems to limit WIP. This means that the Business-IT Alignment activity performed by an Enterprise Architecture organization, and the Resource Optimization activity, performed by the PPM function should work in a one-piece flow rather than a batching mode. Instead of batching demand, Product Backlogs should be seeded for each discrete "business change request". This enables the Just-in-Time pull of IT supply resources. Rather than launching into discrete multi-year batched planning exercises that coincide with budgeting cycles, single Business-IT Alignment requests should continuously flow downstream. Whether the demand results in one or more project's or existing products require adaptive maintenance, demand should flow as fast as possible without incurring the waste of waiting/delay.

To implement Lean Portfolio Management we must enable investment governance such that effort can be aborted early if unfeasible. Leveraging the risk confrontive phase structure such that exit real options can be exercised in a meaningful way is not only a core tenet of any Unified Process lineage, but also from Lean. By tying these phases to the just-in-time allocation of resources, the second value proposition of the Project Management capability can be seen. By facilitating the pragmatic assessment of IT investments across multiple areas of investment concern, expensive and limited IT supply can be leveraged in as optimal a fashion as possible. If an investment has not achieved the expected results for a themed period of time as defined by the UP phases, the investment can be cancelled promptly such that IT resources can be freed up for other investment realization. As such, the phases act as a coarse-grained pull system. Each phase represents a state, and like *Kanban*, resources are pulled in only the quantities required for the upstream "order".

To facilitate reasoned investment decisions in a timely manner, the themes of the investment phases should focus effort on answering stakeholder concerns in a just-in-time fashion. In other words, only those questions that need to be answered at a distinct point in time in the IT investments lifecycle should be in focus during each phase. This concept, also known as *Toll-gates* [151] leverages crisply worded questions during investment review to ensure that the goals of investment management are being met in a timely fashion. Failure to satisfactorily address stakeholder concerns through the answers to the questions enables visibility into the true status of the investment. This enables value in the form of exit real-options. This approach is common within the Lean Six Sigma community. It is also consistent with the focusing approach of *Goal-Question-Metric* – *GQM* [152] leveraged commonly in Project Management measurement circles.

The primary evidence that provides the answers to the questions posed by the various facets of the investment governance community is working software. All other evidence supporting the achievement of Investment governance objectives is intended to be just enough in addition to just-in-time. Lean Governance enabled through carefully worded toll-gate questions guides the team to focus only on what is necessary to deliver answers at the phase checkpoints throughout the product lifecycle. Work Products are grown at a rate and inclusive of the content suggested by the theme of the investment governance phase. During the *Concept and Context* theme, a breadth-oriented perspective is manifested in the working software, high-level requirements and candidate architecture. This is enforced through the time-boxing of what is known in Agile circles as *"Iteration 0"*. Early engagement by concerned parties occurs such that commitment at the last responsible moment is actionable through the necessary participant decisions. This is consistent with such notions as "test-early and often" or "prepare for production early and often". Similar time-boxed iterations are leveraged early in the product lifecycle to determine investment feasibility. Architectural risk mitigation is addressed through the time appropriate assessment of significant design decisions, as well as other aspects of delivery governance related to lead-time preparations.

The key point in leveraging JIT phases of resource expenditure during IT Delivery is that value is not lost due to treating projects as a sunk cost. Instead of discovering late that a projects cost-benefit ratio is unattractive, or that the architectural feasibility remains to be proven after most of the investment is spent, due diligence would suggest terminating these investments earlier. This is the other key value proposition of Project Managers within modern software engineering. Given that teams can self-organize related to detailed work breakdown structure planning (just-in-time), Project Managers can serve a facilitative role in coordinating all aspects of investment governance. As such, other than being "servant leaders" [106] for delivery teams, the role is more akin to Investment Manager / Advisor where a business owner/customer does not wish or is unable to perform all the governance coordination required for large scale IT initiatives. And as a valuable and skilled resource, Project Managers should be leveraged across many instances of demand realization (Projects). This can be viewed as moving up further ahead in the value stream, enabled by team self organization.

Figure 8.13 illustrates the application of toll-gates in relation to themed investment delivery and management activity.

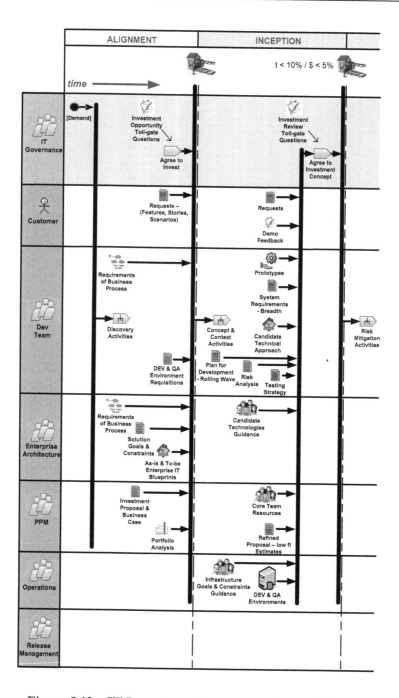

Figure 8.13 – IT Investment Governance through Toll-gates

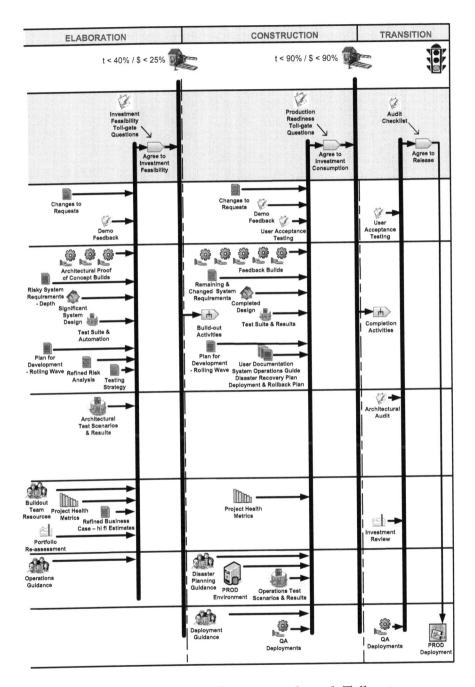

Figure 8.13 – IT Investment Governance through Toll-gates

The use of toll-gates is sometimes viewed as controversial within Agile circles. This is usually driven by the misconception that working, testable software is not developed within each phase. But as discussed above, this serves as the concrete basis for making sound investment decisions. While it is true that the reality is that early investment feasibility iterations will typically not result in deployed software value, such is the reality in most large-scale IT Enterprises.

The interesting thing is that this model for governing a large portfolio of IT investment delivery projects is akin to a Venture Capital (VC) Funding model. Ironically this was the environment where Agile grew-up. The key value proposition, as with 2-stage VC funding gates, is that the investment can be cancelled before all funds are used. What is expected by Venture capitalists should be the norm for Enterprise IT.

8.5 – Lean Release Management

The area where IT Delivery (sometimes referred to as "Apps") meets IT Operations (sometimes referred to as "Ops") is known as Release Management. The purpose of this capability is to reduce the risk of change to the business. The body of knowledge that is typically referenced for Release Management practices is ITIL – the IT Infrastructure Library. This compendium of IT Service Management (ITSM) practices is published by the government of the United Kingdom. ITIL v3 is divided into five "books", namely Service Strategy, Service Design, Service Transition, Service Operations and Continual Service Improvement. While it could be argued that this governmental organization has established a great deal of experience related to IT practices, it would be unreasonable to suggest that the entire value-stream is served by ITIL as the authoritative source of knowledge. Other BOKs have far more insight into certain practices, including for example the three modern software engineering communities or the IEEE SWEBOK when it comes to Service Design. However, when it comes to Service Transition and Service Operations, ITIL is definitely seen as the leading BOK. Figure 8.14 below illustrates the relationship of Release Management as it pertains to ITIL v3's view of changes within a business enterprise.

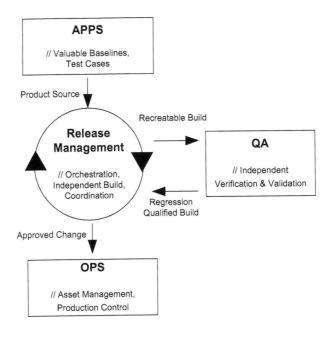

Figure 8.14 –Release Management Orchestration

When it comes to the topic of Lean in relation to Release Management, Toyota's revolutionary step was to take Piggly Wiggly's supermarket replenishment system and drive it back to at least half way through their automobile factories. Their challenge today is to drive it all the way back to their goods-inwards dock. Recognizing JIT could be driven back up the supply chain has reaped Toyota huge benefits and a world dominating position in the auto industry. When one looks at how Toyota ships finished cars to market however, one sees a different decoupled process dynamic. While automobiles are still "pulled" to market via constrained transportation resources (ships), this is done in a batched manner. This is due to the inherent risks associated with the physical barriers of oceans and continents, and the economy of scale that batching yields related to the risk mitigation associated with "deployment". Figure 8.15 shows the use of optimized Roll-on, Roll-off (RORO) ships and the associated queuing docks for staging product for delivery.

Figure 8.15 – Release Batching as Risk Mitigation Approach

Applying this metaphor to Software Product Development, one can extrapolate the notion of a Release Plan to that of the Production Forecast. The rough-order number of Requests is forecast within the Release Plan which is based on known Release "ferry" capacity which reflects current demand trends and customer budget. When Requests are fulfilled, they arrive in the staging area and are "baselined" together; the analogy of this is adding a car's VIN to the ships waybill. Requests that arrive to the "dock" in time are eligible to be included in the baseline, and can therefore be included in the Release. Requests that do not meet minimum lead times for inclusion on the "ship" must wait for the next scheduled departure. One can see that with this analogy, Releases establish a finish-to-finish dependency among Requests, where instead of batching the commencement of work by grouping demand into iterations, batching occurs only when the Requests are fulfilled and are staged.

In Software Development, the parallel to the risks associated with the shipping of product to market in the case of automobiles is related to overall product quality and the risk of regression due to production changes. Regression testing mitigates this risk, but at a cost.

Segregated testing resources and the necessary regression suite maintenance add to the total-cost-of-release. Therefore, release frequencies (ferry departures) are selected to balance the risks of change and the risks of delays of product to market. Note that all changes are not created equal. Delivery of defects and non-risky enhancements can occur more frequently due to the smaller risk mitigation measures. The analogy is the use of smaller, more frequent transport ferries. Figure 8.16 illustrates the notion of smaller batches for smaller risk releases.

Figure 8.16 – Metaphor for right-sizing Release Batches

The matching of transfer batches to the just-in-time downstream process requirements (regression testing) serves as another waste reduction measure. Large idle release equipment should not stand idle where capacity outpaces the incoming realized product requests. Over-processing waste should be avoided where higher ceremony releases and their associated controls are not warranted. And wastes related to delay and waiting on delivery of product to the broader business process should be mitigated through the ability to release in a right-sized way for smaller batches of demand. In this way, total cost of release is balanced with time-to-value considerations using a risk management perspective.

The key practice that supports efficient and effective releases into the production environment has been termed *"process-centric configuration management"* [153]. As will be discussed in Chapter 9, this practice enables informed decisions as to what is being released to production and what acceptance and regression testing is required. By combining change management / request tracking with configuration management versioning and baseline management, automated "waybills" can be produced. Without such a practice in place, it is extremely difficult to know in a time responsive way whether "hazardous cargo" is present.

8.6 – Lean Acquisition-orientation

One of the quickest ways to reduce the amount of waste produced within Enterprise IT is to "build less stuff". Establishing an acquisition-orientation which favors leveraging pre-existing assets over custom development is also consistent with the Lean Product Development practices as seen in the Toyota Product Development System [99]. Leveraging standard, reusable parts enables rapid delivery and responsiveness to market demands with little downside. Conscious limiting of technology choices starts with investment in strategic reuse in the form of product lines (in Toyota's case reusable chasis and power trains for yearly models), or more fine grained reuse through off-the-shelf commodity parts rather than one-off design-from scratch components.

The strategy requires explicit attention to these purposeful constraints by architects. To do this, active consideration of Commercial-Off-the-Shelf "buy" options must be performed in parallel with any build fall-back. And this should be governed as part of the Investment Alignment and Feasibility periods of time. In some environments attempting to make strategic large order reuse a systematic part of solution fulfillment is mandated as policy. The most notable example is the US Federal Government. Through study of the Defense Science Board, the decision was taken to establish policy that mandates the use of commercial technologies instead of internal development, which was viewed as not being a core competency [154].

From study of the experiences within the sometimes very large scale acquisitions, knowledge has been captures as to the subtle differences between development and acquisition. This experience has been harvested by organizations like the Software Engineering Institute at Carnegie Mellon University who publish guidance to industry and government as a result of their research funding. Within the COTS-based Software Engineering initiative (CBSE), one body of knowledge has emerged that mirrors Lean Thinking concepts of set-based, concurrent engineering and real-options theory in its articulation. The Evolutionary Process for Integrating COTS (EPIC) presumably leveraged some of the very same concepts from TPDS as applied to software. Figure 8.17 illustrates this body of knowledge.

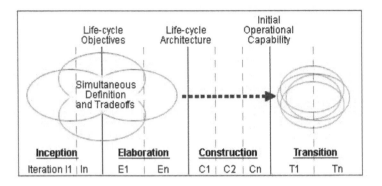

Figure 8.17 – Convergence of decision trade space [134]

The lifecycle framework used to articulate and deliver a governance structure around these concepts was that of the Unified Process. The EPIC body of knowledge is manifested in two forms – a 275 page document that could be argued as being bloated, and as content that is additive to the Rational Unified Process web-delivered product [155].

While some within the Agile community would claim that they "do COTS", the claim is not without skepticism. This is because many of the practices assume a custom development environment. And some of the practices, when strictly interpreted, are inconsistent with the nature of COTS acquisition. Because of the scale typically involved in the large acquisitions that have been studied within the DOD, enforcing a specific frequency of iteration can be problematic. Which wouldn't necessarily be a problem if the intent of the practice was embraced, not the prima facie interpretation. Other realities that are faced with "off-the-shelf" Scrum or XP application can be overcome if one looks at the essence of the practices contained therein.

The best way to describe acquisition is akin to test-driven development as opposed to requirements driven development. This is something that Agile can rally around, but the tests are more like acceptance tests or test scenarios than the typical TDD unit tests. Figure 8.18 illustrates the distinctly different sequence of events in a COTS Acquisition iteration.

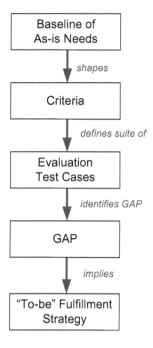

Figure 8.18 – "Test-Driven" Acquisition

When one boils all of the content of EPIC into a practical set of persisted work products and reasoning techniques coherent within an UP-like product lifecycle, one arrives at a workflow articulation like the following in Figure 8.19.

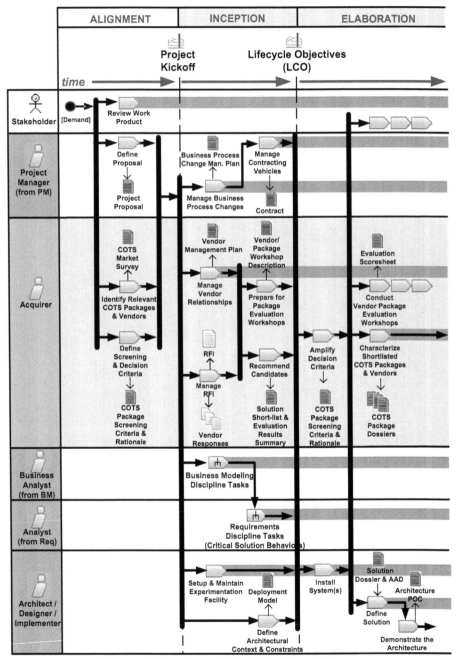

Figure 8.19 – Acquisition Workflow [156]

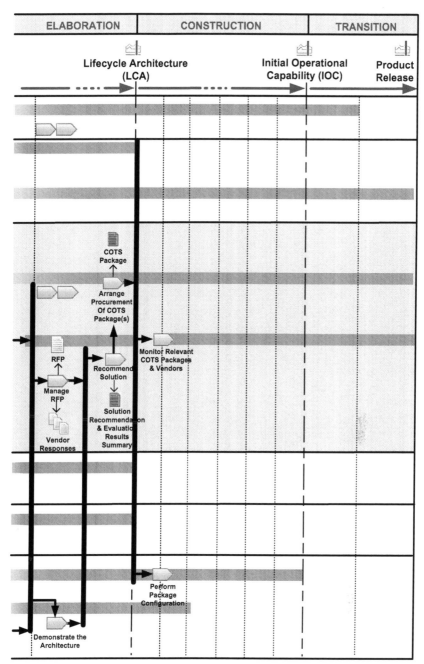

Figure 8.19 – Acquisition Workflow [156]

One criticism with EPIC, which arguably is the best modern software acquisition research that the industry has in terms of reflection within DOD and US Federal Government circles, is that it comes up short in the "how" department. It is left to the practitioner to bring in various experiences and practices to make it actionable and Lean.

Note that placeholder stories will not suffice unless accompanied by their acceptance tests. This is due to the degree of stakeholder concurrence and negotiation that often accompanies COTS acquisition of any scale. This reality occurs because the decision to acquire rather than "require" necessarily involves business process change. And unfortunately Agile is silent on business process analysis and change, as it doesn't amount to code. The upfront reasoning (gap analysis) has nothing to do with coding. In fact, coding of any form is discouraged when an acquisition-orientation is taken, as customization beyond the recommended practice of a vendor has been known to cause large order pain and suffering. This is due to the fact that the Vendor made explicit decisions about what the market requirements were at the outset of building a COTS, and they therefore are in control of not only the requirements but the code that realizes this scope. If they change their mind, or just upgrade, breakage ensues with any customization that is below the radar.

The above discussion implies that tradeoffs are present in relation to the choice to acquire marketplace offerings. This constrains the Lean organization (by design) and requires awareness by everyone involved that full degrees of freedom are a luxury not present in the COTS form factor. Figure 8.20 illustrates the nature of the tradeoffs in play.

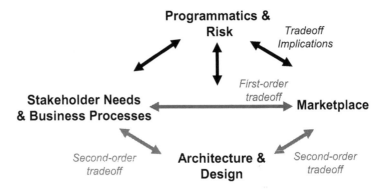

Figure 8.20 – Spheres of influence in Acquisition [156]

The biggest implication of choices made among the various *.Spheres of Influence* on the decision making process is along the axis of Business Process criteria and Marketplace offerings. Choices made among conflicts in this first order dimension and the second order tradeoffs with existing enterprise architectural choices leads to implications in terms of cost, benefit and risk. Figure 8.21 articulates this through the asymmetrical shape in the spheres.

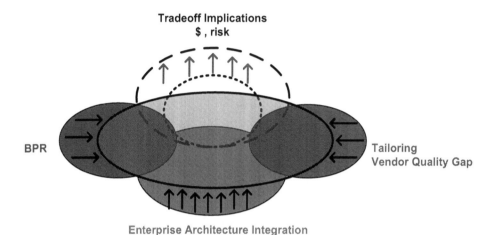

Figure 8.21 – Implications of Convergence on a COTS Solution [156]

It should be noted that not all COTS are equal and there exists a spectrum in which varying degrees of "tailoring" or "configuration" are possible. Here, normal Agile practices find their home. And the focus on working software for feedback is also consistent with the tenets of modern software engineering. Experimentation or test execution is to be established quickly, and the narrowing of the candidate solution space proceeds in an iterative and evolutionary manner.

Because COTS acquisition is performed at a business process level, typically high complexity exists due to the sheer scope of the value streams involved. Here, one technique that can and should be leveraged to facilitate an understanding of gap is visual modeling. Figure 8.22 illustrates the usage of visualization in gap reasoning.

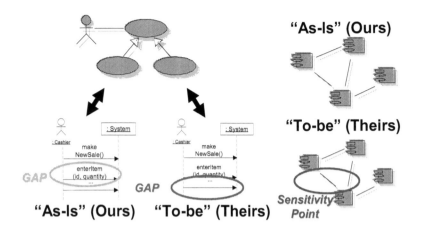

Figure 8.22 – Leveraging Visual Modeling for Gap Analysis [156]

But these efforts cannot degrade into "boil-the-ocean" exercises. One way to prevent this is to leverage pull and one-piece flow from Lean. Visualization is only one tool to leverage in understanding and quantifying gap. Other skills and techniques come from multivariate reasoning approaches such as Multi-attribute Utility Tree analysis [xx], Analytical Hierarchy Process – AHP [121], Kepner Tregoe [157], Cost-Benefit Analysis Method-CBAM [158] in conjunction with Architectural Tradeoff Method – ATAM [159]. An example of how to correlate the spheres of influence to a Multi-attribute Utility Tree - MAUT [122] is shown in Figure 8.23.

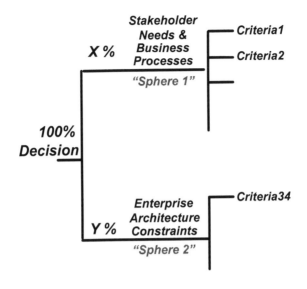

Figure 8.23 – Multi-attribute decision reasoning technique [156]

The results of what are typically open-space testing and evaluation (sometimes called conference-room pilots) are leveraged to enable both visual and economic based evaluation of alternatives through the above techniques, and to enable multi-stakeholder constituency negotiation and collaboration such that convergence on a feasible solution occurs in as Lean and rapid a fashion as possible. In this process, management expertise can play a vital role in delivering leadership. Skills such as vendor management, negotiation and facilitation are critical capabilities of the management specialization.

Chapter 9: SDLC 3.0 Infrastructure

The first value within the Agile Manifesto reads *"Individuals and Interactions over Processes & Tools"*. This represents a bit of a sacred cow when it comes to this community. And it is easy to see why, remembering back to the kinds of tool vendor shenanigans that were present back in the late 1990's. While things have changed in the last 15 years or so, the faithful still hold on to this doctrine very passionately. And while one can agree with the intent of the "process" portion of the Manifesto as was discussed in Chapter 3 related to stochastic systems, the continued bashing of tools is now a bit hypocritical. If you look at some prominent Agile community participants you will see tools front and center. After all, *CruiseControl, XPlanner, Subversion, Mingle* and *Jira* are all tools [160].

When cutting through the rhetoric, it is important to keep in mind a simple concept – "form follows function". While it seems ridiculous with the maturity level of modern SDLC Infrastructure that one would insist on low-tech, it is equally bad to throw tools at a situation "just because". This was arguably the true intent of the value within the Manifesto. Tool usage is contextual, and trying to match modern software engineering practice to the constraints of current technologies was likely the historical beef of the Agile community.

9.1 – Realities of Modern Enterprise IT

There are certain challenges that were discussed in Chapter 7 related to issues of scale. Modern IT Enterprises are more often than not distributed due to disaster recovery, follow-the-sun development or off-shoring strategies. Business-IT separation is a fact of life for business reasons, and SDLC Infrastructure is the only way to overcome geographical distribution. With the maturity of the Internet, practice modifications like "virtual co-location" and "virtual daily stand-ups" are now possible. Instead of labeling these practices as not being "pure", we need to acknowledge the fact that we have been leveraging tools and technology to solve business problems since the emergence of the opposable thumb. Information Technology is the main reason behind the gains in productivity that the world has experienced in the last few decades, and the IT Business should be no different in their exploitation of technology.

While it may seem attractive to draw artificial boundaries around the practices that are willing to be considered, tool aversion is a key reason as to why Agile approaches have unnecessarily had difficulty in very large or complex environments. Where leveraging yellow stickies or index cards makes sense in conjunction with practices like big visible charts and co-location, such formats become ridiculous for a large constituency of challenging projects. For these efforts, necessity typically leads teams to stray from the established doctrine, albeit quietly for fear of being labeled non-conformist. When faced with these challenges, rather than proclaim that Agile won't work or doesn't scale, the preferable approach is to understand and acknowledge the nature of collaboration, the nature of distributed workflow, and the complexity of modern product development. Such a study of the essence of these problems necessarily leads to the conclusion that tools are required if they are to be solved.

Another reality faced by modern IT organizations is related to compliance with such regulations as SOX [80], Basel II [161], HIPAA [162] and the like. The standard of care to comply with these statutes is tested in the case of SOX through application of the Statement of Auditing Standard-70 (SAS-70) audits [81]. IT auditors leverage this standard such that Sarbanes Oxley Sections 302 and 404 can be certified. Whether you agree with the effectiveness of the risk mitigation or not, or deem any compliance-based ERM (Enterprise Risk Management) to be pure waste or not misses the point. Today, firms live in a political and economic reality that has little to do with the term "Agile" or its belief structure. The risks associated with compliance failures can equal those related to a lack of business agility. As such, a balanced treatment of risks is necessary to enable efficient compliance while at the same time not killing agility.

The automation that supports SDLC can preserve Business Agility and IT efficiency and effectiveness. The core capability that achieves this is *process-centric configuration management*. This practice binds the activity of demand management to the outputs from realization activities. This enables the production of automatic and reproducible builds and the associated bill-of-materials. Such integrated traceability information is available to release management, quality assurance and production control organizations to enable informed decisions about the governance and coordination of what is being introduced into the production IT environment. Without such capability, either extensive and error prone manual processes are required or totally ineffective release management practices result. When a lack of configuration management maturity does exist within the IT Delivery organization, the result is either a lack of Business Agility or failed SAS-70 audits. This will only get amplified as the industry continues to mature. The "common law" as to the standard of care expected of IT Organizations is also based on trends in SDLC infrastructure and ongoing audit results. This will have the effect of raising the bar as auditors expect the instantiation of this type of automation.

9.2 – Making Lean Thinking Actionable

One requirement for establishing a Lean Enterprise is to leverage data to make informed decisions about continual process improvement. Without measurement, *Kaizen* is not possible or at best, improvement is made only from anecdotal guesses. If you look closely at Lean Thinking practices, very simple metrics are leveraged for identifying opportunities for waste reduction. And the focus is not on the individual instance of a product delivery, but on the long term viability of sustainable business operations.

Anyone who has been part of a "metrics for the sake of metrics" program knows that these initiatives (usually stemming from a command-and-control management philosophy) fail miserably. These types of initiatives usually start with the rigorous collection of data in an effort to improve visibility and "business intelligence". While some approaches to this attempt to align the metrics selected with some meaningful question that needs to be answered by management to achieve some business operational goal, typically this traceability is established bottom-up with a focus on the available data rather than the business need. This lack of focus on measuring the right things leads to improvement in the wrong area. The improvement does not trace to what the customer values.

If one takes a value stream perspective from Lean, measurement become far simpler and focused on something that is of value to the customer. Specifically, the customer cares about the output of the software delivery organization. We know that this system is complex and adaptive, and it is very difficult to define a causal relationship at an individual agent level between output and agent dynamics. Therefore, the most reasonable thing we can achieve is measurement of the output of this highly dynamic system as a function of input, as both are observable. In essence, we can assess the organizations efficiency over time. We can also understand the effectiveness of the organization through testing. Each of these constituent elements are meaningful to the customer because ultimately they articulate value in the form of productivity. Ultimately, the goal for improvement and therefore the rationale for collecting metrics is to improve productivity. Figure 9.1 illustrates the relationship of these core measurements.

$$Productivity = efficiency \times effectiveness$$

$$= \frac{output}{input} \times \frac{desired\ output}{all\ output}$$

$$= \frac{throughput}{input} \times \%\,valuable\ output$$

Figure 9.1 – Metrics Goals need to trace to Productivity

From the previous equations, it can be seen that Lean metrics focus on the customer view of value that hinges on throughput. This means that we want to understand the cumulative flow of output and we know from Little's law that this depends on cycle time. Therefore our measurement must be focused on cycle time for each unit of output.

Most traditional approaches focus on the decomposition of work in the form of project plans as the primary source of metrics data. However, unless the work breakdown structure is based on units of customer value, the temporal metrics accrued from plans is meaningless. What is needed is a WBS structure which decomposes work based on atomic or minimal increments of value. While each increment has a task breakdown which yields internal measurement data, it is the external or customer-centric measurement that is important. Measuring the output timestamp in relation to the input timestamp for a normalized unit of scope (as opposed to work) enables evaluation and improvement of self organizing teams. This is all the oversight that is needed, as it is this cycle time that is important for the realized scope, not the individual tasks of the team.

With a focus on measuring the right things, the next challenge that metrics programs and measurement have historically run into is a lack of data, specifically automatic data from "natural artifacts". This means that unless tool automation data can be mined such that meaningful information and business intelligence can be discerned, manual creation of the necessary data ensues. Because the creation of this data (in the form of various manual reporting schemes) is separate and apart from the normal course of activity during the day, the manual approach fails. Metrics programs devolve into policing exercises, not a true process improvement culture. This implies the importance of automation. Without workflow automation, Lean Thinking is not possible.

It just so happens that modern, mature tools can serve this purpose if leveraged in an informed way. As described in section 9.1, the key practice that enables this meaningful measurement is process-centric configuration management. If customer demand capture is constrained in such a way as to represent similar granularity across product requests, then automatic timestamps can be leveraged to yield cycle-time metrics and therefore indicate productivity – either overall across a program over time, or among the various teams realizing the requests. Coupling the delivery of work products on an integration branch (which means done-done within the Scrum community) with the automated timestamps of the events representing the lifecycle of the realization of the demand yields all the necessary information. The state-machine of a Product Request represents the start-to-finish lifecycle of the demand, so capturing the work-in-progress transition event and comparing it to the delivery transition event yields cycle-time. Obviously, when looking for root causes in relation to poor throughput, internal timing data can be leveraged. Application of theory of constraints can guide the exploration as to the root cause of poor performance such that improvements can be made.

Figure 9.2 illustrates one example of the process-centric configuration management practice which enables effective metrics programs. The Unified Change Management [163] model from IBM Rational was one of the first instances of this practice.

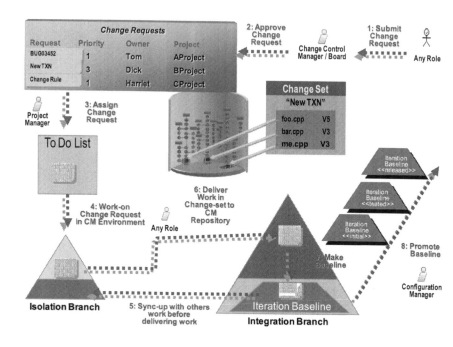

Figure 9.2 – Unified Change Management Model[163]

This key element to bind workflow dynamics with work products that such a workflow produces is a key enabler to implementing Lean at an enterprise level. It represents the fundamental kernel for such aspects as efficient and effective value-stream integration, decision reasoning, compliance and continuous process improvement.

9.3 – Implementing Lean Standard Work

The word "process" has been a dirty word for some time within Agile circles. Based on the era when the values of Agile were codified, it's no wonder. The stories of bloated process-ware are widespread. But if you change the word "process" for the words "standard work" and something interesting happens. The persistence of knowledge related to practices suddenly doesn't seem so offensive. This is because *Standard Work* is a key enabler to *Kaizen* in Lean Thinking. And Lean Thinking and Agile seem to get along.

Standard Work is a practice in which the approach for how work is performed is documented. That means the knowledge of how work is performed is persisted. It does not mean that this is a prescription. Nothing in the Standard Work component of the TPS implies that somehow by documenting procedures or practices is this knowledge static. Rather it is intended to represent a baseline of how work is performed currently. And it is continuously evolving. This is because when combined with Kaizen, the organization consistently strives to improve the standard baseline, and encourages improvement in this snapshot of work "best practice" over time as more is learned. This means that Standard Work as a strategy necessarily leads to a learning organization.

In the world of software engineering, we know that we cannot prescribe a deterministic process. It is in conflict with the nature of tacit knowledge and its relationship to the complex adaptive system we call a project. But persisting generally accepted practices in a general way can have a stabilizing effect. This is because of the delay due to the learning curve for new agents of the project related to how "our organization develops software". At a *type* level rather than a specific *instance*, the knowledge of how work should be approached adds value such that further non-linearities are not introduced into the delivery. Approaching method knowledge management in this manner is contrary to the detailed work-breakdown structure approaches of the past which historically have degraded into prediction exercises. Instead, practice-oriented approaches attempt to abstract the general attributes of experience that has proven to yield success.

One immediate benefit of leveraging this approach within modern large-scale enterprise environments is a more cost effective knowledge transfer mechanism. In the absence of persisted forms of knowledge related to software delivery guidance, an over-reliance on coaches or mentors can occur. While the coaching and mentoring of personnel is a required element for traversing the knowledge transfer curve [xx], focusing solely on this component of knowledge management can result in reliance on costly "master" level resources. To avoid vendor lock-in, tacit knowledge must be extracted over time at a reasonable pace to eventually replace external real-time coaching with internal mentoring candidates. Coaching is only one component in knowledge transfer and should be supplemented with book learning and classroom training.

Historically, "process-ware" has been in the form of printed documents, typically in sets of binders that sit on shelves only to collect dust. Modern approaches however replace this paradigm with online delivery. Modern process and practice management capability typically involves web published content in some sort of structure such that retrieval of knowledge is unimpeded and rapid. Early attempts at this approach include the RUP from IBM Rational and Process Continuum from Platinum Systems [164]. Unfortunately the misapplication of these knowledge assets has resulted in a perception similar to document based process descriptions. Anti-patterns include "Ivory Tower" process groups who seem to develop process for the sake of process with no real connection to how software is developed. Also contributing has been a lack of understanding of these assets as frameworks to be instantiated. However, nothing in leveraging these approaches necessarily implies predictive and rigid sequencing of work breakdown.

Rapidly maturing tools like the IBM Rational Method Composer (RMC) [165] implement a non-prescriptive software delivery knowledge management facility for establishing Standard Work. This tool has a robust feature set, and enables a rapid assembly of standard work configurations drawn from extensive libraries. The process management capabilities of RMC are enabled through the manifestation of industry standards related to the meta-model of process description. The most mature of these standards is the Software Process Engineering Meta-model (SPEM) which is maintained by the Object Management Group (OMG) [166]. The specific instantiation of this standard by IBM Rational is called the "Unified Method Architecture – UMA", and is the basis for how RMC is structured.

Figure 9.3 illustrates the core aspects of the SPEM.

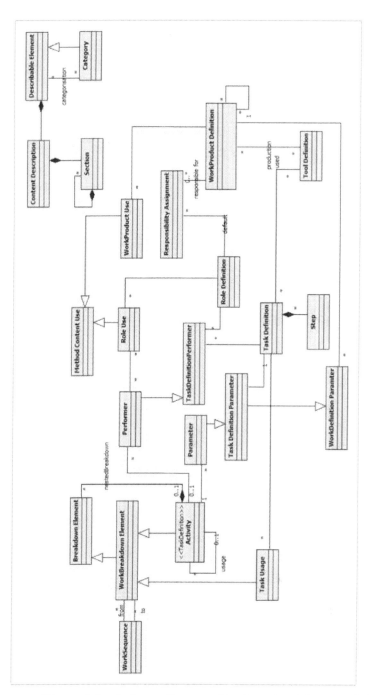

Figure 9.3 – Software Process Engineering Meta-model

Recent trends in leveraging the SPEM standard and tooling to make software development knowledge management real and actionable indicate a shift towards a practice-based approach [167]. This is consistent with the domain model presented in Chapter 4. The key challenge in leveraging RMC is to rapidly enable the assembly of the right practices for a delivery based on context. RMC Asset libraries that deliver an actionable form of SDLC 3.0 system of patterns exist [168]. These libraries enable Lean IT supported by finite cycles of coaching when introduced into an IT Enterprise.

Figure 9.4 illustrates a portion of the SDLC 3.0 Standard Work definition.

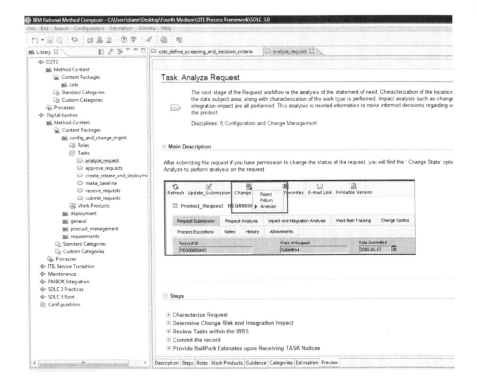

Figure 9.4 – IBM Rational Method Composer [168]

Additionally, integration of practice description capability with the process enactment capabilities of RMC is emerging. Such stronger forms of practice definition enable robust guidance for teams in the face of such a complex system of patterns, and enable effective governance to achieve compliance objectives. The vision of collaborative process enactment technology is evolving as of the time of this writing.

9.4 – Collaborative ALM Trends

One of the root causes related to the opposition to the usage of tools in software development within the Agile community stems from the common strategy employed by vendors. Typically, tool vendors strive for selling all the tools that make up SDLC infrastructure. They attempt to win all the business even if they are not in the best position to fulfill the need. As such they drive a "best of brand" message. This sales strategy typically stems from the "Microsoft Office" pattern. Microsoft pioneered the notion of a suite of products that are sold as a set to yield attractive savings over the purchase of individual products incrementally. The tool vendors have leveraged this pattern for the most part and continue to strive for full lifecycle penetration to this day. To enable bundled solutions to be sold, most vendors are forced to acquire emerging or failing competitor products to fill gaps in their offering. This in no way means that the best product or technology is acquired. It just means that they have to have an offering without which they cannot compete. This leads to the same kinds of system-of-system integration problems that occur within Enterprises, but when left to the vendors, it results in vendor lock-in.

Historically, this has led to much frustration by firms who have bona fide needs in terms of supporting development activity. The typical scenario is where a tool vendor gets a meeting at one or more levels of the organization and attempt to make a case for their assets. They usually claim to have "all the bases covered" and can offer capability in all the various disciplines that realize software product delivery. And they deliver somewhat of a magic show in terms of razzle-dazzle demonstrations of their products from *their* view of the software engineering world. After these initial conversations and meetings conclude, either one of two things occurs. The purchasing organization is so confused that they buy the pitch - lock stock and barrel. The tools are purchased en-masse so as to get the biggest discount and it is left to the purchasing organization to figure out what to do with the new acquisition. The other more mature eventuality is that they launch into a detailed gap analysis, treating the tool vendors like any other COTS and focus on deferring decisions until enough information is present to make the least risky decisions. This usually involves "bake-offs" or "conference room pilots", something the tool vendors typically try to avoid as it leads to a lengthy sales cycle. While the tool vendor company executives would like to see fitness-for-purpose for their offerings and would like to "do the right thing", other levels of their organizations feel the pressures of Wall Street related to making their number.

The new industry buzzword is "Application Lifecycle Management – ALM". Built from a foundation of *process-centric configuration management*, a workflow-centric view is starting to guide tool vendor strategy. It is a sign of a maturing industry where the variable nature of projects and organizations is now understood such that accommodation of such variability is a key component of recent tool offerings. The ability to define the practices or processes to be leveraged first, and then match the tooling second is a giant step in the evolution of SDLC infrastructure. Instead of being burned by vendors whose integration and customizability claims fall short, modern trends are to enable the application of vendor technologies reflective of the customers' needs.

Coincidental within the ALM space is more openness related to integration among competing products. With the evolution of integration technologies like web services based on SOAP or REST, vendor product architectures are changing. While far from perfect, the trend is showing more of a desire on the part of vendors to abandon a philosophy of being all things to all people. Some vendors are exposing integration interfaces faster than others, but most are being driven by the realities of modern service-orientation within their architectures. This will ultimately lead to service enablement and thereby enabling vendor integrations.

Another trend that is related to the evolution of technology is the application of collaboration technologies along-side the traditional SDLC infrastructure capabilities. An example of this includes "Collaboration-in-Context" as delivered by IBM Rational Team Concert, where meaningful contextual information is made available on a specific artifact within the workflow such that team interaction is simpler and more effective. And because the collaboration is facilitated through the use of technology, the Agile challenges of scale and geographical distribution are removed.

9.5 – IT Delivery Enactment Architecture (IDEA)

Once a vendor service enables their product capabilities, a more robust strategy for providing a scalable, integrated and independent SDLC Infrastructure becomes available to IT Enterprises. This strategy, while attempted in the past, is arguably only recently feasible. The *Best-of Breed* strategy represents the composition of a system of tools (system-of-systems) which support the workflow in the best possible way from whichever vendor can best deliver. Instead of shaping delivery practice and approaches around the constraints of a single vendors' offering due to the fear of integration breakage when the independent vendors release new versions, a composite system approach is taken. This is no different than that taken for business systems based on current trends. Identifying the services necessary to realize a delivery organizations workflow at an interface level ensures that vendor lock-in is avoided. The best tool offering is selected to realize the service interface, and this can change over time as new opportunities present themselves.

The discussion that follows represents an experienced based reasoning of the abstractions and workflow involved in modern software engineering. To support SDLC 3.0, multiple vendor offerings are necessary based on current capabilities. For the purposes of generic discussion, detailed analysis of vendor fitness for the various components is out of scope for this book. Industry analysts constantly assess the evolution of the vendor offerings and strategies [169, 170] and can be referenced when making choices for the various service realizations described in this section.

The IT Delivery Enactment Architecture (IDEA) articulates multiple views that facilitate the reasoning about significant decisions to be made related to vendor offerings. Given the Business Use Case View presented in Chapter 8 for a modern IT enterprise, a "Business Logical View" articulates the main abstractions that realize the core business missions and supporting capabilities/disciplines. This view is typically developed concurrently with views that illustrate the dynamic workflows, some of which were also illustrated in Chapter 8. Figure 9.5 shows the Logical View for the IT Business. Commonly there are three types of abstractions in this structural view when leveraging "Object-oriented Business Engineering" techniques [171]. These are *Business Workers, Business Entities and Business Systems.*

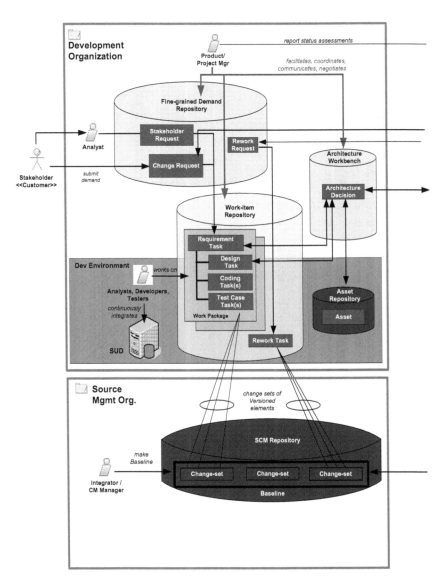

Figure 9.5 – IDEA Process Enactment Logical View

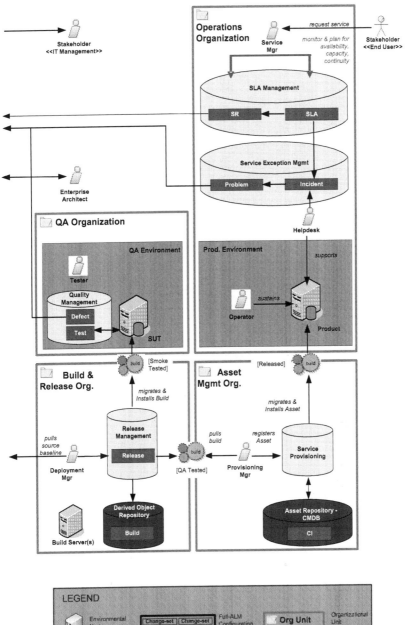

Figure 9.5 – IDEA Process Enactment Logical View

The tools that are the subject of this discussion are Business Systems, as the IT Enterprise is a business system no different than "normal" businesses. Therefore we can apply the same techniques that we apply to engineer system-of-systems for typical business domains.

An IT Enterprise typically consists of a structural decomposition based on synergies related to skill-sets. And increasingly, a formal segregation of these discipline-centric organizations is required due to compliance. This has caused controversy within the Agile community, but shouldn't necessarily be seen as bad practice or ceremony for the sake of ceremony. The segregation of duties that are commonly required within SOX and other compliance standards make reasonable sense. The problems start occurring due to root cause issues related to automation. When automation is insufficient or lacking (also becoming a standard of care within compliance norms), agility suffers due to manual and error prone practices. Figure 9.5 shows six segregated support organizations – *Development Services, Software Configuration Management Services, Build & Release Management Services, Independent Quality Assurance Services, Asset Management Services, and Operations.*

The context boundary of the IT organization is defined by what is outside – namely the Business Actors. For IT Enterprises, the actors are stakeholders typically referred to as *Customers*, and *End Users*. Business stakeholders acting in the role of a Customer submit demand to the IT organization, whereas End Users are the Business Workers who leverage systems once they are deployed. Demand for the implementation of software systems is captured through a queuing system. Such systems are typically called *Request Tracking Systems*, and represent the entry point for IT Demand. Note that the demand for IT system's development can be new or can be the result of existing system operation, and as such represents change requests for existing systems. Changes to existing systems identified by End Users can be fed from other IT infrastructure systems closer to operations like that from Service Management infrastructure (Problem or Incident Management, Capacity Management, Performance Management, Availability Management and the like). But to facilitate efficient prioritization of IT demand for service, the multiple entry points for Product Requests should be managed in a single Request Tracking System. All demand for a single Product represents the Product Backlog, and lives beyond projects during the Products' potentially multi-generational lifecycle.

Various specialized roles (also Business Workers) within the IT Enterprise serve as the supply chain required to realize the demand. Analysts serve the useful role of helping to clarify the IT demand in such a way as to help Customers understand when demand has been fulfilled, or to help articulate demand in such a manner that solution domain realization is efficient and effective. As such they serve to facilitate the extraction of tacit knowledge in what are typically "Requirements". The first amplification of the demand as worded from the Customer starts the Request workflow. High-level characterization of the Request sets the stage for evaluation by a representative cross-section of the stakeholder community. This ensures that system impacts are assessed and that the demand is prioritized in relation to its relative importance with other IT system demand. This is similar to the Meta Scrum approach taken in Agile, and if change is embraced as reality within traditional organizations, is known as a Change Advisory Board.

Once demand is prioritized, it remains in queue and potentially subject to changes in prioritization. The elements of demand will have been shaped to resemble either User Stories, Scenarios or Features if they are well formed and actionable. The Analyst helps to ensure that either of these are minimal and will result in valuable capability upon completion and leave the system in a stable state. With iterative development, an entire project team will tackle a batch of approved demand from this queue. With Lean, only single elements of demand (also known as micro-increments) are addressed per realization team. Depending upon the organizational configuration, similar amounts of demand may be worked on simultaneously as that of teams leveraging timeboxed iterations and their batch of demand. Limits enforced on the work in progress per team implements the practice of "Digital Kanban".

For a Request that is changed from the *Approved* state to the *In-Progress* state, the first thing to be done by a self organizing team is to define the work breakdown for the Request. This task planning occurs just-in-time, and only for a single Request. This avoids the waste of performing predictive planning for an entire project or iteration. Also, the true measure of progress comes from comparing the burn-down of the Product Backlog over time. Task progress information is used by the self organizing team to aid in managing the risk to delivery and to identify and reason about work improvement.

If the demand captured at a high level and leveraged for characterization and prioritization is not actionable for the team to fulfill the Request, one of the Tasks will leverage the specialized skills of the Analyst. Analysts are tasked with elaborating demand into a form that is actionable by developers. This knowledge extraction of the problem domain does not necessarily mean documents. Requirements can be persisted within the process enactment infrastructure in the form of database records such that documentation can be printed in the form of a report or view at any time. This form of Requirements storage is more valuable, as other interesting attributes (also known as Requirements Attributes) can be coupled with the textual description of the demand such that separate traceability, prioritization or effort attribution is not necessary.

With only a small lead time to elaborate requirements, Analysts immediately switch to developing tests acting in the role of "Test Designer". Some self organizing teams like to elaborate requirements into such a form as to equate to acceptance tests instead, such that two differing work products are combined into one. Developers then begin the work to realize the Request with the necessary source code and builds. Developers within these self organizing teams possess both design and implementation skill-sets, similar to the multi-hat wearing of the Analysts. Each role whether it be Analyst or Developer works in the context of Tasks, with one Request containing multiple realization Tasks. Tasks represent not only the work breakdown, but serve as the linkage with configuration management infrastructure. The output from a Task is one or more Work Products. Work Product versions are collected in what are known as "change sets". All the versions of files for whatever configuration item type are collected in the Task change-set. When all work is complete for a Task, the entire change set is "delivered" or merged into the shared or integration branch. During this stage of a Task's workflow, any parallel development merge conflicts are resolved due to the fact that many workers may be changing the same configuration artifact (source code unit, document, etc.) at the same time. Once all the versions of files within the change set are delivered to the integration branch, these versions are then visible to the rest of the teams for the product. Typically, a policy requires a re-sync by team members on a periodic basis to ensure that merge conflicts do not occur too frequently.

The action of delivering a developer change-set should trigger a build of the Product through the application of the continuous integration practice. This build and execution of unit tests is on a near-continuous basis for large scale Products. Continuous frequency builds can occur depending on the branching structure leveraged as well.

When all Tasks for a Request are complete, the Request can be transitioned to the *Complete* state. This enables the inclusion of the Request in a Release. Depending on the Release frequency this can occur immediately, or can be batched to coincide with a useful and sustainable Release window. When included in a Release workflow, it is labeled or "baselined" together with other Requests and signaled as ready for independent testing. The Build and Release organization oversees the independent and re-creatable build of the Product from source code. Following a successful build, this organization is also responsible for deployment of the build to the segregated QA environment once it is ready to receive the new target of test. In mature organizations, this typically initiates full automatic regression test suite execution. Results are evaluated by a Tester or Test Manager, typically with signoffs associated for later use in determining production readiness of the Release baseline. If quality is within established risk tolerances, the baseline becomes a valuable asset. This asset is ready to be secured in a Definitive Media Library and a Configuration Management Database (CMDB).

The final stage of the overall workflow for a Request occurs when approvals are collected by the various stakeholders for the change event. Not only must the Business organization signify readiness to accept the change, but the Operations organization must acknowledge their ability to support the Release deployment and the operational support after the change is made. This includes the Service Operations activities of Helpdesk, service monitoring and system administration.

From the discussion above, it can be seen that there are many moving parts that more or less are reasonable things that must occur for software to be released into an organization of any reasonable complexity, scale or risk tolerance. What some Agilist's might claim as being and event of "just go and install it" does not reflect reality in most non-trivial organizations. But for this level of sustainable maturity to be efficient and effective and not kill business agility, all of the systems involved must be seamlessly integrated into an overall value stream. This requires that each component of the system must be locally-optimized, ignorant of this overall orchestration. Rather, the systems that are leveraged for each stage of this complex workflow must work together.

Figure 9.6 describes the dynamic view of the scenario described above. The diagram represents a UML interaction diagram, and shows the sequence in instantiation of the entities involved in the collaboration.

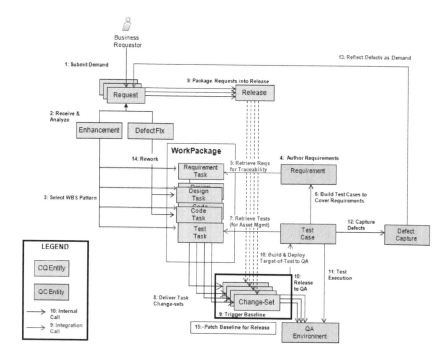

Figure 9.6 – IDEA Request-to-Release Scenario

The challenge with modern SDLC infrastructure is that vendors are in competition with each other. As discussed in section 9.4, this usually leads to a drive to win business related to all capabilities. But it is unrealistic to think that a single vendor can deliver the best capability across the ALM spectrum. Therefore, it is reasonable to assume that vendors like HP, IBM and BMC will have to co-exist. The good news is that integration mechanisms are starting to mature. For example, if one recognizes that IBM Rational is the leader in Enterprise Change and Configuration Management capability [172], and HP Quality Center (QC) is the leader in Test Automation and Management [173], then the need quickly emerges for integrating these two infrastructure components. Differing strategies for each of the technologies require integration approaches based on the constraints of each vendor. We wish to be able to push Defects as a work request type back to our Product Backlog workflow system, so HP Quality Center must be able to call the exposed REST-based API of IBM Rational ClearQuest or IBM Rational Team Concert. If this capability is not available easily from the server side, a pull-oriented integration is necessary, where scheduled scripts will facilitate the integration with the QC Visual Basic based API. Also to be considered is the fact that most CQ based implementations leverage Perl as the scripting language such that cross-platform Windows and Unix development can occur seamlessly.

Similarly, integration between BMC's Remedy platform (arguably the leader in the ITSM space [174]) and IBM Rational ClearQuest or Team Concert requires that Remedy make RESTful calls such that production incidents that are deemed to be recurring problems can be fed back to the development organization. The Remedy platform is more robust than the constraints of QC, so server-side integration is possible between the two components.

The key point to take away from these examples is that integration is possible and for the most part is trivial in terms of code. The API's are reasonably stable, so the fear instilled from some tool vendors as to integration breakage is for the most part non-existent. This enables the workflow practices leveraged by the development organization in the context of specific process problems to drive the technology and not the other way around. All that is necessary is some higher level reasoning about the rationale for the integrations based on an understanding of why certain practices make sense.

Bibliography:

Chapter 1:

[1] Kent Beck, et al. *"Manifesto for Agile Software Development"*, 2001.

[2] Michael Polanyi, *"The Tacit Dimension"*. University of Chicago Press, 1967.

[3] Information Systems Audit and Control Association (ISACA), *"Control Objectives for IT – COBIT"*. www.isaca.org.

[4] Project Management Institute, *"A Guide to the Project Management Body of Knowledge (PMBOK®)"* Fourth Edition, 2008.

[5] Office of Government Commerce (UK), Majid Iqbal, Michael Nieves, *"IT Infrastructure Library (ITIL) Service Strategy"*; and Vernon Lloyd ,Colin Rudd, *"ITIL Service Design"*; and Shirley Lacy, Ivor Macfarlane, *"ITIL Service Transition"*; and David Cannon, David Wheeldon , *ITIL Service Operation."*; and George Spalding, Gary Case, *"ITIL Continual Service Improvement"*. The Stationery Office, 2007.

[6] David Anderson, *"Future directions of Agile"*, Agile Alliance Conference 2008.

[7] Gartner Inc. *"The Gartner Hype Cycle for Application Development – 2008"*, Gartner Group Inc.

[8] Standish Group, *"The Standish Group Report- Chaos"*, www.standishgroup.com 1994-2009.

[9] National Hurricane Center – National Oceanic and Atmospheric Administration (NHC-NOAA) *"Hurricane Katrina Public Advisory 10"* and *"Hurricane Katrina Public Advisory 23"* , August 2005.

Chapter 2:

[10] W. Royce, *"Managing the Development of Large Software Systems"*, Proc. Westcon, IEEE CS Press.1970, pp. 328-339.

[11] Mary Poppendieck, Tom Poppendieck *"Lean Software Development: An Agile Toolkit"*. Addison-Wesley, 2006.

[12] J. P. Womack, D. T. Jones, (1996). *"Lean Thinking: Banish waste and create wealth in your corporation"*. New York: Free Simon & Schuster.

[13] T. Ohno, (1988). *"Toyota Production System: Beyond Large-Scale Production"*. New York:Productivity Press.

[14] W. Edwards Deming, *"Out of the Crisis"*, MIT Press, 1986.

[15] Jay W. Forrester, *"System Dynamics and the Lessons of 35 Years"*. Sloan School of Management - Massachusetts Institute of Technology 1991.

[16] E. Goldratt, *"The Goal: A Process of Ongoing Improvement"*, North River Press, 1992.

[17] Clinger-Cohen, *"Information Technology Management Reform Act"*, *"Federal Acquisition Reform Act"*, 104th Congress, Washington D.C. , February 1996.

[18] Internal memorandum from US Undersecretary of Defense.

[19] B. Boehm, *"A Spiral Model of Software Development and Enhancement"*, Proceedings of Int'l Workshop Software Process and Software Environments; ACM Press, 1985.

[20] T. Gilb, *"Evolutionary Development"* ACM Software, Eng. Notes, Apr. 1981.

[21] James Rumbaugh, Michael Blaha, William Premerlani, Frederick Eddy, William Lorensen, *"Object Oriented Design and Modeling"*, Prentice Hall, 1991.

[22] G. Booch, *"Object Oriented Analysis & Design with Applications"*, Benjamin-Cummings, 1993.

[23] Ivar Jacobson, Magnus Christerson, Patrik Jonsson, Gunnar Ovargaard, *"Object Oriented Software Engineering – a Use Case Driven Approach"*, Addison Wesley, 1992.

[24] Philippe Kruchten, *"The Rational Unified Process: – An Introduction"*, Addison Wesley, 2000.

[25] Ivar Jacobson, Grady Booch, James Rumbaugh, *"The Unified Software Development Process"*, Addison Wesley Object Technology Series, 1999.

[26]Object Management Group – OMG, *"The Unified Modeling Language (UML)"*, 1997.

[27] B. Boehm, *"Anchoring the Software Process"*, IEEE Software, Jul. 1996.

[28] Eclipse Foundation, "OpenUP", http://epf.eclipse.org/wikis/openup/ 2005

[29] Ivar Jacobson, *"The Essential Unified Process"* at www.ivarjacobson.com

[30] S. Ambler, J. Nalbon, M. Visdos, *"The Enterprise Unified Process: Extending the Rational Unified Process"*. Prentice Hall PTR, 2005.

[31] M. Beedle, et al., *"SCRUM: A Pattern Language for Hyper-productive Software Development, in Pattern Languages of Program Design"*, N. Harrison, Editor. 1999, Addison-Wesley. p. 637-651. 1994. 308(6942): p. 1499-.

[32] K. Beck, *"eXtreme Programming Explained: Embrace Change"*, Addison Wesley, 1999.

[33] J. Donovon Wells, *"Extreme Programming: A Gentle Introduction."* www.ExtremeProgramming.org .

[34] Elton Mayo, *The Human Problems of an Industrialized Civilization* (1933).

[35] S. R. Palmer, J. M. Felsing, *"A Practical Guide to Feature-Driven Development"*. Prentice Hall 2002.

[36] James P. Womack, Daniel T. Jones, Daniel Roos; *"The Machine that Changed the World : The Story of Lean Production"*, Harper Perennial, 1991.

[37] Jeffrey Liker, *"The Toyota Way"*. New York: McGraw-Hill, 2004.

[38] www.limitedWIPsociety.org.

[39] Toyota Motor Corp. *"The Toyota Production System"*, http://www.toyota.co.jp/en/vision/production_system

[40] Scott Ambler, *"Agile UP"*, www.ambysoft.com 2002-2005.

[41] Craig Larman, *"An Agile UP"*, www.scribd.com. Valtech 2002.

[42] D. D'Souza, A. Cameron Wills,*"Objects, Components, and Frameworks with UML: The Catalysis_SM Approach"*. Addison-Wesley Professional, 1998.

[43] Corey Ladas, *"Scrumban - Essays on Kanban Systems for Lean Software Development"*, Modus Cooperandi Press 2009.

Chapter 3:

[44] Frederick W. Taylor *"The Principles of Scientific Management"*, New York: Harper Bros., 1911.

[45] Gantt, Henry L., *"Organizing for Work"*, Harcourt, Brace, and Howe, New York, 1919. Dupont *"Critical Path Method"*, 1957.

[46] Defense Systems Management College, *Earned Value Management Textbook, Chapter 2*. Defense Systems Management College, EVM Dept.,1997.

[47] Paul Solomon, *"Performance Based Earned Valuet"*. IEEE Computer Society Press, November , 2006.

[48] American National Standards Institute/ Information Technology Association of America/Electronics Industry Association, *"Systems Engineering Capability Model – EIA 731"*. 2002.

[49] B. Boehm, C. Abts, A.W. Brown, S. Chulani, B. K. Clark, E. Horowitz, R. Madachy, D. Reifer and B. Steece. *"Software Cost Estimation with COCOMO II"*. Prentice Hall PTR, July 2000.

[50] Ludwig von Bertalanffy, *"General System theory: Foundations, Development, Applications"*, George Braziller, 1968.

[51] W. Buckley, *"Sociology and Modern Systems Theory"* New Jersey: Englewood Cliffs 1967; .and A.W. Steiss, *"Urban Systems Dynamics.* Toronto: Lexington Books*, 1967.*

[52] Jay Wright Forrester, *"Industrial Dynamics"*. Pegasus Communications, 1961.

[53] Jay Wright Forrester, *"Urban Dynamics"*. Pegasus Communications, 1969.

[54] Jay Wright Forrester, *"World Dynamics"*. Wright-Allen Press, 1973.

[55] Peter Senge, *"The Fifth Discipline: The Art and Practice of the Learning Organizations"*. Doubleday Business, 1994.

[56] John Sterman,. *"Business Dynamics: Systems Thinking and Modeling for a Complex World"*, McGraw-Hill, 2000.

[57] John Holland, *"Adaptation in Natural and Artificial Systems: An Introductory Analysis with Applications to Biology, Control, and Artificial Intelligence"*, MIT Press, 1992.

[58] Wikipedia, *"System"*. http://en.wikipedia.org/wiki/System

[59] Complex Adaptive Systems Group, *"Hurricane-Galaxy Similarities"*. http://www.cas-group.net/similarities.htm#hurricanes

[60] Jim Highsmith, *"Adaptive Software Development: A Collaborative Approach to Managing Complex Systems"*, Dorset House, 1999.

[61] John Holland, *"Hidden Order: How Adaptation Builds Complexity"*. Helix Press, 1996.

[62] Dee Hock, *"One from Many: VISA and the Rise of Chaordic Organization"*. Berrett-Koehler Publishers, 2005.

[63] EDS, *"Herding cats"*. Superbowl Commercial, 2000.

[64] M. Waldrop, *"Complexity: the emerging science at the edge of order and chaos"*. London Viking, 1992.

[65] Dan Vergano, *"Hurricane-calming technology? Bill Gates has a plan"*, USA Today, July 2009.

[66] Charles Darwin, *"The Origin of Species by Means of Natural Selection"*. London: John Murray, Albemarle Street, 1859.

[67] Grady Booch, *"Object Solutions: Managing the Object Oriented Project"*, Addison Wesley Professional, 1995.

[68] William S. Levine et al, *"The Control Handbook"*, IEEE Press, 1995.

[69] Bernardo Huberman, Dennis Wilkinson, *"Performance Variability and Project Dynamics"*, Computational & Mathematical Organization Theory, 2005.

[70] Mathworks Tutorial, *"Non-linear Black-box Identification of Hammerstein-Wiener Models"*, http://www.mathworks.com / access/helpdesk /help/toolbox/ident/ug/bq2ix15.html

[71] Bernt Oksendal, *"Stochastic Differential Equations – An Introduction with Applications"*, Springer, 2003.

[72] Frederick Brooks, *"The Mythical Man-Month, Essays on Software Engineering – Anniversary Edition"*, Addison Wesley, 1995.

[73] H. Rahmandad, J. Sterman, *"Heterogeneity and Network Structure in the Dynamics of Diffusion: Comparing Agent-Based and Differential Equation Models"*. MANAGEMENT SCIENCE Vol. 54, No. 5, May 2008.

[74] Putnam, L. and Myers, W. , "Measures for Excellence", Yourdon Press Computing Series, 1992.

[75] H. Rahmandad, N. Repenning, J. Sterman, *"Effects of Feedback Delay on Learning"*. "System Dynamics Review Vol. 25, No. 4; Oct.-Dec. 2009.

Chapter 4:

[76] IEEE Computer Society, *"Guide to the Software Engineering Body of Knowledge – SWEBOK"*, IEEE Press, 2004

[77] Mitre Corporation, *"Guide to the (Evolving) Enterprise Architecture Body of Knowledge – EABOK"*:, Mitre Case No. 04-0104, 04-0105, 2004.

[78] The Open Group, *"The Open Group Architecture Framework – TOGAF"*, http://en.wikipedia.org.

[79] Jim Womack, Mike Rother, John Shook, *"Learning to See: Value Stream Mapping to Add Value and Eliminate Muda"*, Productivity Press, 1999.

[80] Paul Sarbanes, Michael Oxley, *"'Corporate and Auditing Accountability and Responsibility Act"*, United States House of Representatives, 2002.

[81] Auditing Standards Board of the American Institute of Certified Public Accountants (AICPA), *"Statement of Auditing Standards-70: Service Organizations"* and *"Statemenn of Auditing Standards – 94: The Effect of Information Technology on the Auditor's Consideration of Internal Control in a Financial Statement Audit"* AICPA AU Section 324 para. 02, 1993-2006.

Chapter 5:

[82] Stewart Myers, *"Determinants of Capital Borrowing"*, Journal of Financial Economics, Vol..5, 1977.

[83] Karl Scotland; *"Minimum Marketable Features"*, Availagility Blog 2008.

[84] Hakan Ergdogmus, *"Valuation of Learning Options in Software Development Under Private and Market Risk"*, National Research Council of Canada, 2002.

[85] Barry Boehm, Richard Turner, *"Balancing Agility & Discipline: A Guide for the Perplexed"*, Addison Wesley, 2003.

[86] Michael Porter, *"Competitive Strategy: Techniques for Analyzing Industries and Competitors"*. Free Press, 1998.

[87] Lowell Lindstrom; Carmen Zannier; Erdogmus, Hakan (2004). *Extreme Programming and Agile Methods"* - XP/Agile Universe 2004: 4th Conference on Extreme Programming and Agile Methods, Calgary, Canada, 2004.

[88] John, Bicheno, Holweg Matthias, *"The Lean Toolbox"*. PICSIE Books, 2009.

[89] James Duggan, *"The Hall Pass has been Repealed: The Evolution of Application Lifecycle Management"*, Gartner ITxpo Symposium 2008.

[90] G. Weinberg, *"Quality Software Management Vol. 4: Anticipating Change"*. 1997: Dorset House.

[91] David H. Freedman, *"Corps Business: The 30 Management Principles of the US Marines"*, Collins 2000.

[92] IEEE Architecture Working Group, *"IEEE Recommended Practice for Architectural Description of Software-Intensive Systems"*, IEEE Std 1471-2000, IEEE, 2000.

[93] IEEE Architecture Working Group, *"IEEE Recommended Practice for Software Requirements Specifications"*, IEEE Std 830-1998, IEEE, 1998.

[94] Scott Ambler, *"Examining the 'Big Requirements Up Front (BRUF) Approach'"*, Agile Modeling 2006-2009

[95] Robert E. Quinn, John Rohrbaugh, *"A Competing Values Framework to Organizational Effectiveness"*, Public Productivity Review, 1981.

[96] Patrick Lencioni. *"The Five Dysfunction of a team – A Leadership Fable"*, Jossey Bass, 2002.

[97] George Miller, *"The magical number seven, plus or minus two: Some limits on our capacity for processing information"* Psychological Review 63 (2): 81-97. 1956.

[98] Charles Spearman, Jenkins, James J. (Ed); Paterson, Donald G. *"The Abilities of Man. Studies in individual differences: The search for intelligence"*. (Ed). (1961). Studies in individual differences: The search for intelligence. (pp. 241-266). East Norwalk, CT, US: Appleton-Century-Crofts. xiv, 774 pp.

[99] James Morgan, Jeffrey Liker, *"The Toyota Product Development System: Integrating People, Process, and Technology"*. Productivity Press, 2006.

Chapter 6:

[100] H. Takeuchi and I. Nonaka, *"The New New Product Development Game"*, Harvard Business Rev., Jan.1986, pp. 137-146.

[101] Cyril Northcote Parkinson, *"Parkinson's Law"*, The Economist, 1955.

[102] http://www.agilemodeling.com/essays/changeManagement.htm.

[103] Wilbur Schramm, *"The Process and Effects of Mass Communication"*, Urbana: University of Illinois Press, 1954.

[104] Douglas McGregor, *"The Human Side of Enterprise"*, New York: McGraw-Hill, 1960, p. 132.

[105] David H. Freedman, *"Corps Business: The 30 Management Principles of the US Marines"*, Collins 2000.

[106] R. Greenleaf, L. Spears, *"Servant Leadership: A Journey into the Nature of Legitimate Power and Greatness 25th Anniversary Edition"*, Paulist Press, 2002.

[107] J. Fritz Roethlisberger, W. J. Dickson, *"Management and the Worker"*. Cambridge, Mass.: Harvard University Press, 1939.

[108] Martin Fowler, *"Continuous Integration"*, martinfowler.com/articles/continuousIntegration.html, 2006.

[109] Larry Constantine, *"Constantine on Peopleware"*, Prentice Hall, 1995.

[110] David West, *"Case Study: Microsoft Speeds Tool Delivery with Agile Development"*, Forrester Research, March 2009.

[111] Bruce W. Tuckman, *"Forming, Storming, Norming & Performing Team lifecycle"*, 1965.

[112] Bertrand Meyer, *"Object-oriented Software Construction"*, Prentice Hall PTR, 2000.

[113] Joe Morgenstern, *"The Fifty-Nine Story Crisis"*, The New Yorker pp 45-53, May 1995.

[114] *Chernobyl Disaster*, Wikipedia.

[115] *"Report to the Royal Commission on the Ocean Ranger Marine Disaster"*, 1984.

[116] Rogers Commission, *"Report of the Presidential Commission on the Space Shuttle Challenger Accident"*, June 1986.

[117] *"Tacoma narrows Bridge failure"*, Wikipedia Commons.

[118] W. Royce, *"Software Project Management"*, Addison-Wesley, 1998.

[119] Nick Rozanski, Eoin Woods, *"Software Systems Architecture with Stakeholders Using Viewpoints and Perspectives"*, Addison-Wesley, 2005.

[120] Mario Barbacci et al, *"Quality Attributes"*, Technical Report CMU/SEI-95-TR-021 ESC-TR-95-021, Software Engineering Institute, Carnegie Mellon University, 1995.

[121] Thomas Saaty, *"The Analytic Hierarchy Process"*, McGraw-Hill, New York, NY, 1980.

[122] D. Winterfeld, W. von and Edwards, *"Decision Analysis and Behavioral Research"*, Cambridge University Press, Cambridge, England, 1986.

[123] Ivar Jacobson, Pan Wei Ng, *"Aspect-Oriented Software Development with Use Cases"*, Addison Wesley, 2005.

[124] Len Bass, Paul Clements, Rick Kazman, *"Software Architecture in Practice"*, Addison-Wesley Professional, 1997.

[125] Santiago Comella-Dorda et al, *"A Process for COTS Software Product Evaluation"*, Software Engineering Institute at CMU/National Research Council of Canada/ TECHNICAL REPORT CMU/SEI-2003-TR-017 ESC-TR-2003-017, July 2004.

[126] Mark Kennaley, *"The 3+1 Views of Architecture – in 3D"*. Working IEEE Conference on Software Architecture -WICSA 2008.

[127] Richard J Schonberger. *"Japanese Manufacturing Techniques: Nine Hidden Lessons in Simplicity"*, Free Press, (1982).

[128] J. D. C. Little, *"A Proof of the Queuing Formula L= λW"* Operations Research, 9, 383-387 (1961).

[129] H. Chen, D. Yao, *"Optimal intensity control of a queuing system with state dependent capacity limit"*. IEEE 1990.

[130] George S. Patton, *"Perfect enemy of good enough"*.

[131] Vinay Datar, Scott Matthews, Boeing, *"Datar-Mathews Method for Quantitative Real Option Valuation"*, US Patent #6862579.

[132] Mathews, Scott H., Datar, Vinay T. and Johnson, Blake. *"A Practical Method for Valuing Real Options"*. Journal of Applied Corporate Finance, Spring 2007, (19), No. 2, pp. 95-104.

[133] JD Powers & Associates Initial Quality Study Awards, 2009.

[134] Cici Albert, Lisa Brownsword, *"Evolutionary Process for Integrating COTS-based Systems - An Overview"*, Technical Reports CMU/SEI-2002-TR-009, Software Engineering Institute, Carnegie Mellon University, 2002.

[135] L. Brownsword, P. Clements, *"A case study in successful product line development"*, Technical Report CMU/SEI-96-TR-016, October 1996.

Chapter 7:

[136] Alistair Cockburn's blog *"Are Iterations Hazardous to your Project?"*. 2005.

[137] Tim Brown, *"Strategy by Design"*, Fast Company Magazine, June 2005.

[138] Frederick Brooks, *"The Mythical Man-Month, Essays on Software Engineering – Anniversary Edition"*, Addison Wesley, 1995.

[139] Craig Larman, *"Scaling Lean Thinking and Agile Methods to Offshore Development"*, Valtech TV, 2006.

[140] Peggy Kenna, Sondra Lacy, *"Business Japan: A Practical Guide to Understanding Japanese Business Culture (Paperback)"*, MacGraw-Hill, 1994.

[141] Rolf Nelson, *"Offshore Development: making it a success with agile practices and team collaboration"*, IBM Rational 2008 Presentation.

[142] The System Company. 1911. *"How Scientific Management is Applied"*. London: A. W. Shaw Company, Ltd.

[143] Kenji Hiranabe, *"Kanban Applied to Software Development: from Agile to Lean"*. InfoQ, January 2008.

[144] Craig Larman, *"Applying UML and Patterns"*, Prentice Hall PTR 2004.

Chapter 8:

[145] Software Engineering Institute. *"CMMI for Development, Version 1.2"*. CMMI-DEV (Version 1.2, August 2006). Carnegie Mellon University Software Engineering Institute. 2006.

[146a,b] IEEE *"Standard for Software Engineering Software Life Cycle Processes"*, ISO/IEEE Std 12207, IEEE, 1998. IEEE *"Standard for Software Engineering Software Life Cycle Processes Maintenance"*, ISO/IEEE Std 14764, IEEE, 2006.

[147] Scott W. Ambler, John Nalbone, and Michael J. Vizdos, *"The Enterprise Unified Process: Extending the Rational Unified Process"*, Prentice Hall PTR 2005.

[148] The Open Group *"TOGAF v9"*. www.opengroup.org/togaf , 2009.

[149] J. Zachman, *"A Framework for Information Systems Architecture"*, IBM Systems Journal Vol 26, No 3, 1987.

[150] P. Kruchten, *"The 4+1 View Model of Architecture"*, IEEE Software, volume 12, issue 6, 1995.

[151] Michael L. George, *"Lean Six Sigma: Combining Six Sigma Quality with Lean Production Speed"*, MacGraw-Hill, 2002.

[152] V. Basili, G. Caldiera, H. Dieter Rombach, *"The Goal Question Metric Approach"*. 1994

[153] Carey Schwaber, *"The Forrester Wave: Process Centric Configuration Management"*. Forrester Research Q4 2005.

[154] Defense Science Board, *"Acquiring Defense Software Commercially"*, Office of the Undersecretary of Defense For Acquisition and Technology, Washington D.C. , June 1994.

[155] Cecile Peraire., *"An Introduction to IBM Rational Unified Process for Package Delivery"*, IBM DeveloperWorks Article, IBM, August 2005.

[156] Mark Kennaley, *"EPIC+ : An amplification of Package Acquisition Best Practices"*. www.fourth-medium.com.

[157] C. Kepner, B. Tregoe, *"KT Rational Process"*. www.kepner-tregoe.com. 1958.

[158] Rick Kazman, Jai Asundi, Mark Klein, *"Making Architecture Design Decisions: An Economic Approach"*, Technical Reports CMU/SEI-2002-TR-035 ESC-TR-2002-035, Carnegie Mellon University, 2002.

[159] Rick Kazman, Mark Klein, Paul Clements, *"ATAM: Method for Architecture Evaluation"*, Technical Reports CMU/SEI-2000-TR-004, Software Engineering Institute, Carnegie Mellon University, 2000.

Chapter 9:

[160] Socially acceptable Agile tools - *Jira, Mingle, XPlanner, VersionOne, Cruise-control, Subversion*.

[161] Basel Committee on Banking Supervision, *"Basel II: International Convergence of Capital Measurement and Capital Standards: A Revised Framework"*, November 2005.

[162] HIPAA, *"The Health Insurance Portability and Accountability Act (HIPAA) of 1996 (P.L.104-191)"*, 104th Congress, Washington D.C. , August 1996.

[163] IBM Redboook, *"Software Configuration Management – A Clear Case for IBM Rational Clearcase and ClearQuest UCM"*, IBM Rational 2004.

[164] Margo Visitacion and Liz Barnett, *"CA Process Continuum: Greater Depth, Lower Cost, but Still a Big Product"*. Forrester Research June 2001.

[165] IBM Rational, *"IBM Rational Method Composer 7.5"*, www.ibm.com/software/awdtools/rmc/

[166] Object Management Group, *"Software Process Engineering Meta-model Specification"*. www.omg.org 2005.

[167] Ivar Jacobson, Pan Wei Ng, and Ian Spence, *"Enough of processes – Lets do practices"*. Journal of Object Technology, 6(6):41-67, 2007.

[168] Mark Kennaley, Carson Holmes, *"SDLC 3.0 delivered in IBM Rational Method Composer"*, Fourth Medium Consulting Inc. 2010.

[169] Gartner Inc., *"The Gartner Magic Quadrant"*. http://www.gartner.com/technology/research/methodologies/researc h_mq.jsp08.

[170] Forrester Research, *"The Forrester Wave"*, www.forrester.com/wave

[171] Ivar Jacobson, Maria Ericsson, Agneta Jacobson, "The Object Advantage: Business Process Reengineering with Object Technology", ACM Press, 1995.

[172] Forrester Research, *"The Forrester Wave: Software Change and Configuration Management"*. Q2 2007.

[173] Forrester Research, *"The Forrester Wave: Functional Testing Solutions"*. Q3 2008.

Index

Q

R

V

W

X

Y

Z

17125081R00155

Made in the USA
Lexington, KY
01 September 2012